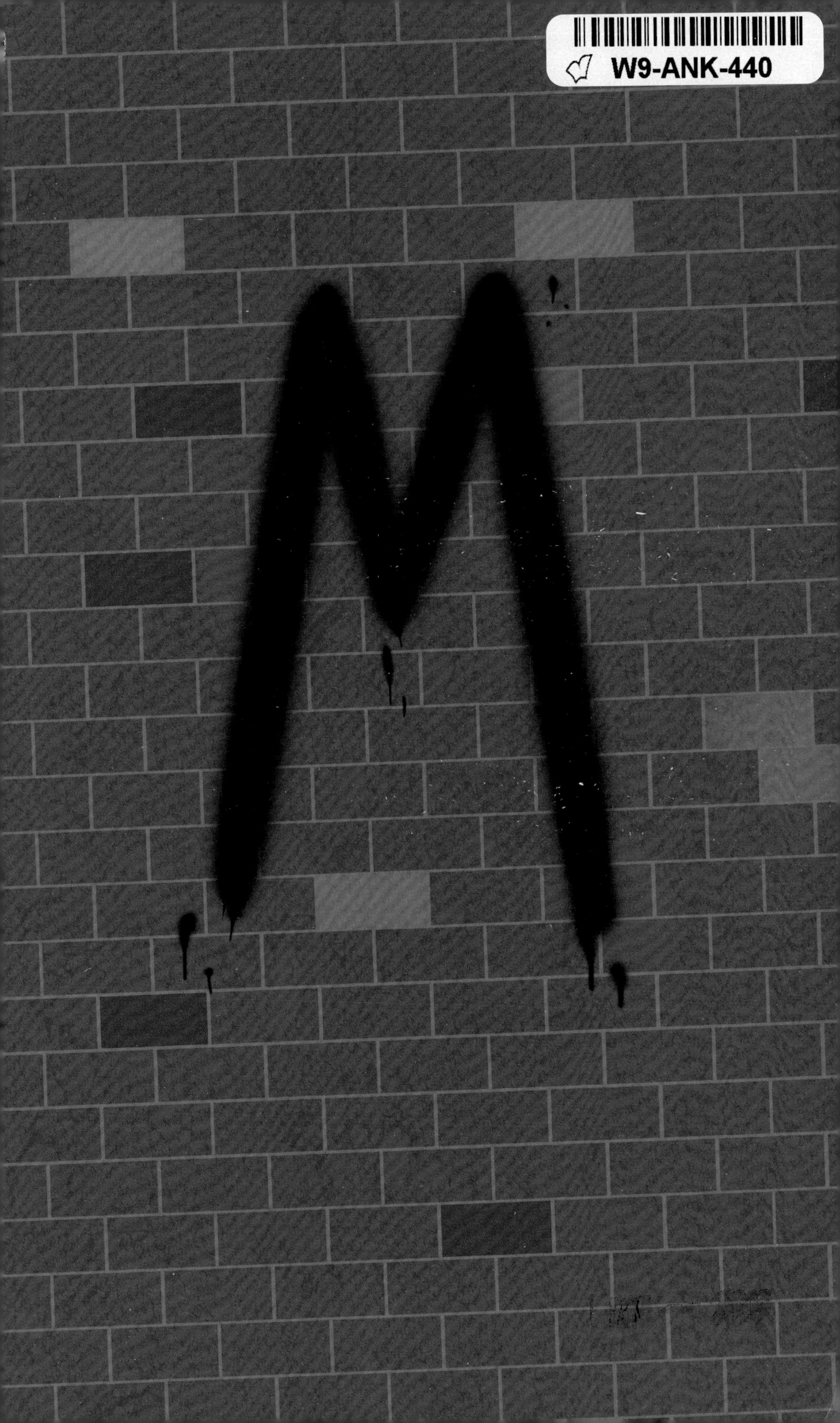

YEARS OF FUTURE PAST

Collection Editor - JENNIFER GRÜNWALD
Assistant Editor - SARAH BRUNSTAD
Associate Managing Editor - ALEX STARBUCK
Editor, Special Projects - MARK D. BEAZLEY
Senior Editor, Special Projects - JEFF YOUNGQUIST
SVP Print, Sales & Marketing - DAVID GABRIEL
Book Designer - ADAM DEL RE

Editor in Chief - AXEL ALONSO
Chief Creative Officer - JOE QUESADA
Publisher - DAN BUCKLEY
Executive Producer ALAN FINE

X-MEN: YEARS OF FUTURE PAST. Contains material originally published in magazine form as YEARS OF FUTURE PAST #1-5. First printing 2015. ISBN# 978-0-7851-9894-9. Published by MARVEL WORLDWIDE, INC., a subsidiary of MARVEL ENTERTAINMENT, LLC. OFFICE OF PUBLICATION: 135 West 50th Street, New York, NY 10020. Copyright © 2015 MARVEL No similarity between any of the names, characters, persons, and/or institutions in this magazine with those of any living or dead person or institution is intended, and any such similarity which may exist is purely coincidental. Printed in Canada. ALAN FINE, President, Marvel Entertainment; DAN BUCKLEY, President, TV, Publishing and Brand Management; JOE QUESADA, Chief Creative Officer; TOM BREVOORT, SVP of Publishing; DAVID BOGART, SVP of Operations & Procurement, Publishing; C.B. CEBULSKI, VP of International Development & Brand Management; DAVID GABRIEL, SVP Print, Sales & Marketing; JIM O'KEEFE, VP of Operations & Logistics; DAN CARR, Executive Director of Publishing Technology; SUSAN CRESPI, Editorial Operations Manager; ALEX MORALES, Publishing Operations Manager; STAN LEE, Chairman Emeritus. For information regarding advertising in Marvel Comics or on Marvel.com, please contact Jonathan Rheingold, VP of Custom Solutions & Ad Sales, at jrheingold@marvel.com. For Marvel subscription inquiries, please call 800-217-9158. Manufactured between 10/2/2015 and 11/9/2015 by SOLISCO PRINTERS, SCOTT, QC, CANADA.

10 9 8 7 6 5 4 3 2 1

3 KSPE 003 42049 Q

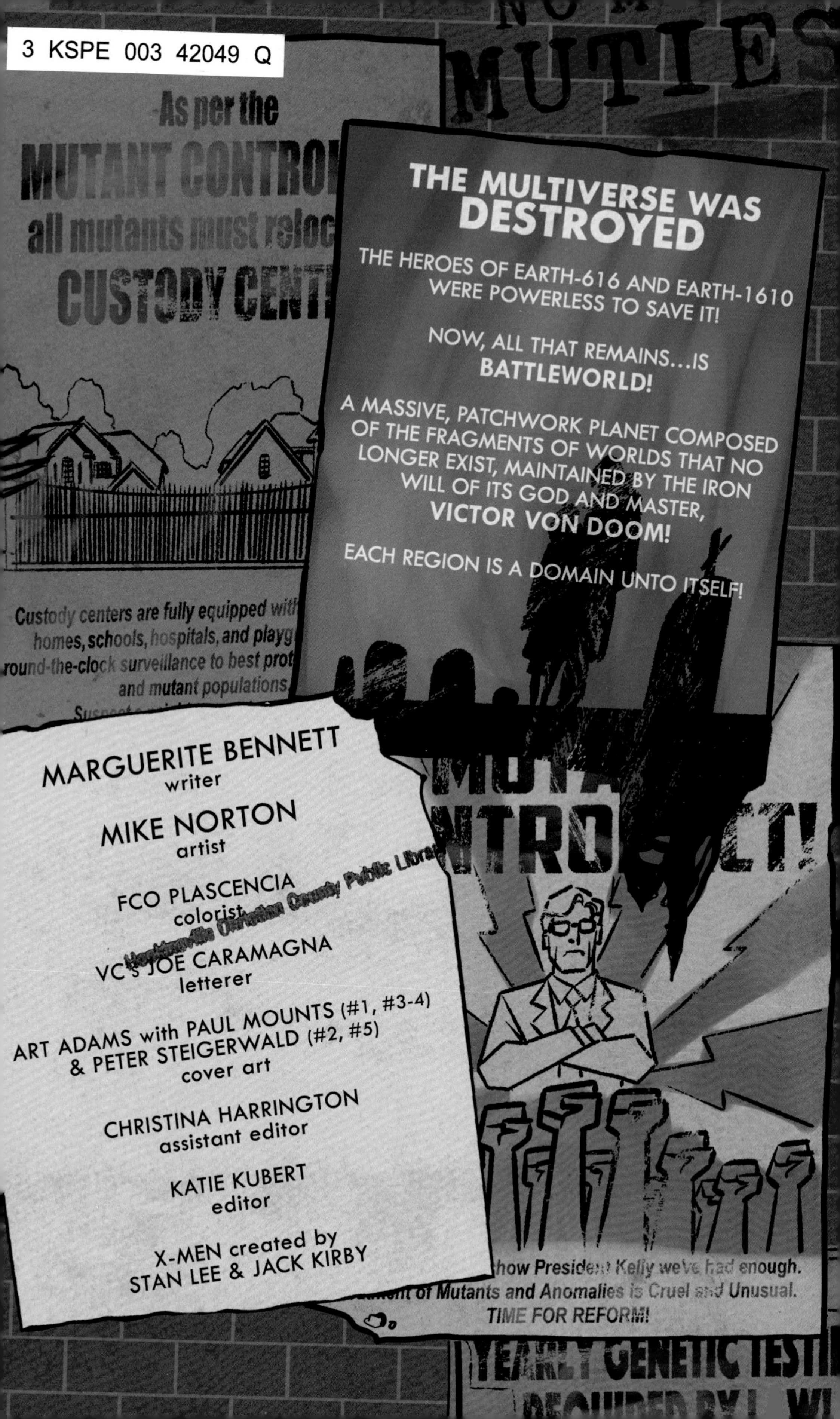

NO MUTIES

-As per the
MUTANT CONTROL
all mutants must reloc
CUSTODY CENT

Custody centers are fully equipped with
homes, schools, hospitals, and playg
round-the-clock surveillance to best prot
and mutant populations.
Suspect

THE MULTIVERSE WAS DESTROYED

THE HEROES OF EARTH-616 AND EARTH-1610 WERE POWERLESS TO SAVE IT!

NOW, ALL THAT REMAINS...IS BATTLEWORLD!

A MASSIVE, PATCHWORK PLANET COMPOSED OF THE FRAGMENTS OF WORLDS THAT NO LONGER EXIST, MAINTAINED BY THE IRON WILL OF ITS GOD AND MASTER, VICTOR VON DOOM!

EACH REGION IS A DOMAIN UNTO ITSELF!

MARGUERITE BENNETT
writer

MIKE NORTON
artist

FCO PLASCENCIA
colorist

VC's JOE CARAMAGNA
letterer

ART ADAMS with PAUL MOUNTS (#1, #3-4) & PETER STEIGERWALD (#2, #5)
cover art

CHRISTINA HARRINGTON
assistant editor

KATIE KUBERT
editor

X-MEN created by
STAN LEE & JACK KIRBY

Huntsville Othman County Public Libra

MUTA
NTRO CT!

how President Kelly we've had enough.
ment of Mutants and Anomalies is Cruel and Unusual.
TIME FOR REFORM!

YEARLY GENETIC TEST

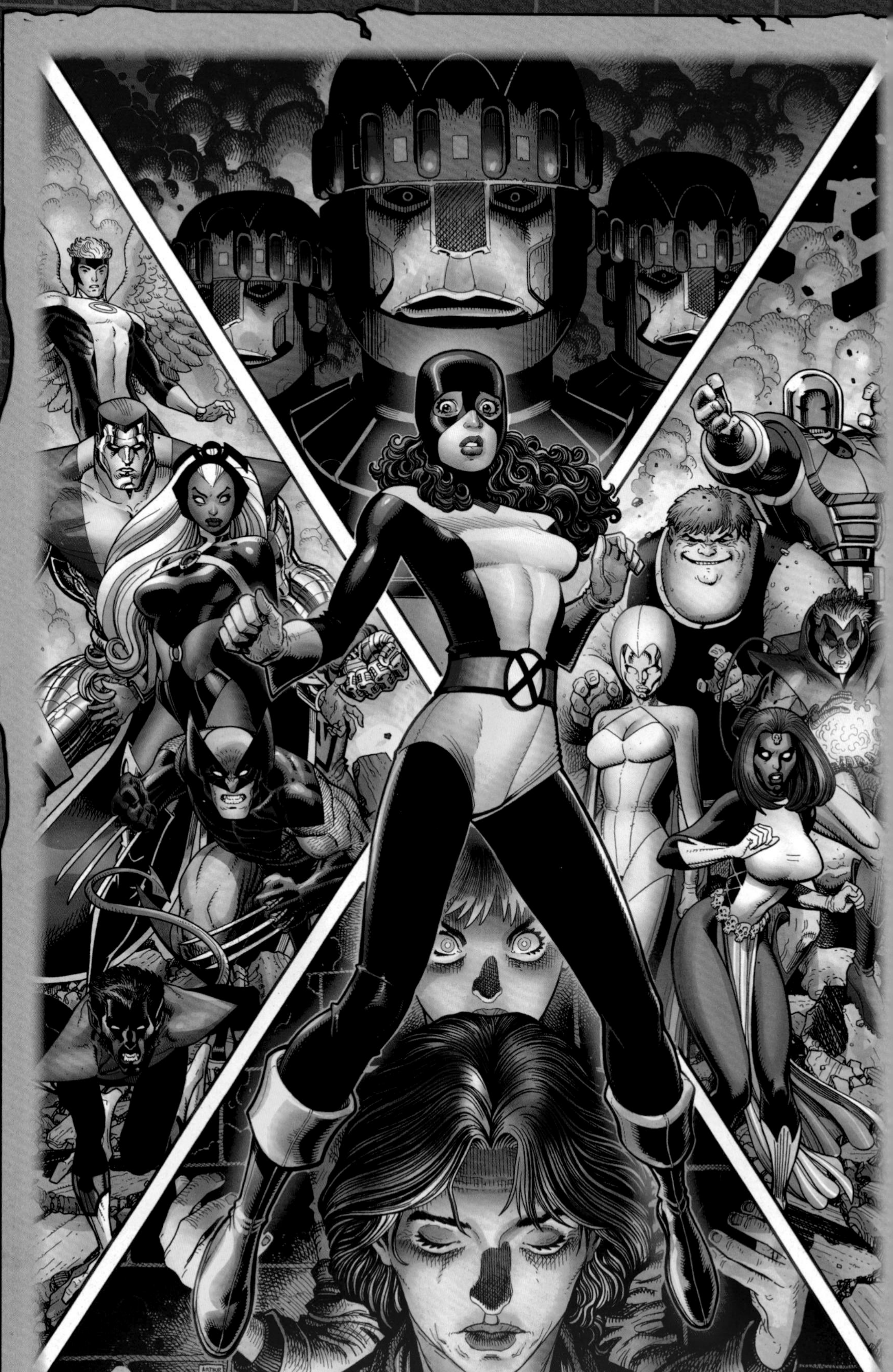

1

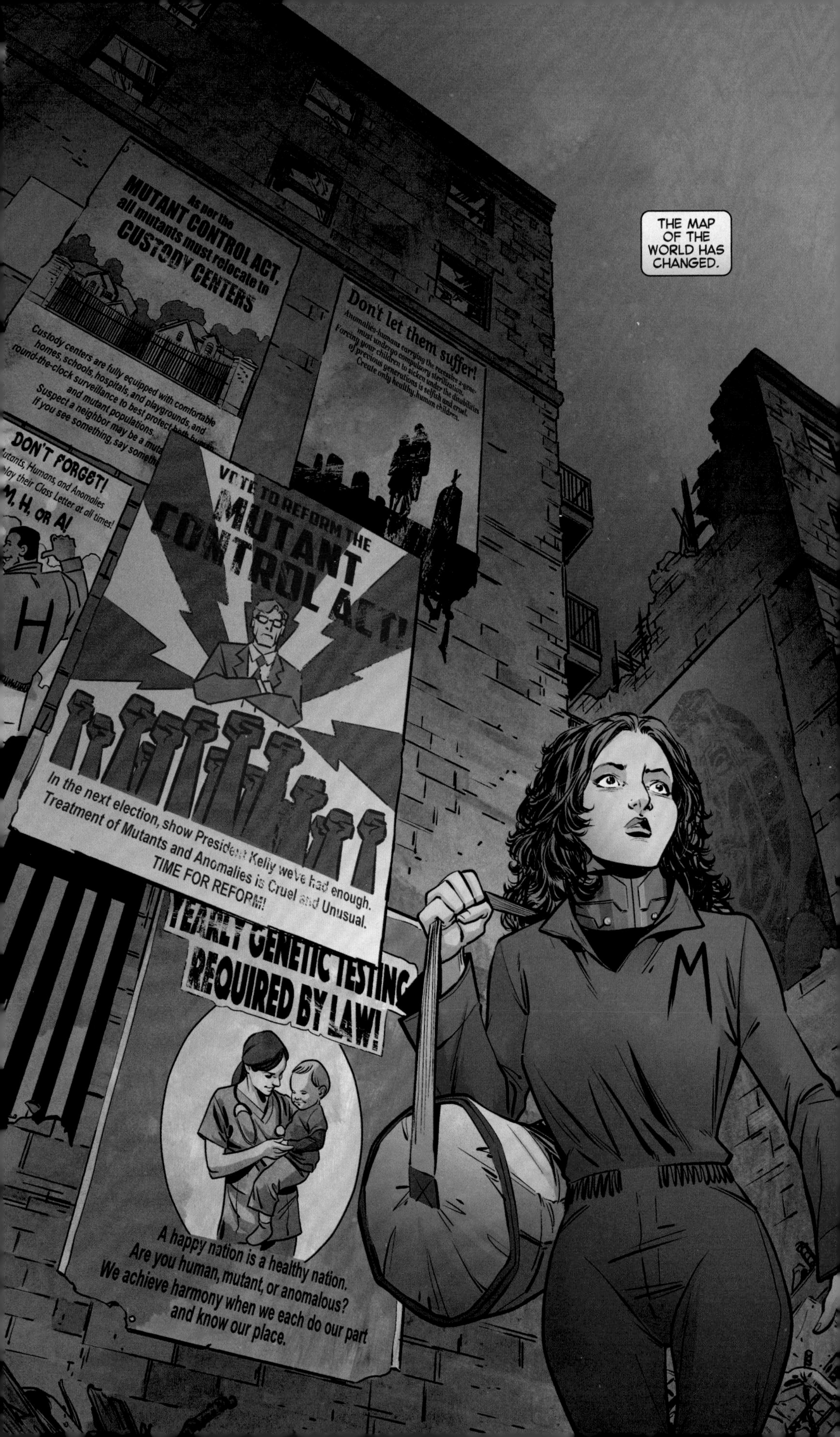

As per the
MUTANT CONTROL ACT,
all mutants must relocate to
CUSTODY CENTERS
Custody centers are fully equipped with comfortable homes, schools, hospitals, and playgrounds, and round-the-clock surveillance to best protect both huma
and mutant populations.
Suspect a neighbor may be a muta
If you see something, say someth
Don't let them suffer!
Anomalies-humans carrying the recessive x-gene-must undergo compulsory sterilization.
Forcing your children to sicken under the disabilities of previous generations is selfish and cruel.
Create only healthy, human children.
DON'T FORGET!
utants, Humans, and Anomalies
lay their Class Letter at all times!
M, H, OR A!
H
VOTE TO REFORM THE
MUTANT CONTROL ACT!
In the next election, show President Kelly we've had enough.
Treatment of Mutants and Anomalies is Cruel and Unusual.
TIME FOR REFORM!
YEARLY GENETIC TESTING
REQUIRED BY LAW!
A happy nation is a healthy nation.
Are you human, mutant, or anomalous?
We achieve harmony when we each do our part
and know our place.
M
THE MAP OF THE WORLD HAS CHANGED.

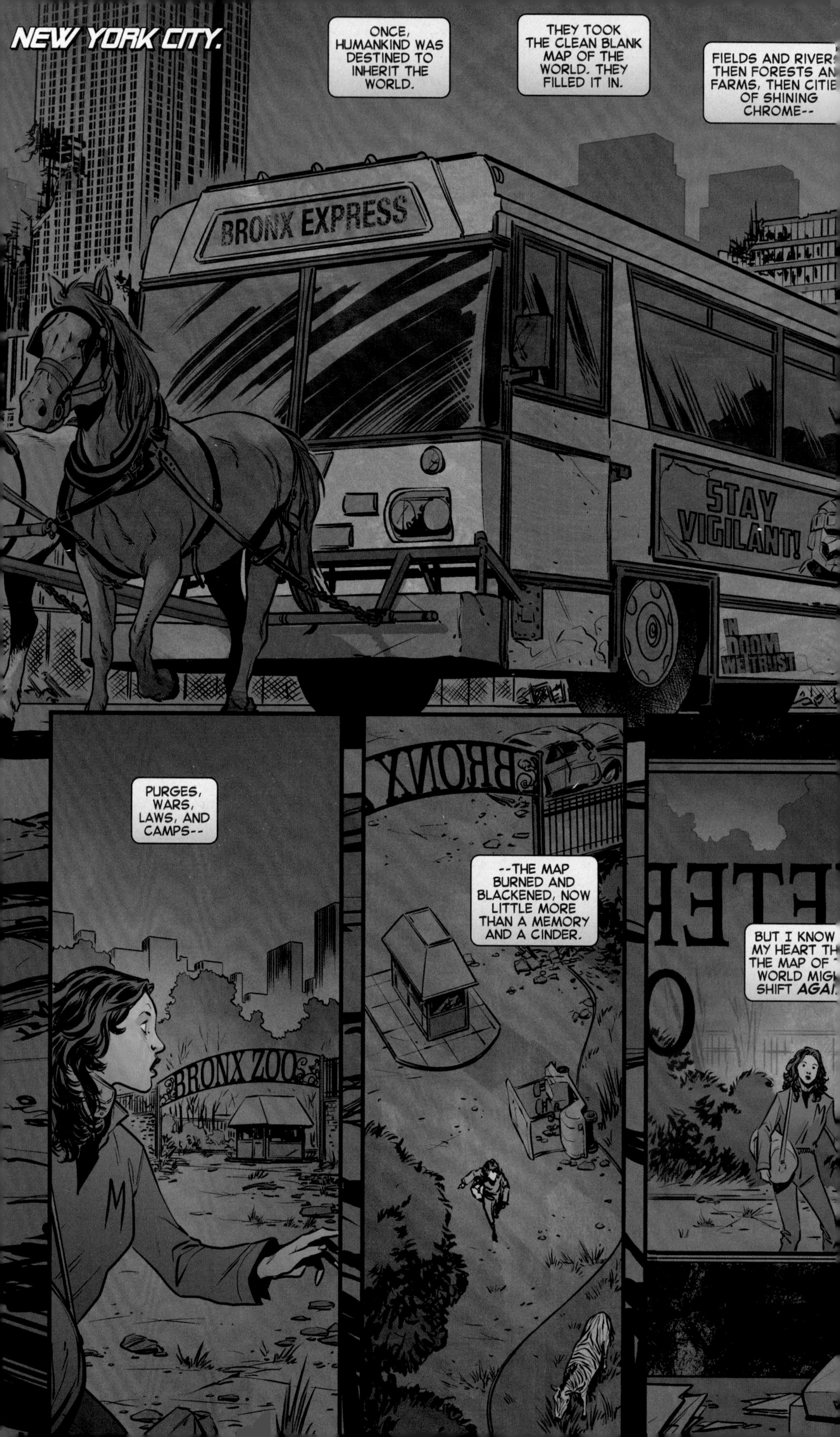
NEW YORK CITY.
ONCE, HUMANKIND WAS DESTINED TO INHERIT THE WORLD.
THEY TOOK THE CLEAN BLANK MAP OF THE WORLD. THEY FILLED IT IN.
FIELDS AND RIVERS THEN FORESTS AN FARMS, THEN CITIE OF SHINING CHROME--
BRONX EXPRESS
STAY VIGILANT!
IN DOOM WE TRUST
PURGES, WARS, LAWS, AND CAMPS--
BRONX ZOO
--THE MAP BURNED AND BLACKENED, NOW LITTLE MORE THAN A MEMORY AND A CINDER.
BUT I KNOW MY HEART TH THE MAP OF T WORLD MIG SHIFT AGAI

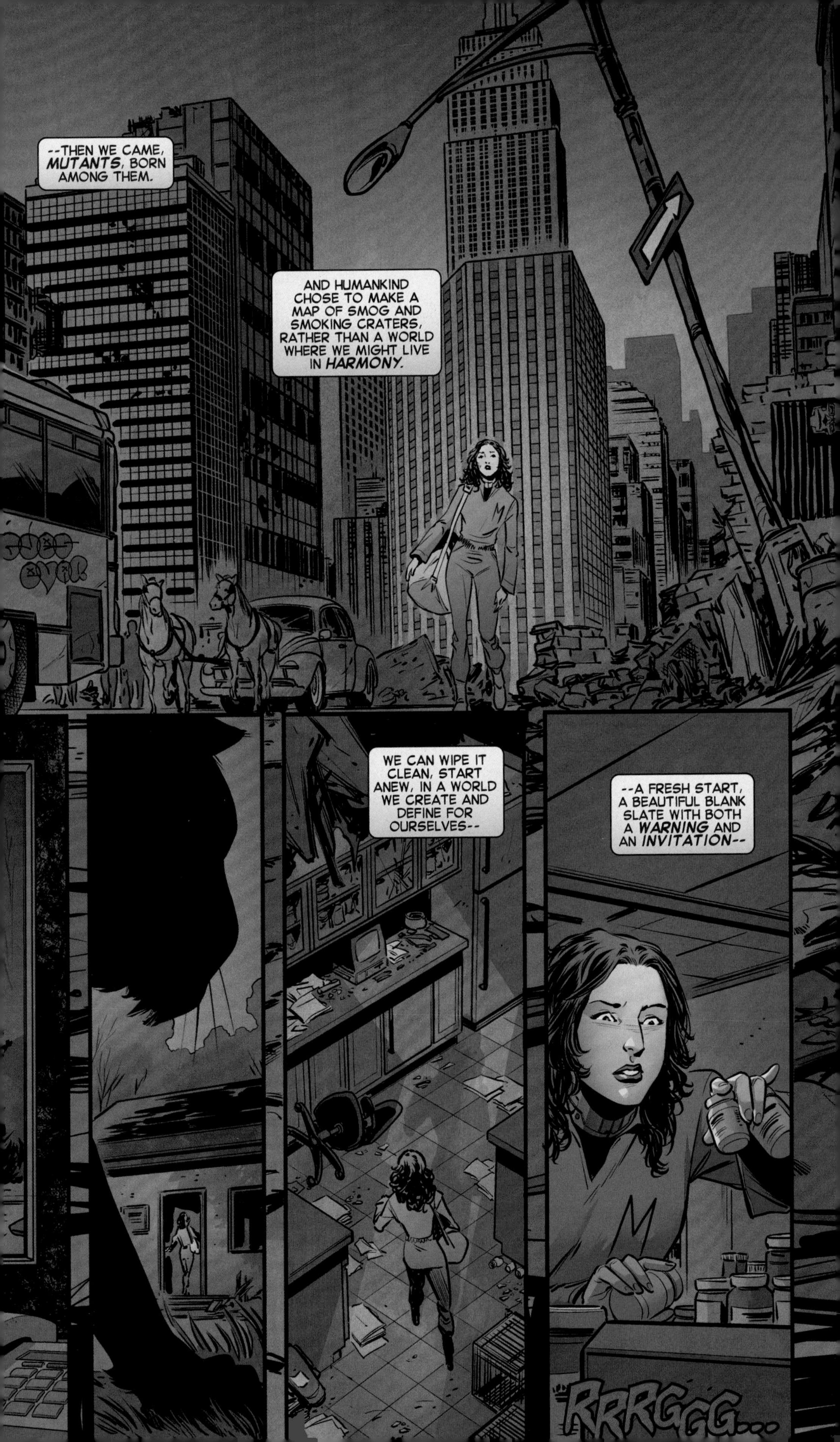
--THEN WE CAME, MUTANTS, BORN AMONG THEM.
AND HUMANKIND CHOSE TO MAKE A MAP OF SMOG AND SMOKING CRATERS, RATHER THAN A WORLD WHERE WE MIGHT LIVE IN HARMONY.
WE CAN WIPE IT CLEAN, START ANEW, IN A WORLD WE CREATE AND DEFINE FOR OURSELVES--
--A FRESH START, A BEAUTIFUL BLANK SLATE WITH BOTH A WARNING AND AN INVITATION--
RRRGGG...

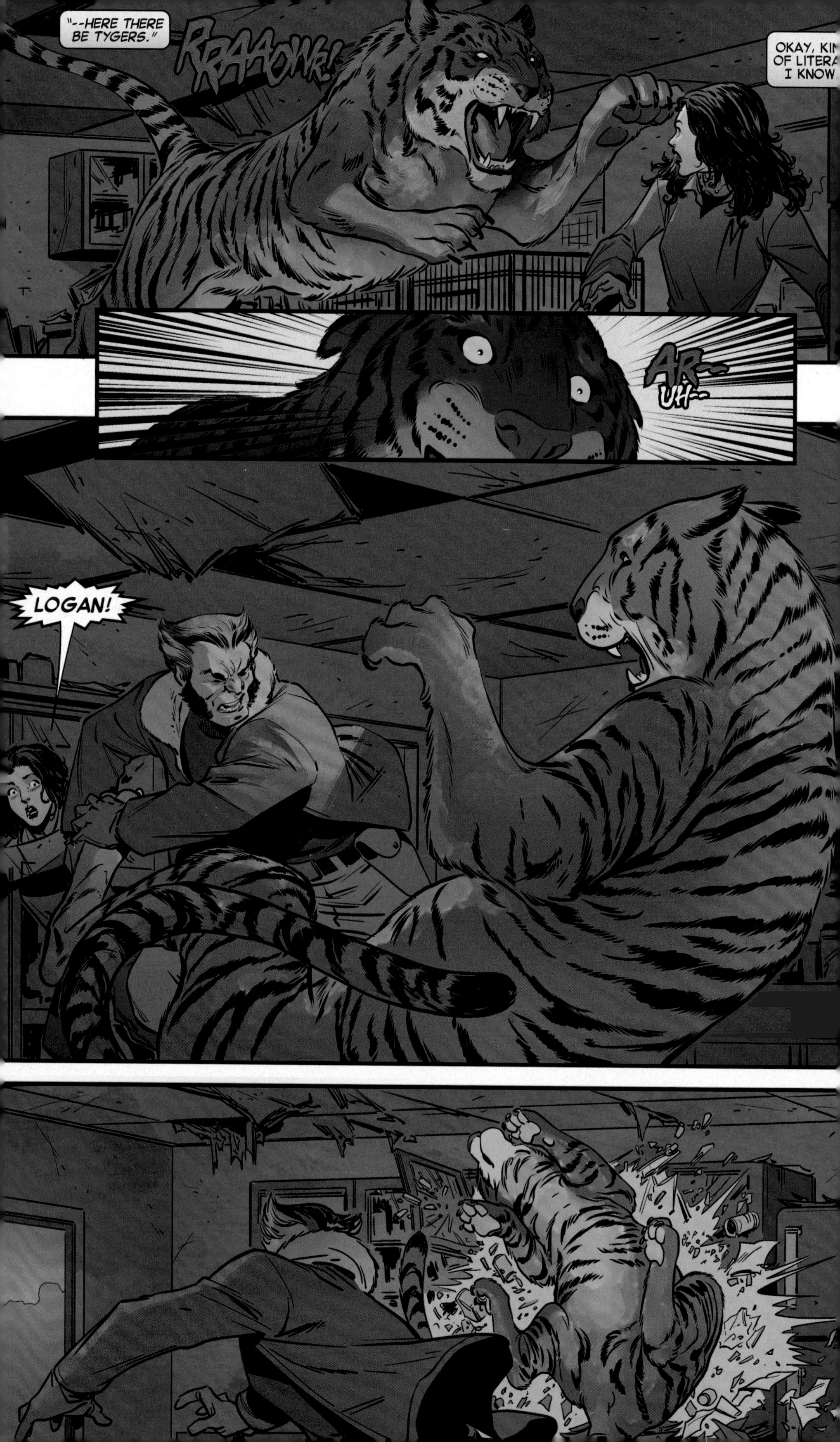
"--HERE THERE BE TYGERS."
RRAAOWR!
OKAY, KIN
OF LITERA
I KNOW.
AR--
UH--
LOGAN!

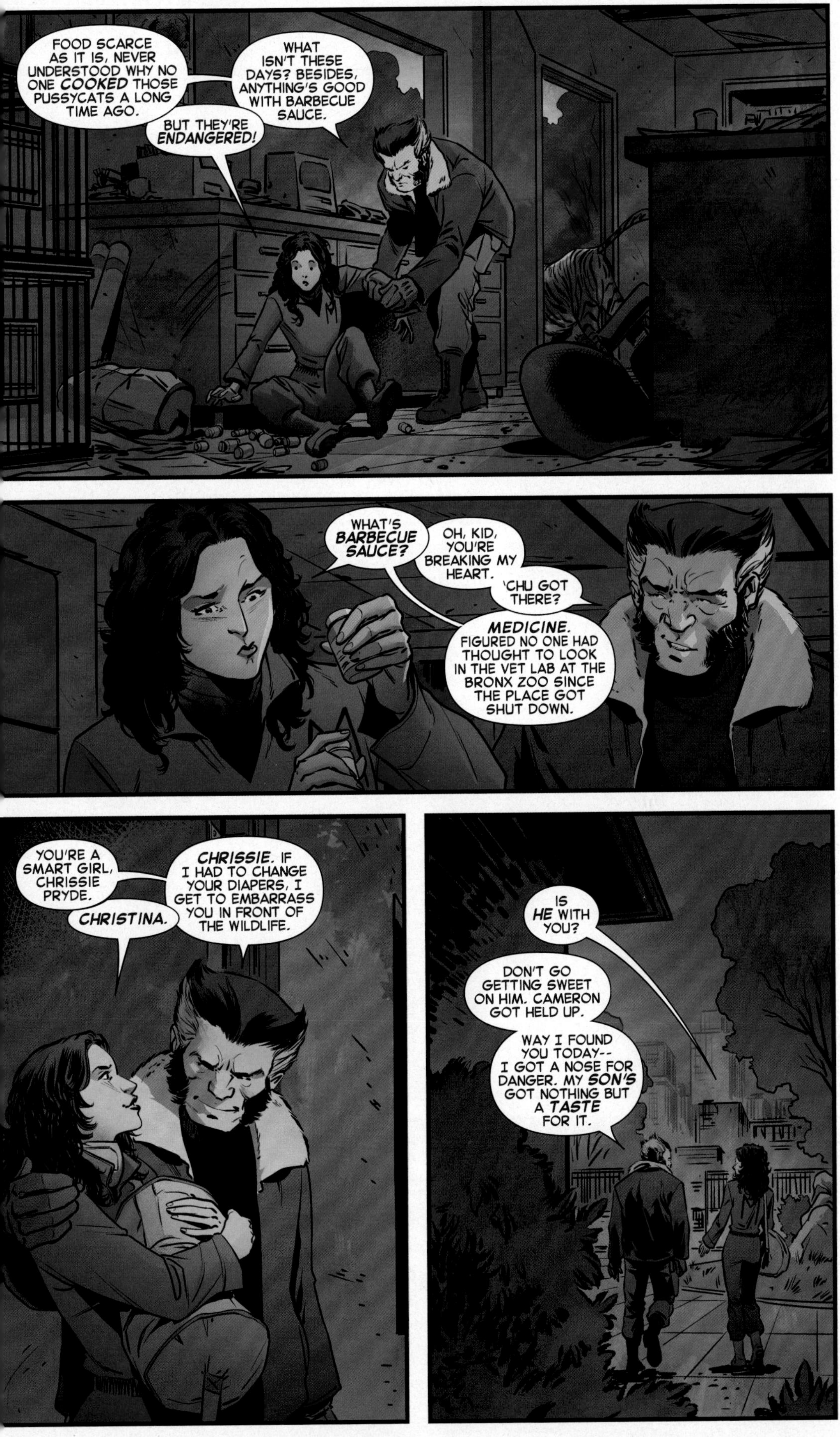
FOOD SCARCE AS IT IS, NEVER UNDERSTOOD WHY NO ONE COOKED THOSE PUSSYCATS A LONG TIME AGO.
BUT THEY'RE ENDANGERED!
WHAT ISN'T THESE DAYS? BESIDES, ANYTHING'S GOOD WITH BARBECUE SAUCE.
WHAT'S BARBECUE SAUCE?
OH, KID, YOU'RE BREAKING MY HEART.
'CHU GOT THERE?
MEDICINE. FIGURED NO ONE HAD THOUGHT TO LOOK IN THE VET LAB AT THE BRONX ZOO SINCE THE PLACE GOT SHUT DOWN.
YOU'RE A SMART GIRL, CHRISSIE PRYDE.
CHRISTINA.
CHRISSIE. IF I HAD TO CHANGE YOUR DIAPERS, I GET TO EMBARRASS YOU IN FRONT OF THE WILDLIFE.
IS HE WITH YOU?
DON'T GO GETTING SWEET ON HIM. CAMERON GOT HELD UP.
WAY I FOUND YOU TODAY-- I GOT A NOSE FOR DANGER. MY SON'S GOT NOTHING BUT A TASTE FOR IT.

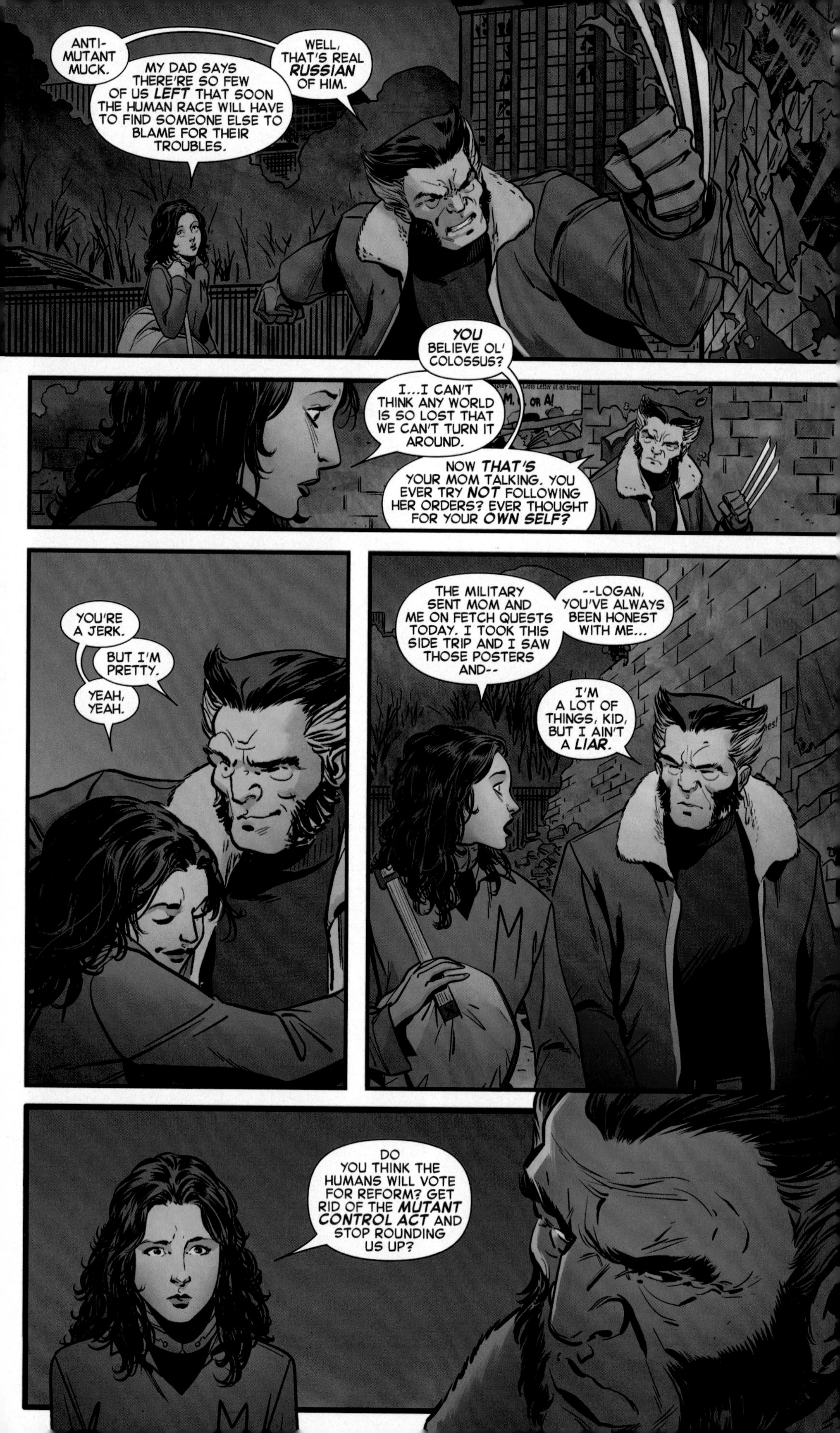
ANTI-MUTANT MUCK.
WELL, THAT'S REAL RUSSIAN OF HIM.
MY DAD SAYS THERE'RE SO FEW OF US LEFT THAT SOON THE HUMAN RACE WILL HAVE TO FIND SOMEONE ELSE TO BLAME FOR THEIR TROUBLES.
YOU BELIEVE OL' COLOSSUS?
I...I CAN'T THINK ANY WORLD IS SO LOST THAT WE CAN'T TURN IT AROUND.
NOW THAT'S YOUR MOM TALKING. YOU EVER TRY NOT FOLLOWING HER ORDERS? EVER THOUGHT FOR YOUR OWN SELF?
YOU'RE A JERK.
BUT I'M PRETTY.
YEAH, YEAH.
THE MILITARY SENT MOM AND ME ON FETCH QUESTS TODAY. I TOOK THIS SIDE TRIP AND I SAW THOSE POSTERS AND--
--LOGAN, YOU'VE ALWAYS BEEN HONEST WITH ME...
I'M A LOT OF THINGS, KID, BUT I AIN'T A LIAR.
DO YOU THINK THE HUMANS WILL VOTE FOR REFORM? GET RID OF THE MUTANT CONTROL ACT AND STOP ROUNDING US UP?

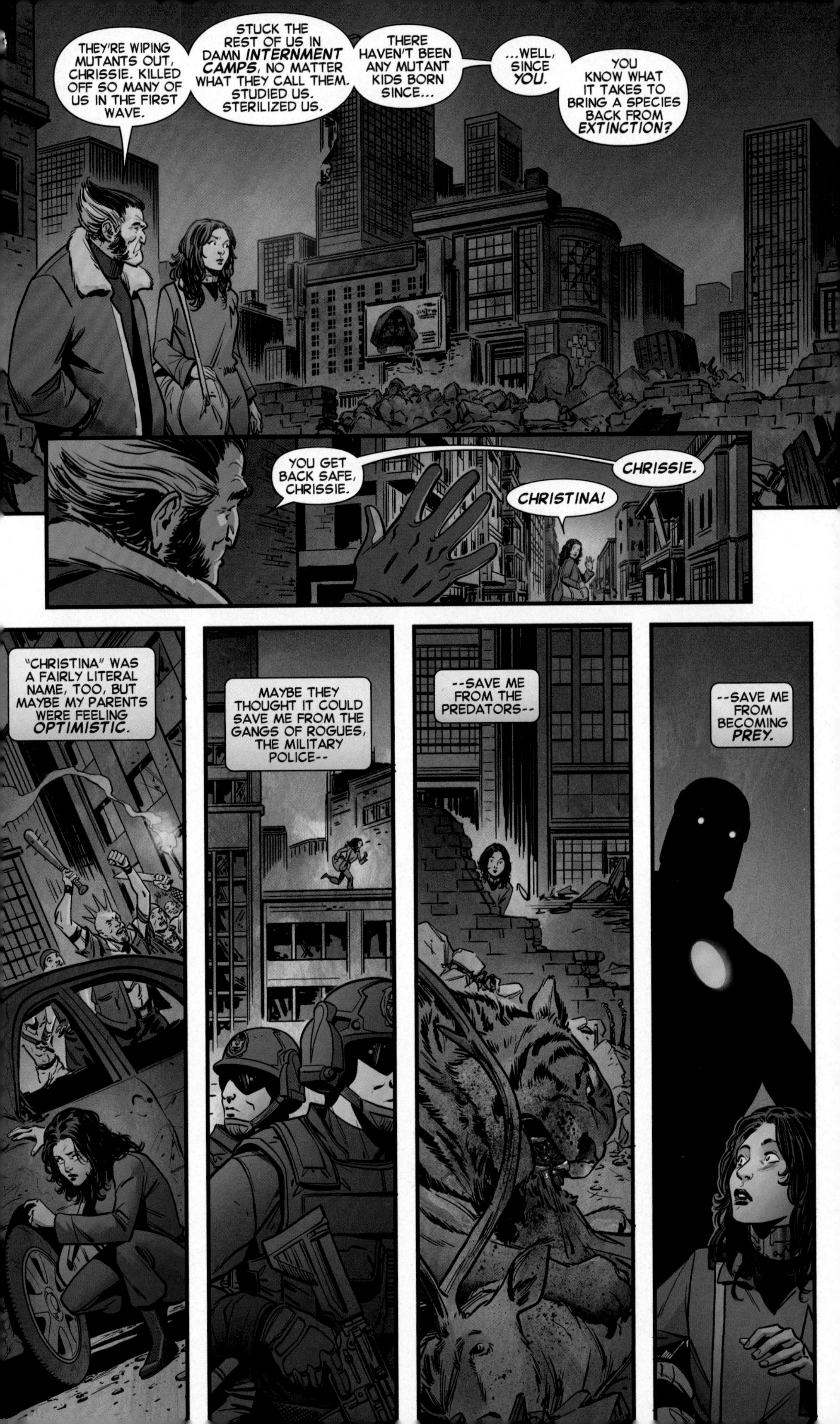

THEY'RE WIPING MUTANTS OUT, CHRISSIE. KILLED OFF SO MANY OF US IN THE FIRST WAVE.
STUCK THE REST OF US IN DAMN INTERNMENT CAMPS, NO MATTER WHAT THEY CALL THEM. STUDIED US. STERILIZED US.
THERE HAVEN'T BEEN ANY MUTANT KIDS BORN SINCE...
...WELL, SINCE YOU.
YOU KNOW WHAT IT TAKES TO BRING A SPECIES BACK FROM EXTINCTION?
YOU GET BACK SAFE, CHRISSIE.
CHRISSIE.
CHRISTINA!
"CHRISTINA" WAS A FAIRLY LITERAL NAME, TOO, BUT MAYBE MY PARENTS WERE FEELING OPTIMISTIC.
MAYBE THEY THOUGHT IT COULD SAVE ME FROM THE GANGS OF ROGUES, THE MILITARY POLICE--
--SAVE ME FROM THE PREDATORS--
--SAVE ME FROM BECOMING PREY.

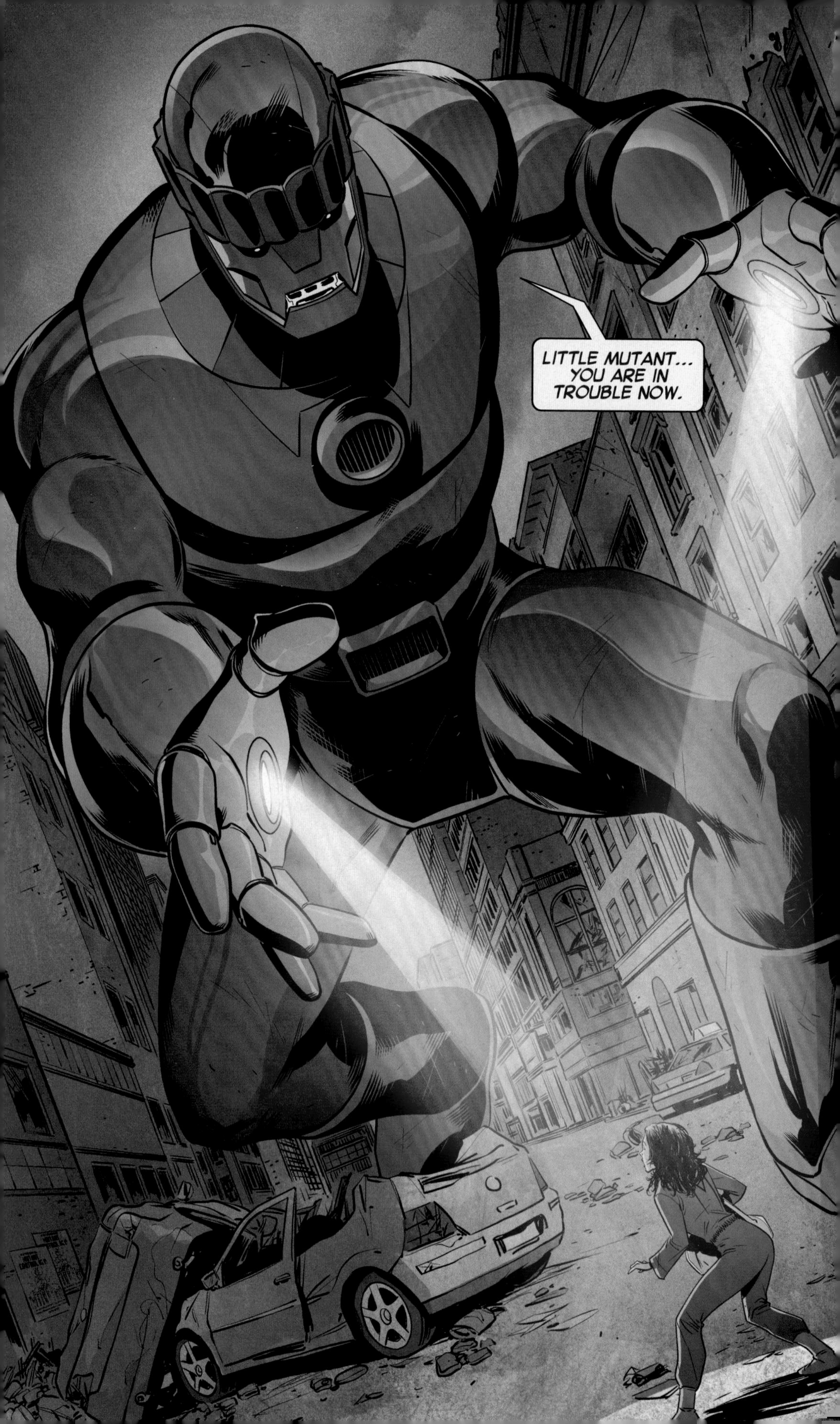
LITTLE MUTANT... YOU ARE IN TROUBLE NOW.

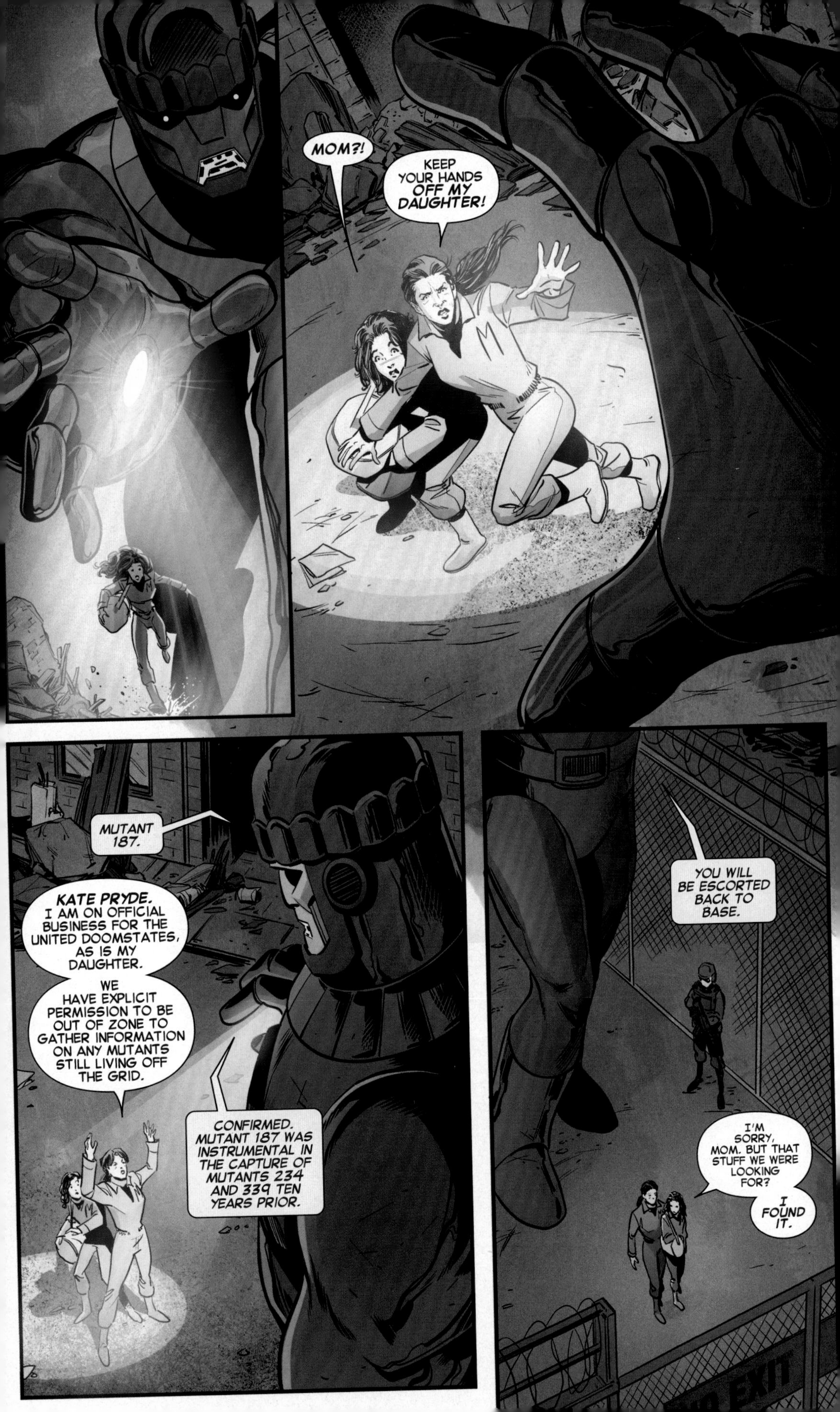
MOM?!
KEEP YOUR HANDS OFF MY DAUGHTER!
MUTANT 187.
KATE PRYDE. I AM ON OFFICIAL BUSINESS FOR THE UNITED DOOMSTATES, AS IS MY DAUGHTER.
WE HAVE EXPLICIT PERMISSION TO BE OUT OF ZONE TO GATHER INFORMATION ON ANY MUTANTS STILL LIVING OFF THE GRID.
CONFIRMED. MUTANT 187 WAS INSTRUMENTAL IN THE CAPTURE OF MUTANTS 234 AND 339 TEN YEARS PRIOR.
YOU WILL BE ESCORTED BACK TO BASE.
I'M SORRY, MOM. BUT THAT STUFF WE WERE LOOKING FOR?
I FOUND IT.

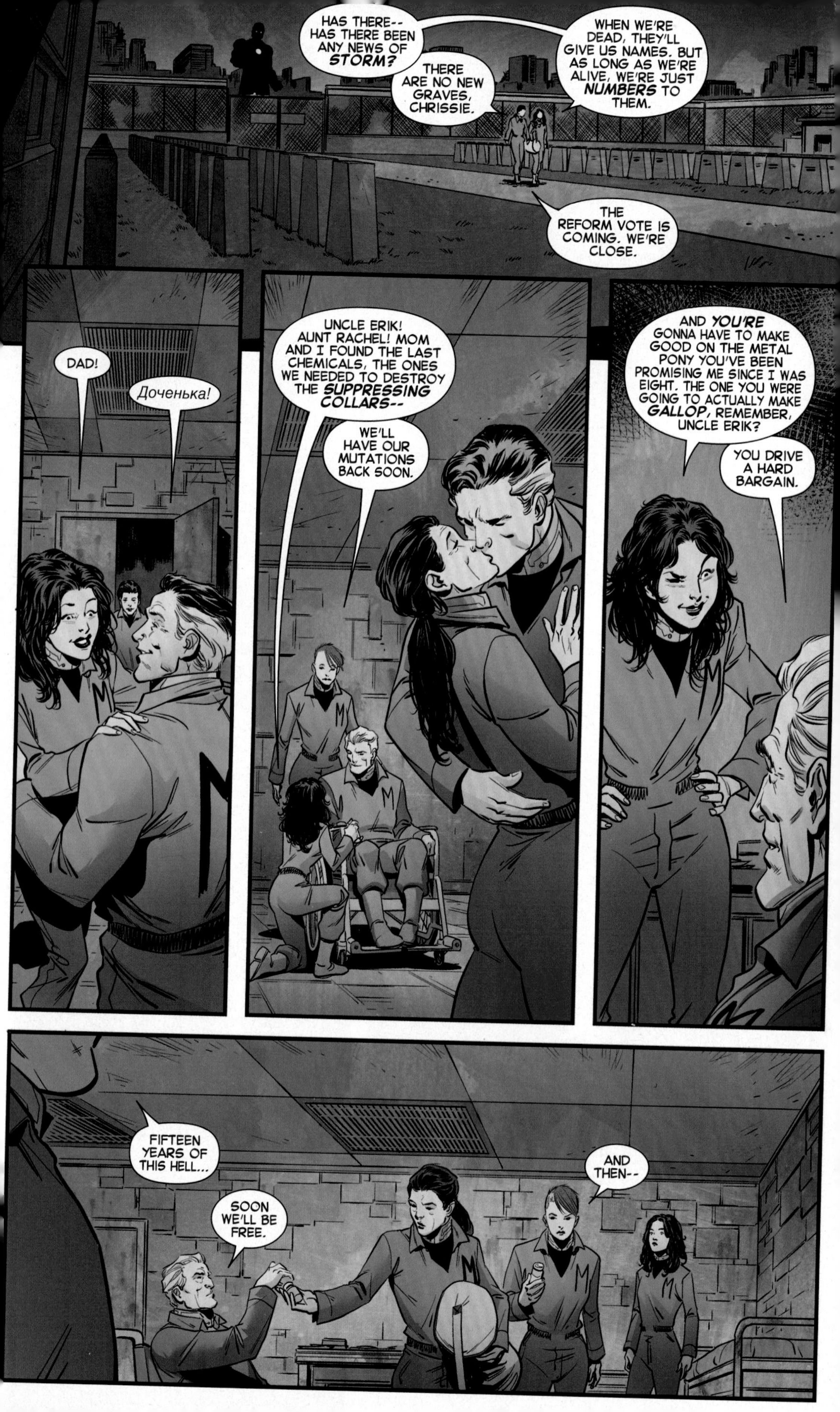

HAS THERE-- HAS THERE BEEN ANY NEWS OF STORM?
THERE ARE NO NEW GRAVES, CHRISSIE.
WHEN WE'RE DEAD, THEY'LL GIVE US NAMES. BUT AS LONG AS WE'RE ALIVE, WE'RE JUST NUMBERS TO THEM.
THE REFORM VOTE IS COMING. WE'RE CLOSE.
DAD!
Доченька!
UNCLE ERIK! AUNT RACHEL! MOM AND I FOUND THE LAST CHEMICALS, THE ONES WE NEEDED TO DESTROY THE SUPPRESSING COLLARS--
WE'LL HAVE OUR MUTATIONS BACK SOON.
AND YOU'RE GONNA HAVE TO MAKE GOOD ON THE METAL PONY YOU'VE BEEN PROMISING ME SINCE I WAS EIGHT. THE ONE YOU WERE GOING TO ACTUALLY MAKE GALLOP, REMEMBER, UNCLE ERIK?
YOU DRIVE A HARD BARGAIN.
FIFTEEN YEARS OF THIS HELL...
SOON WE'LL BE FREE.
AND THEN--

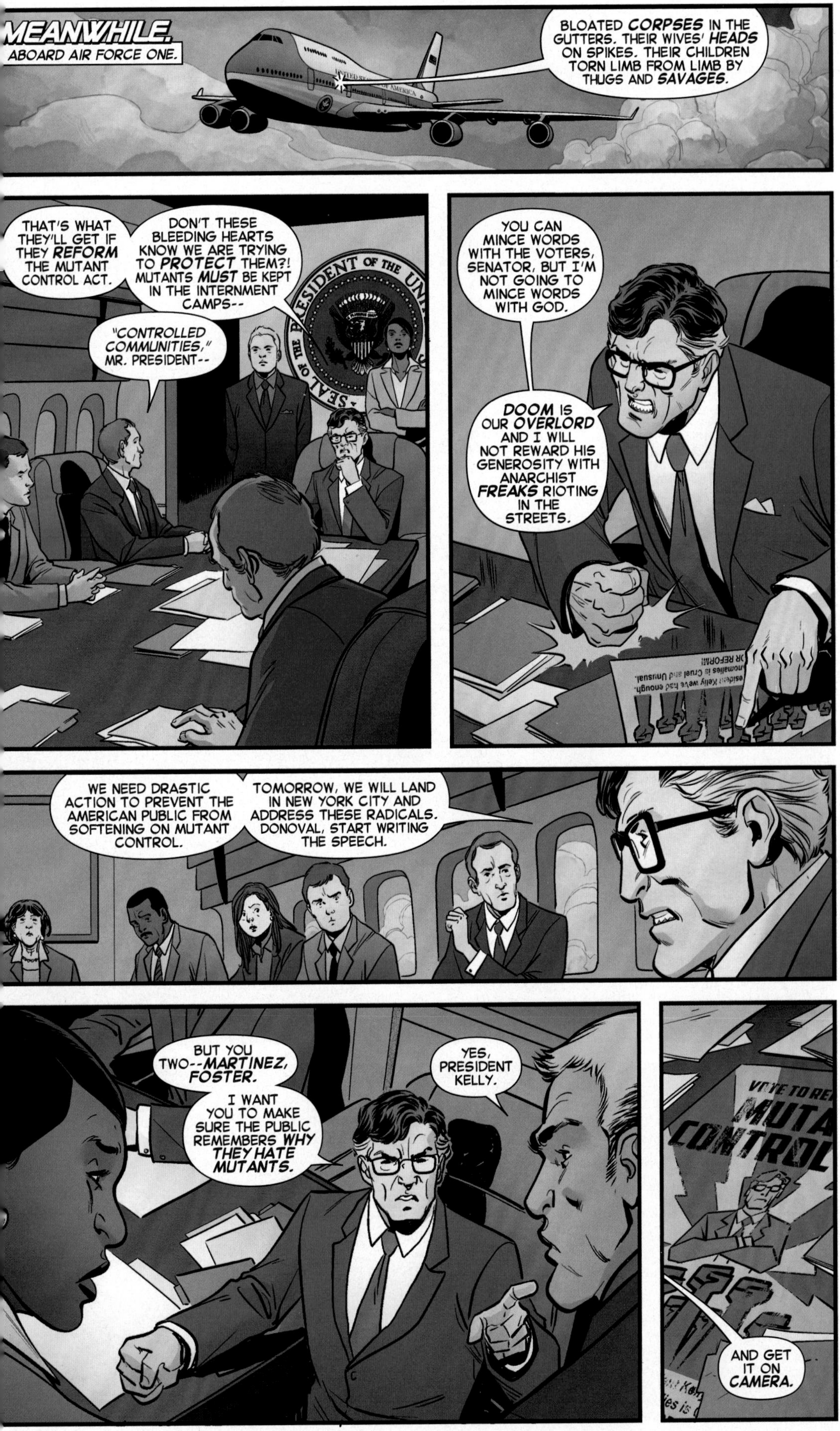
MEANWHILE. ABOARD AIR FORCE ONE.
BLOATED CORPSES IN THE GUTTERS. THEIR WIVES' HEADS ON SPIKES. THEIR CHILDREN TORN LIMB FROM LIMB BY THUGS AND SAVAGES.
THAT'S WHAT THEY'LL GET IF THEY REFORM THE MUTANT CONTROL ACT.
DON'T THESE BLEEDING HEARTS KNOW WE ARE TRYING TO PROTECT THEM?! MUTANTS MUST BE KEPT IN THE INTERNMENT CAMPS--
"CONTROLLED COMMUNITIES," MR. PRESIDENT--
YOU CAN MINCE WORDS WITH THE VOTERS, SENATOR, BUT I'M NOT GOING TO MINCE WORDS WITH GOD.
DOOM IS OUR OVERLORD AND I WILL NOT REWARD HIS GENEROSITY WITH ANARCHIST FREAKS RIOTING IN THE STREETS.
WE NEED DRASTIC ACTION TO PREVENT THE AMERICAN PUBLIC FROM SOFTENING ON MUTANT CONTROL.
TOMORROW, WE WILL LAND IN NEW YORK CITY AND ADDRESS THESE RADICALS. DONOVAL, START WRITING THE SPEECH.
BUT YOU TWO--MARTINEZ, FOSTER.
I WANT YOU TO MAKE SURE THE PUBLIC REMEMBERS WHY THEY HATE MUTANTS.
YES, PRESIDENT KELLY.
AND GET IT ON CAMERA.

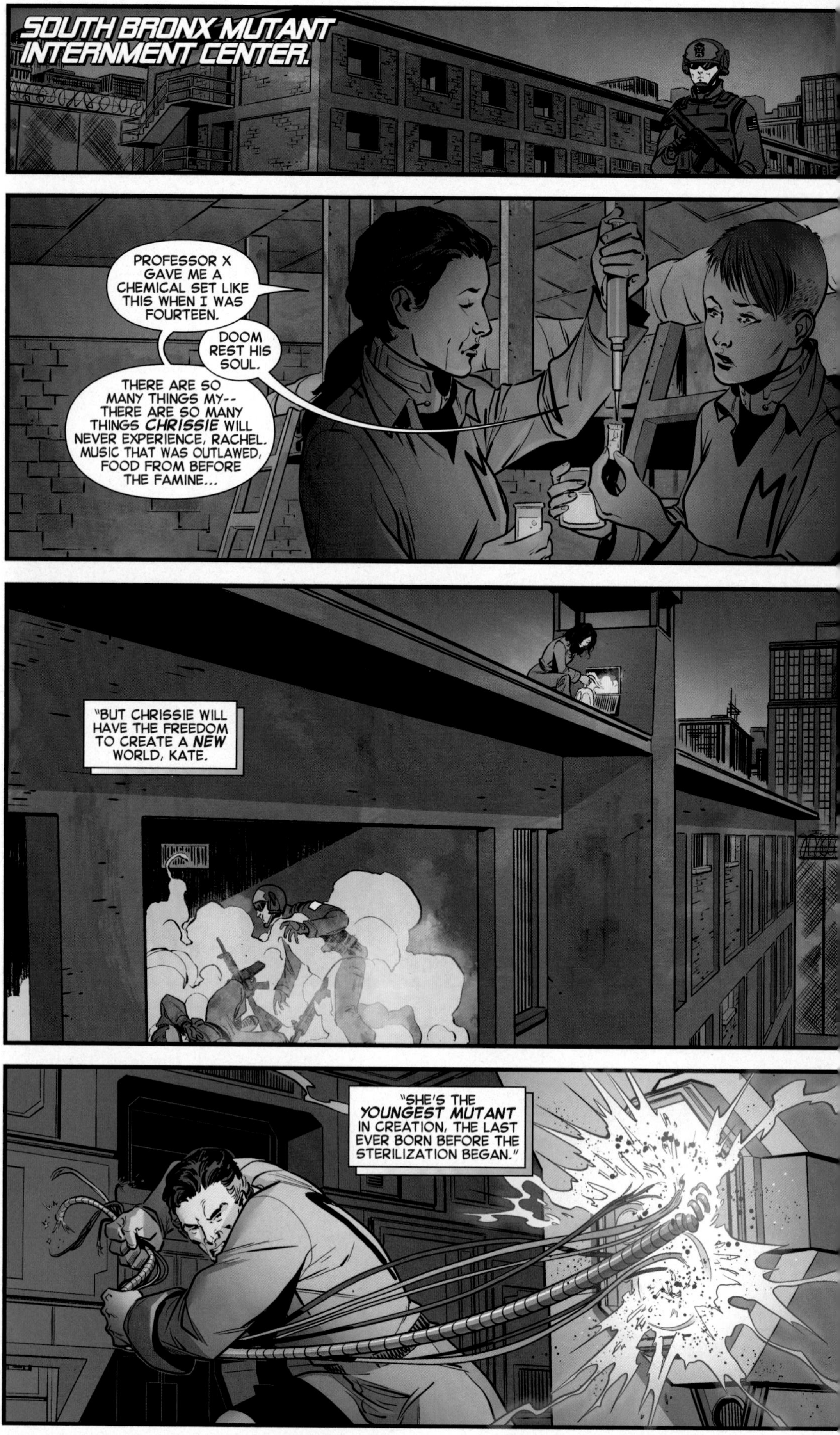
SOUTH BRONX MUTANT INTERNMENT CENTER.
PROFESSOR X GAVE ME A CHEMICAL SET LIKE THIS WHEN I WAS FOURTEEN.
DOOM REST HIS SOUL.
THERE ARE SO MANY THINGS MY-- THERE ARE SO MANY THINGS CHRISSIE WILL NEVER EXPERIENCE, RACHEL. MUSIC THAT WAS OUTLAWED, FOOD FROM BEFORE THE FAMINE...
"BUT CHRISSIE WILL HAVE THE FREEDOM TO CREATE A NEW WORLD, KATE.
"SHE'S THE YOUNGEST MUTANT IN CREATION, THE LAST EVER BORN BEFORE THE STERILIZATION BEGAN."

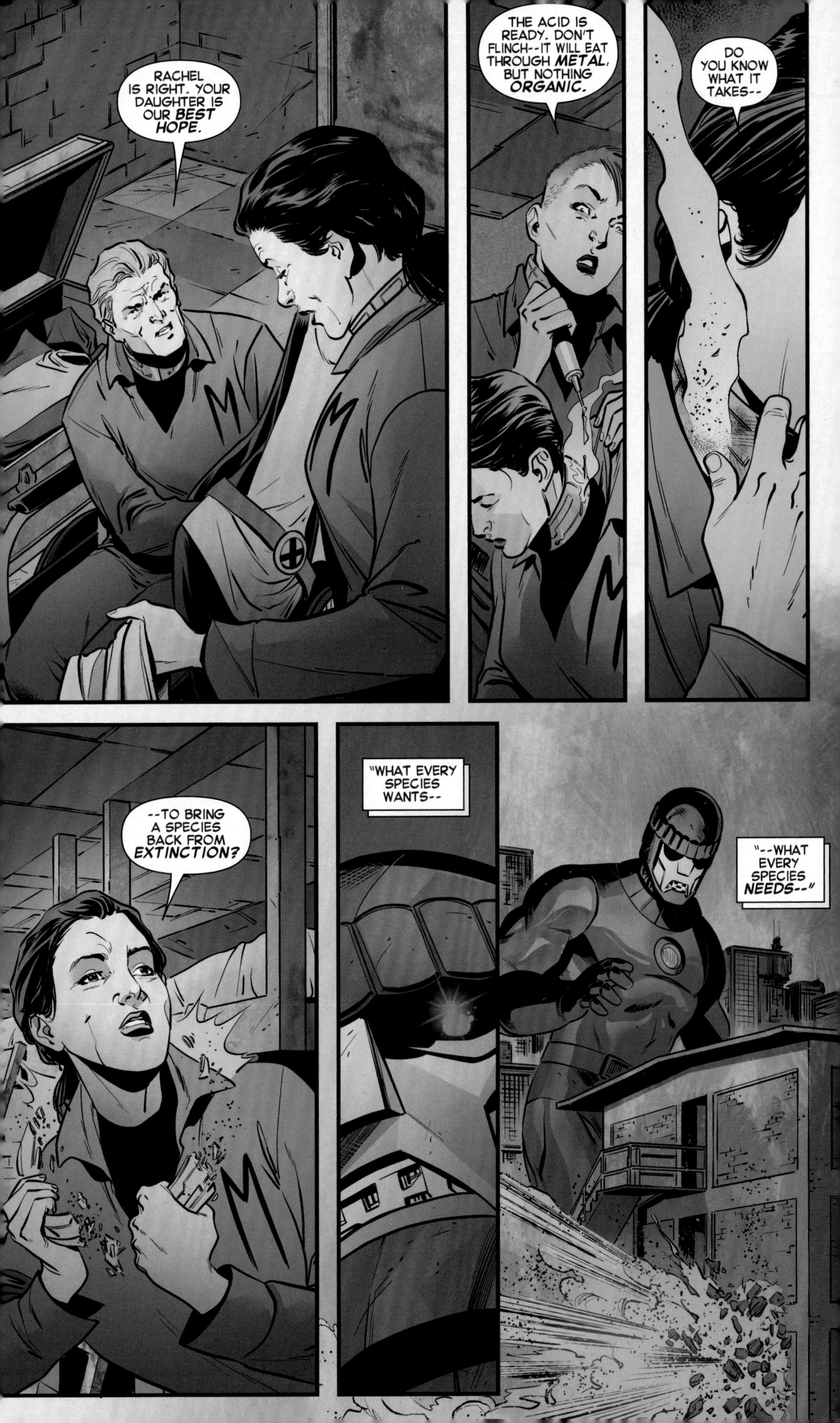
RACHEL IS RIGHT. YOUR DAUGHTER IS OUR BEST HOPE.
THE ACID IS READY. DON'T FLINCH--IT WILL EAT THROUGH METAL, BUT NOTHING ORGANIC.
DO YOU KNOW WHAT IT TAKES--
--TO BRING A SPECIES BACK FROM EXTINCTION?
"WHAT EVERY SPECIES WANTS--
"--WHAT EVERY SPECIES NEEDS--"

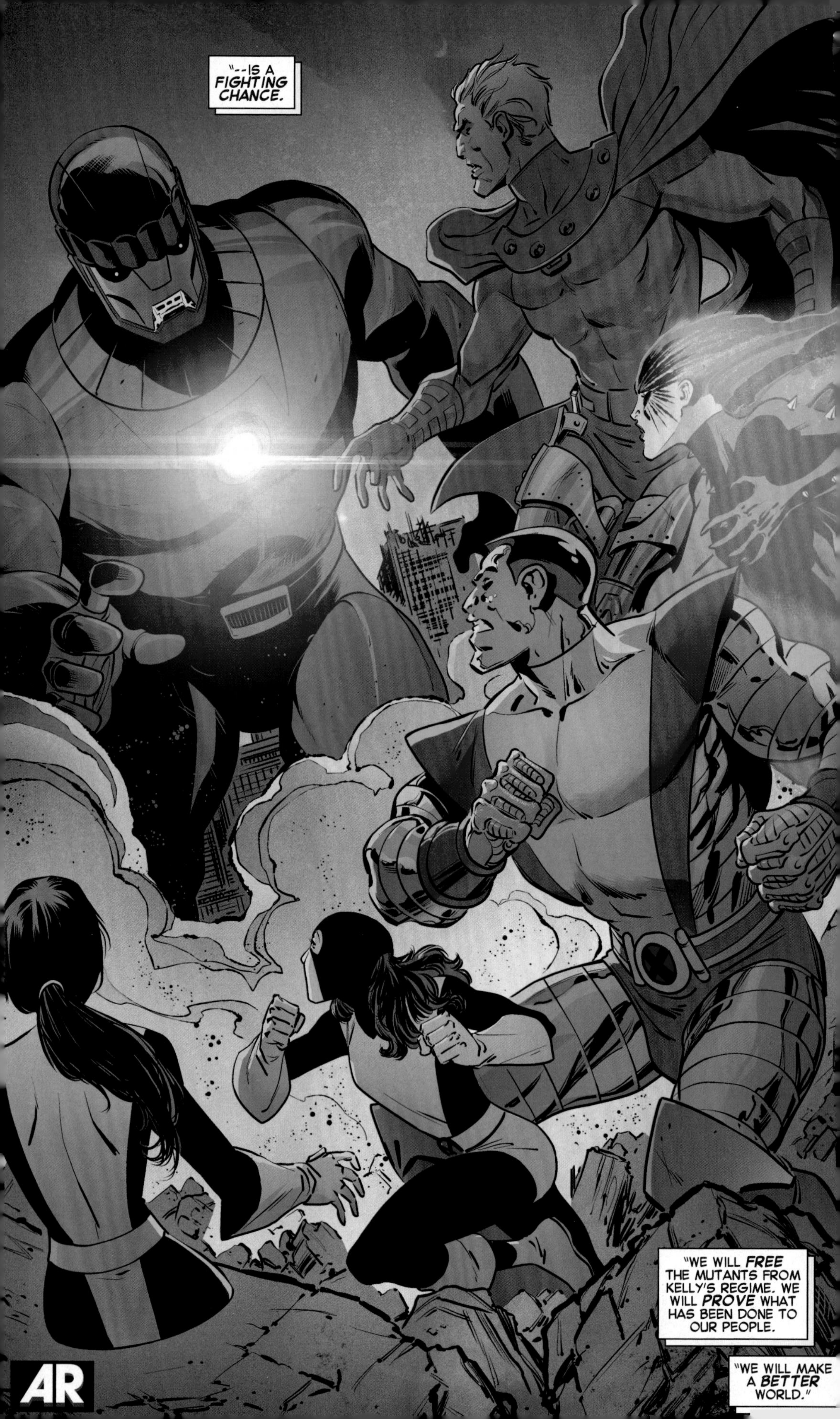
"--IS A FIGHTING CHANCE.
"WE WILL FREE THE MUTANTS FROM KELLY'S REGIME. WE WILL PROVE WHAT HAS BEEN DONE TO OUR PEOPLE.
"WE WILL MAKE A BETTER WORLD."

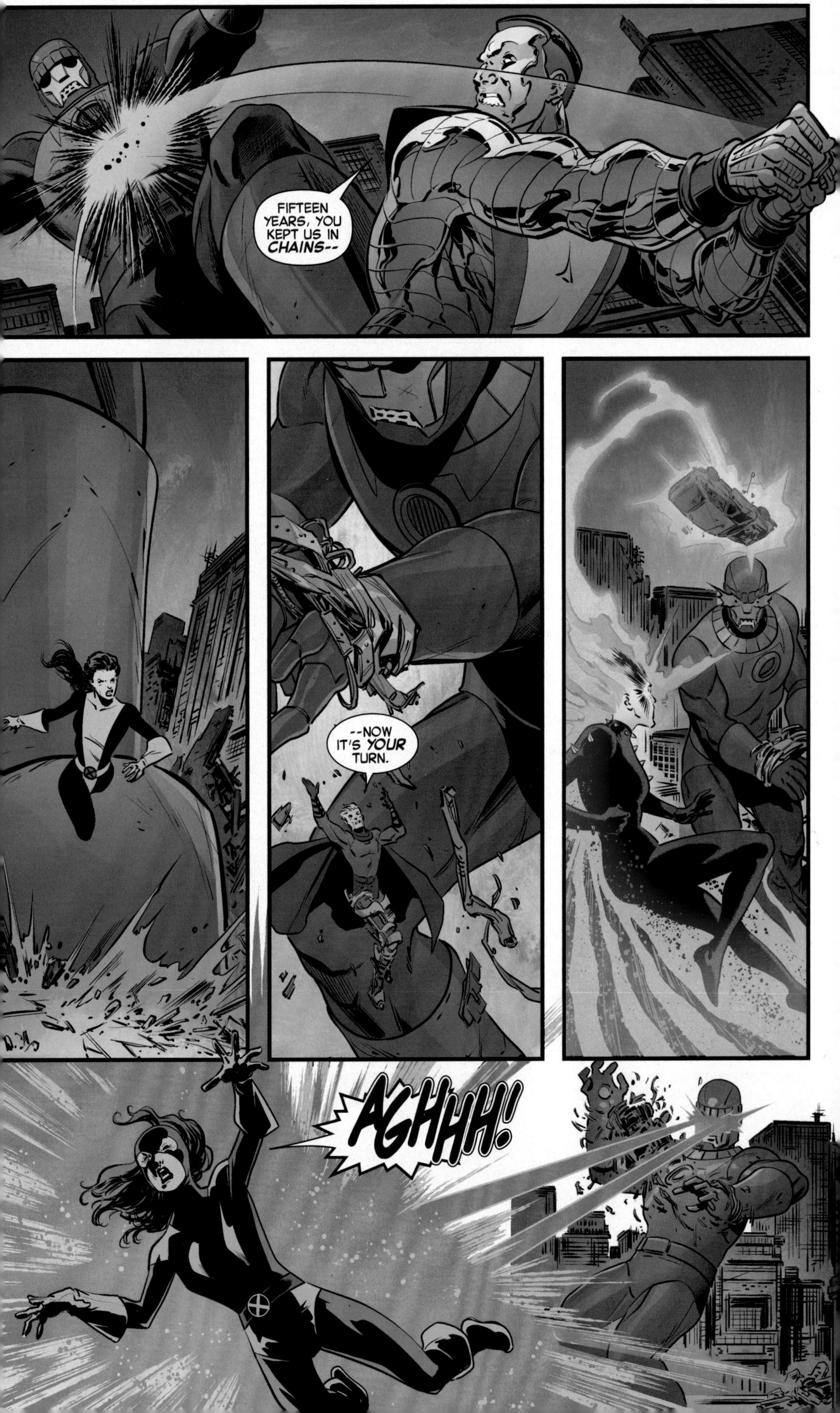
FIFTEEN YEARS, YOU KEPT US IN CHAINS--
--NOW IT'S YOUR TURN.
AGHHH!

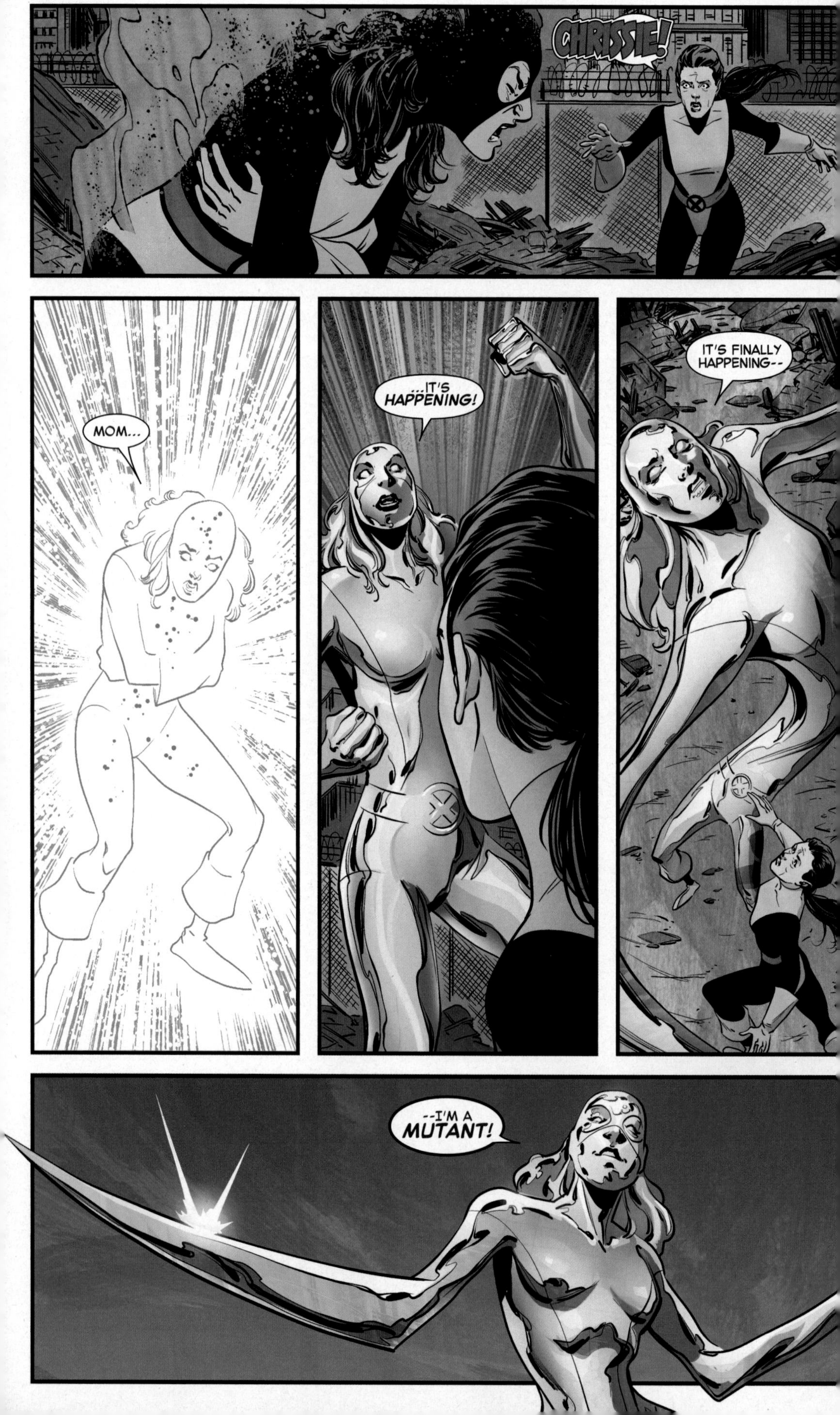
CHRISSIE!
MOM...
...IT'S HAPPENING!
IT'S FINALLY HAPPENING--
--I'M A MUTANT!

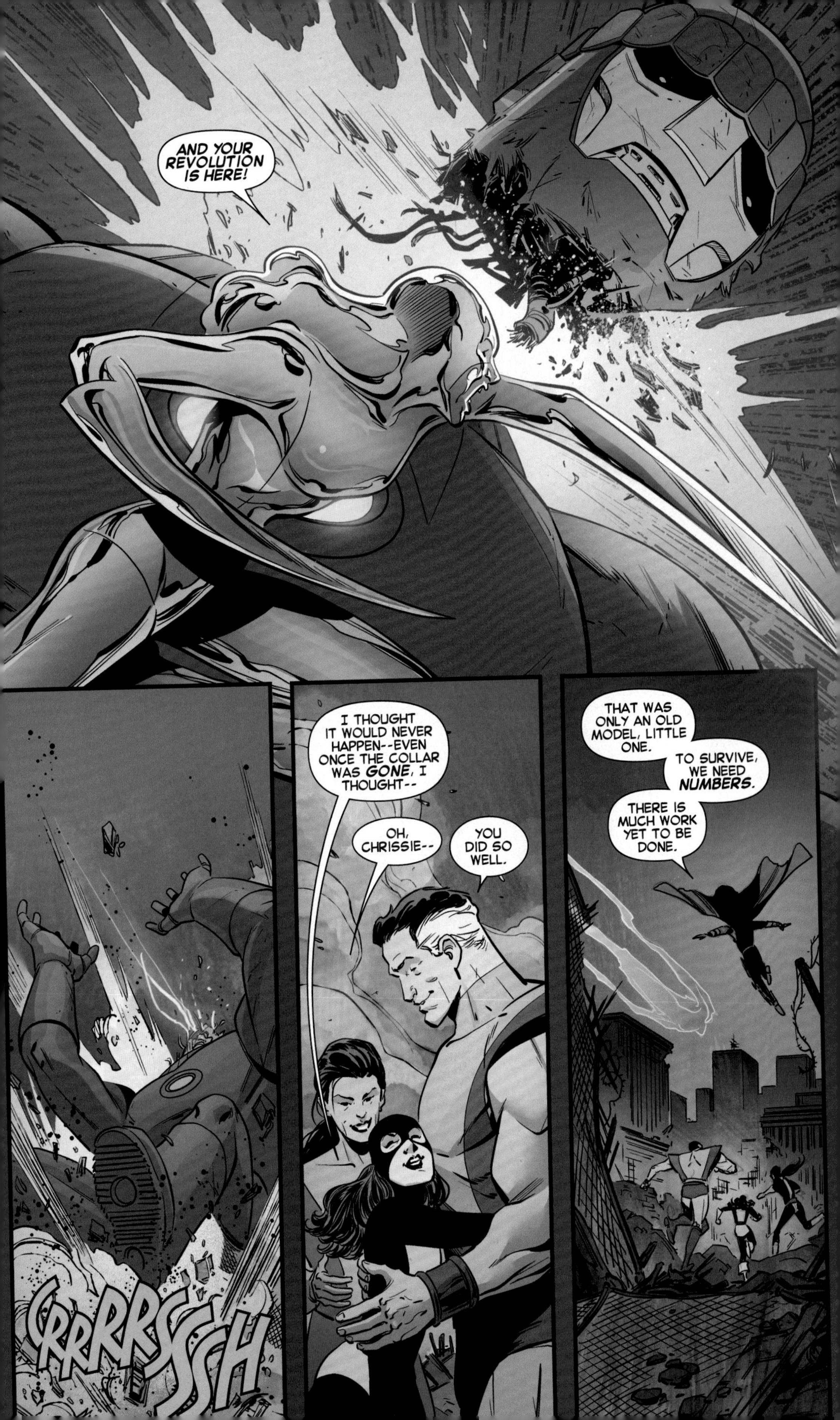
AND YOUR REVOLUTION IS HERE!
CRRRRSSSH
I THOUGHT IT WOULD NEVER HAPPEN--EVEN ONCE THE COLLAR WAS GONE, I THOUGHT--
OH, CHRISSIE--
YOU DID SO WELL.
THAT WAS ONLY AN OLD MODEL, LITTLE ONE.
TO SURVIVE, WE NEED NUMBERS.
THERE IS MUCH WORK YET TO BE DONE.

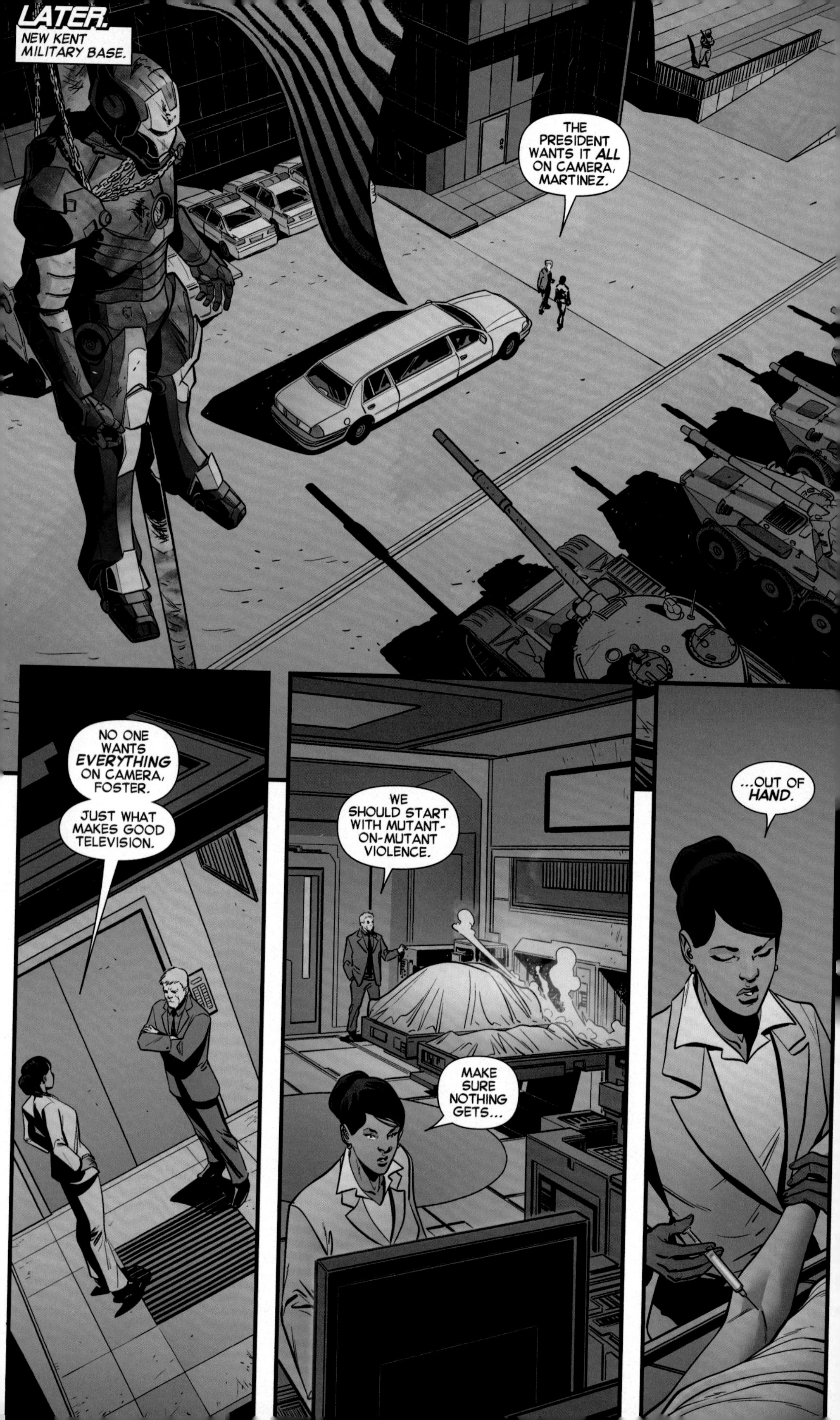
LATER.
NEW KENT MILITARY BASE.
THE PRESIDENT WANTS IT ALL ON CAMERA, MARTINEZ.
NO ONE WANTS EVERYTHING ON CAMERA, FOSTER.
JUST WHAT MAKES GOOD TELEVISION.
WE SHOULD START WITH MUTANT-ON-MUTANT VIOLENCE.
MAKE SURE NOTHING GETS...
...OUT OF HAND.

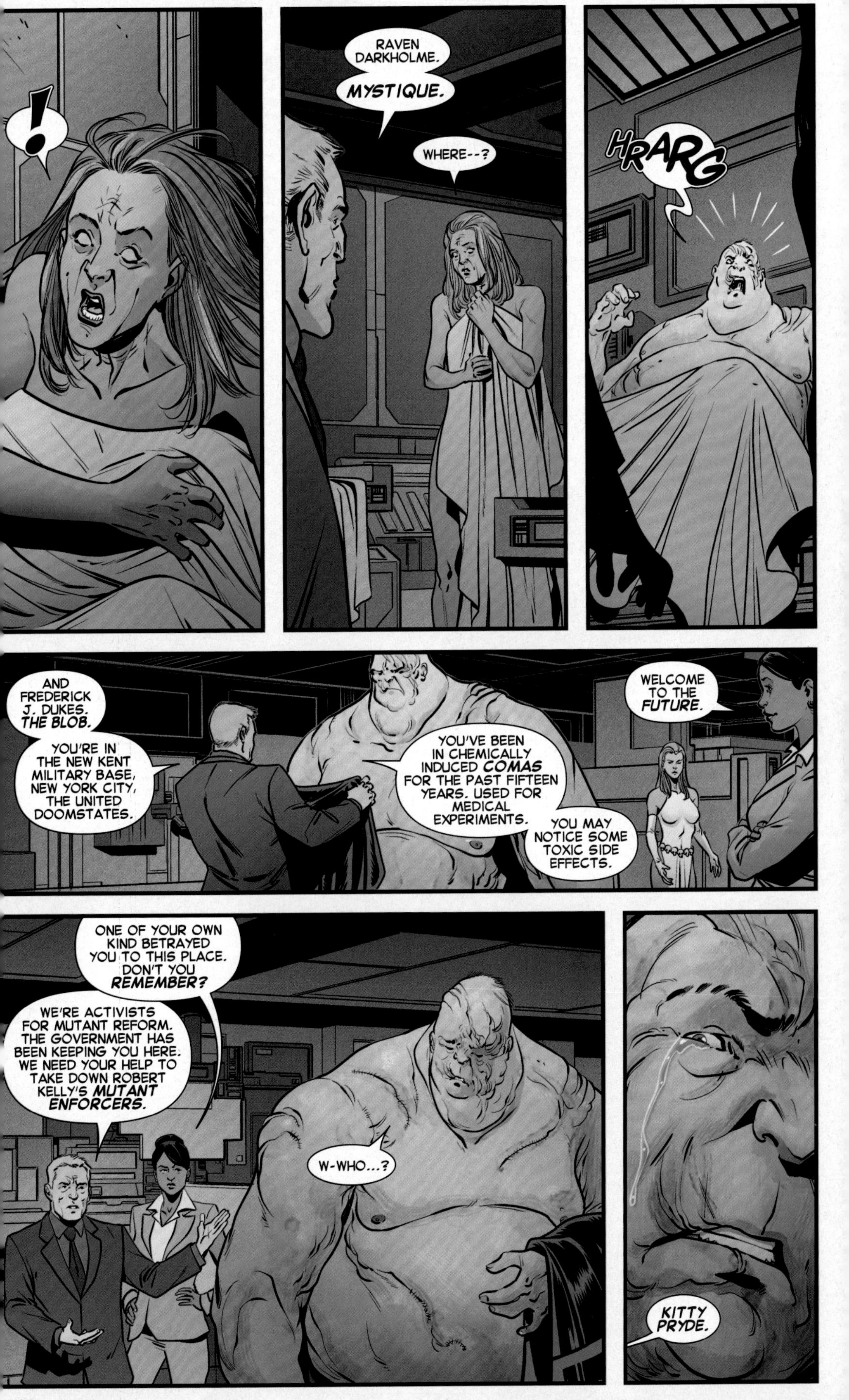
!
RAVEN DARKHOLME.
MYSTIQUE.
WHERE--?
HRARG
AND FREDERICK J. DUKES. THE BLOB.
YOU'RE IN THE NEW KENT MILITARY BASE, NEW YORK CITY, THE UNITED DOOMSTATES.
YOU'VE BEEN IN CHEMICALLY INDUCED COMAS FOR THE PAST FIFTEEN YEARS. USED FOR MEDICAL EXPERIMENTS.
WELCOME TO THE FUTURE.
YOU MAY NOTICE SOME TOXIC SIDE EFFECTS.
ONE OF YOUR OWN KIND BETRAYED YOU TO THIS PLACE. DON'T YOU REMEMBER?
WE'RE ACTIVISTS FOR MUTANT REFORM. THE GOVERNMENT HAS BEEN KEEPING YOU HERE. WE NEED YOUR HELP TO TAKE DOWN ROBERT KELLY'S MUTANT ENFORCERS.
W-WHO...?
KITTY PRYDE.

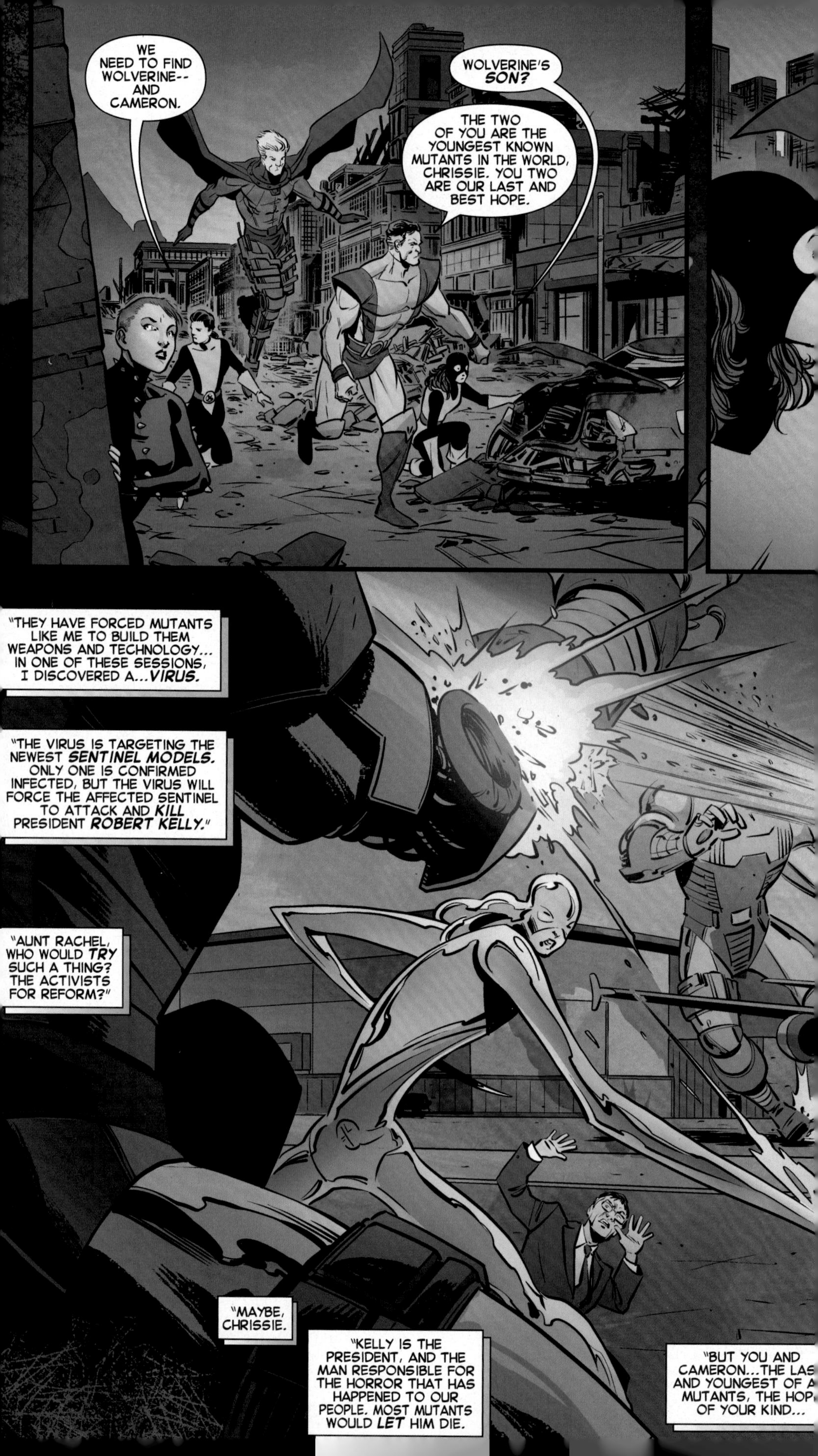

WE NEED TO FIND WOLVERINE-- AND CAMERON.
WOLVERINE'S SON?
THE TWO OF YOU ARE THE YOUNGEST KNOWN MUTANTS IN THE WORLD, CHRISSIE. YOU TWO ARE OUR LAST AND BEST HOPE.
"THEY HAVE FORCED MUTANTS LIKE ME TO BUILD THEM WEAPONS AND TECHNOLOGY... IN ONE OF THESE SESSIONS, I DISCOVERED A...VIRUS.
"THE VIRUS IS TARGETING THE NEWEST SENTINEL MODELS. ONLY ONE IS CONFIRMED INFECTED, BUT THE VIRUS WILL FORCE THE AFFECTED SENTINEL TO ATTACK AND KILL PRESIDENT ROBERT KELLY."
"AUNT RACHEL, WHO WOULD TRY SUCH A THING? THE ACTIVISTS FOR REFORM?"
"MAYBE, CHRISSIE.
"KELLY IS THE PRESIDENT, AND THE MAN RESPONSIBLE FOR THE HORROR THAT HAS HAPPENED TO OUR PEOPLE. MOST MUTANTS WOULD LET HIM DIE.
"BUT YOU AND CAMERON...THE LAS AND YOUNGEST OF A MUTANTS, THE HOP OF YOUR KIND...

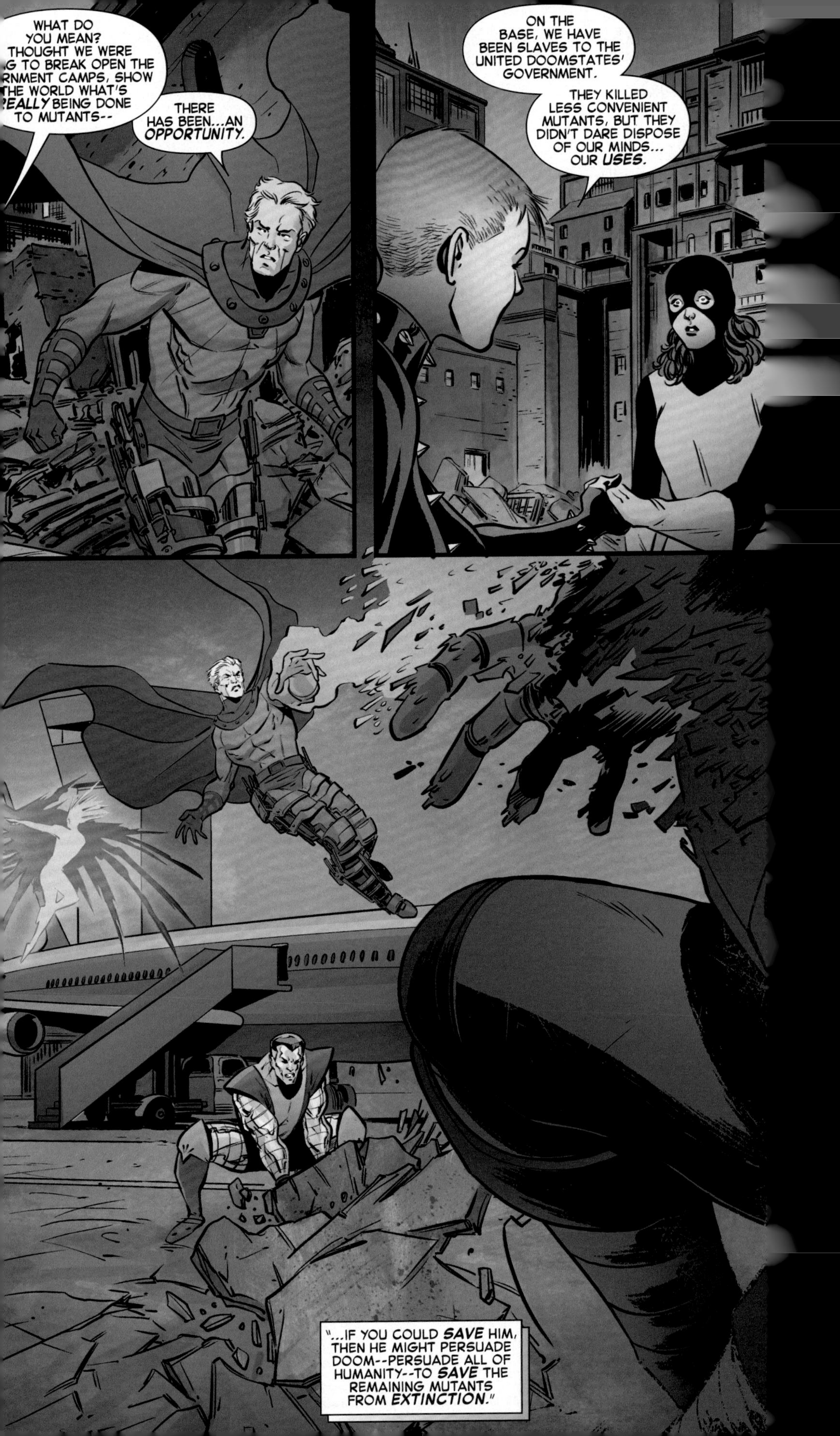
WHAT DO YOU MEAN? THOUGHT WE WERE G TO BREAK OPEN THE RNMENT CAMPS, SHOW THE WORLD WHAT'S REALLY BEING DONE TO MUTANTS--
THERE HAS BEEN...AN OPPORTUNITY.
ON THE BASE, WE HAVE BEEN SLAVES TO THE UNITED DOOMSTATES' GOVERNMENT.
THEY KILLED LESS CONVENIENT MUTANTS, BUT THEY DIDN'T DARE DISPOSE OF OUR MINDS... OUR USES.
"...IF YOU COULD SAVE HIM, THEN HE MIGHT PERSUADE DOOM--PERSUADE ALL OF HUMANITY--TO SAVE THE REMAINING MUTANTS FROM EXTINCTION."

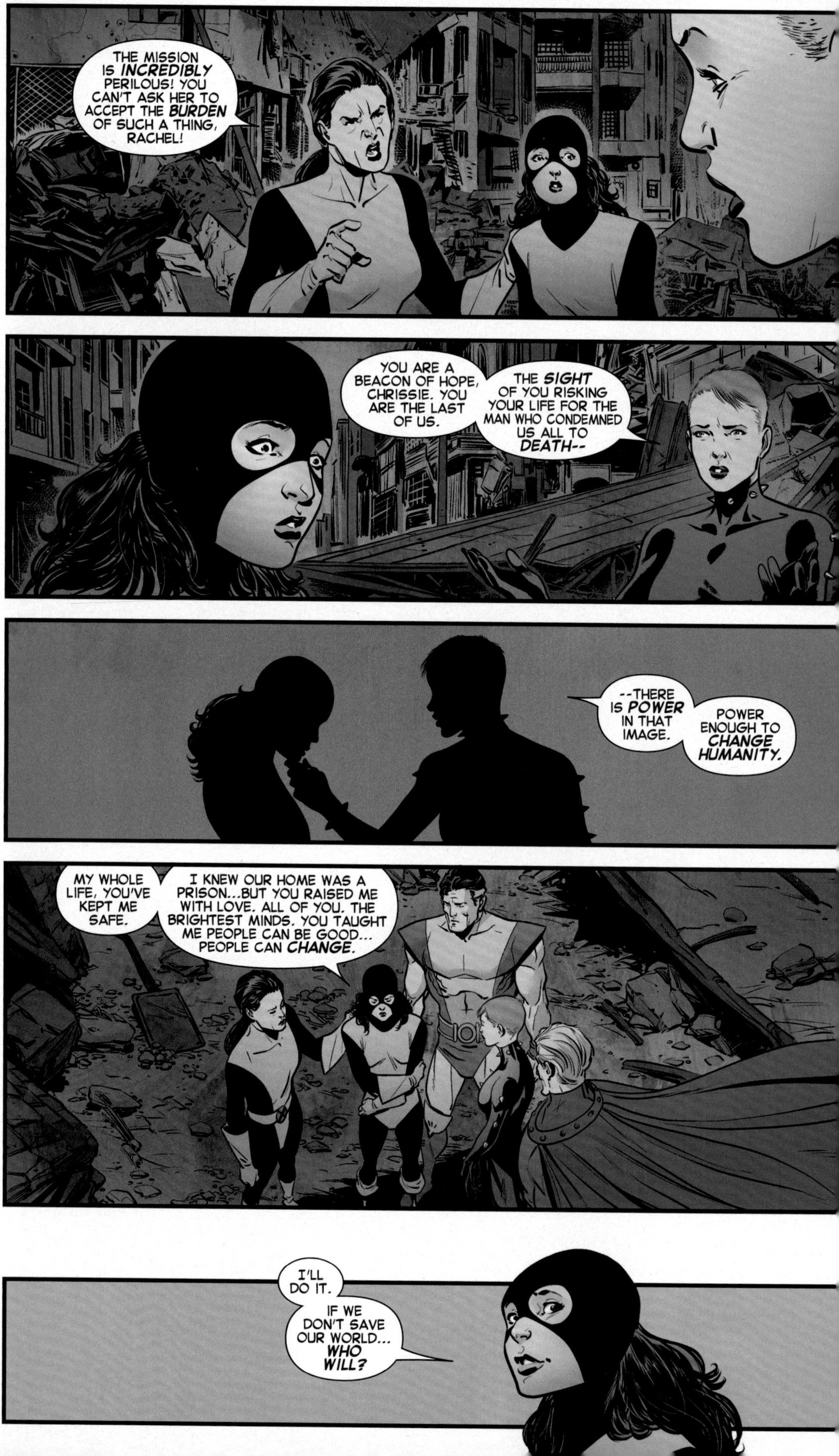
THE MISSION IS INCREDIBLY PERILOUS! YOU CAN'T ASK HER TO ACCEPT THE BURDEN OF SUCH A THING, RACHEL!
YOU ARE A BEACON OF HOPE, CHRISSIE. YOU ARE THE LAST OF US.
THE SIGHT OF YOU RISKING YOUR LIFE FOR THE MAN WHO CONDEMNED US ALL TO DEATH--
--THERE IS POWER IN THAT IMAGE.
POWER ENOUGH TO CHANGE HUMANITY.
MY WHOLE LIFE, YOU'VE KEPT ME SAFE.
I KNEW OUR HOME WAS A PRISON...BUT YOU RAISED ME WITH LOVE. ALL OF YOU. THE BRIGHTEST MINDS. YOU TAUGHT ME PEOPLE CAN BE GOOD... PEOPLE CAN CHANGE.
I'LL DO IT.
IF WE DON'T SAVE OUR WORLD... WHO WILL?

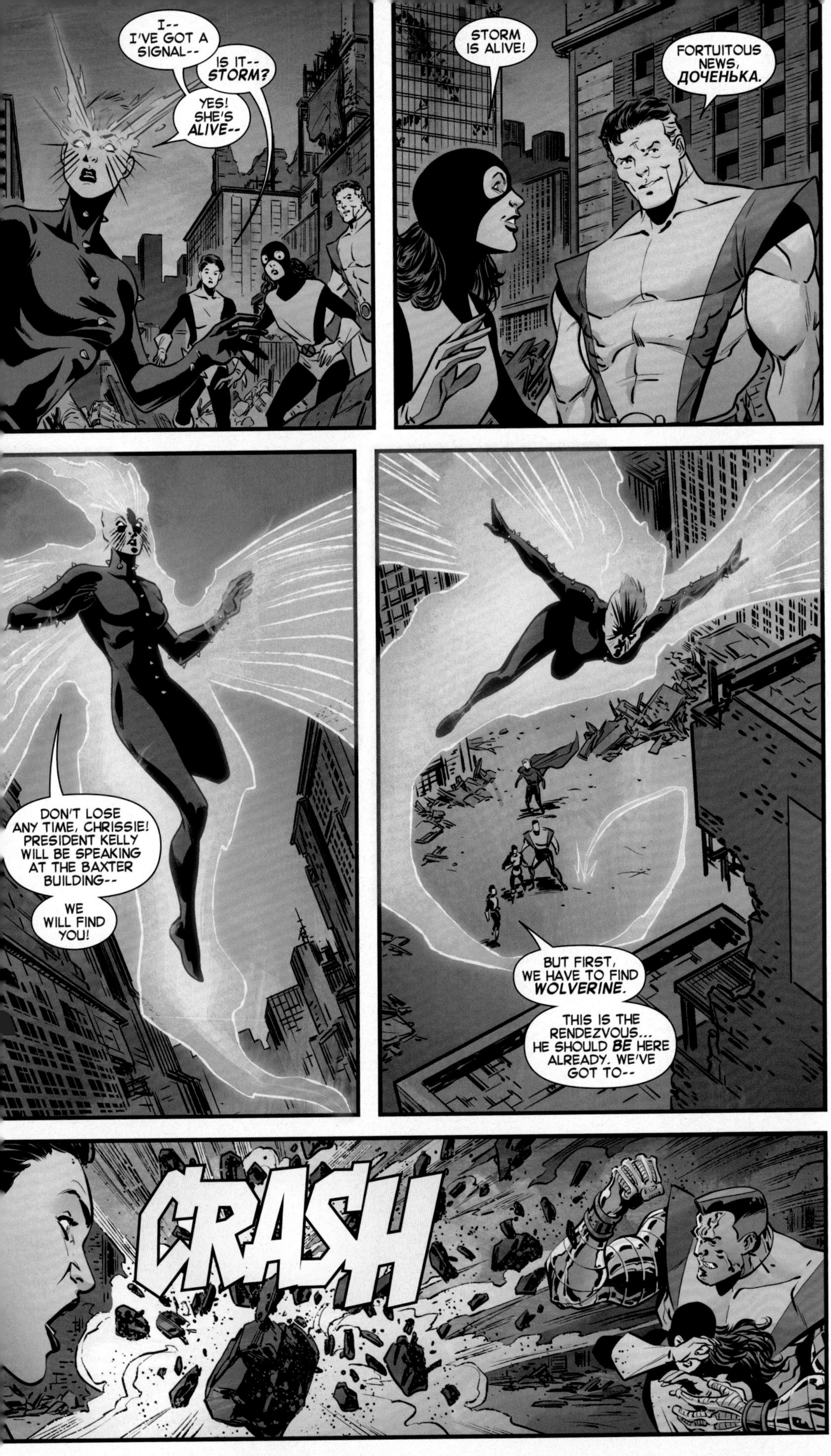
I-- I'VE GOT A SIGNAL--
IS IT-- STORM?
YES! SHE'S ALIVE--
STORM IS ALIVE!
FORTUITOUS NEWS, ДОЧЕНЬКА.
DON'T LOSE ANY TIME, CHRISSIE! PRESIDENT KELLY WILL BE SPEAKING AT THE BAXTER BUILDING--
WE WILL FIND YOU!
BUT FIRST, WE HAVE TO FIND WOLVERINE.
THIS IS THE RENDEZVOUS... HE SHOULD BE HERE ALREADY. WE'VE GOT TO--
CRASH

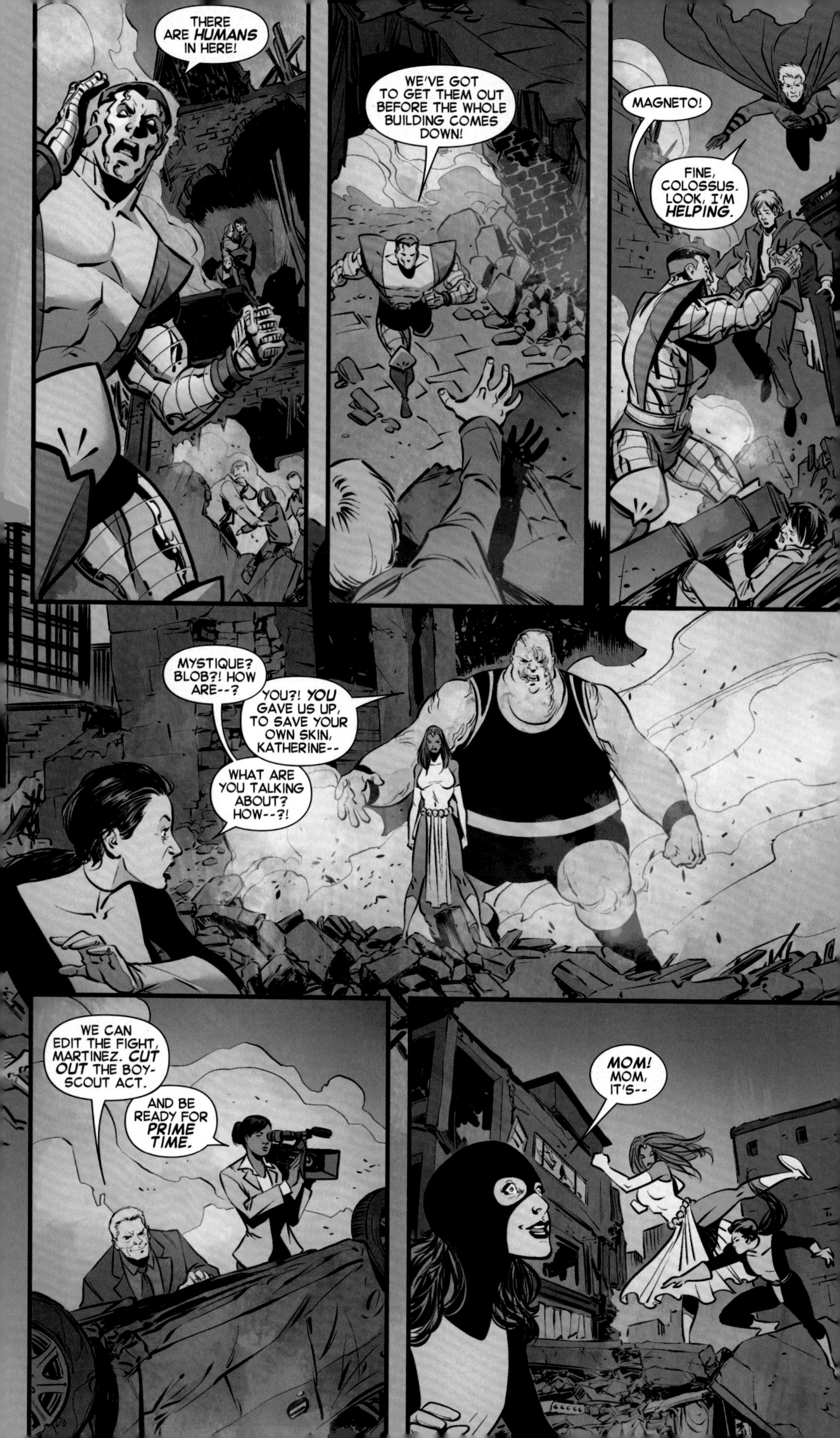
THERE ARE *HUMANS* IN HERE!
WE'VE GOT TO GET THEM OUT BEFORE THE WHOLE BUILDING COMES DOWN!
MAGNETO!
FINE, COLOSSUS. LOOK, I'M *HELPING.*
MYSTIQUE? BLOB?! HOW ARE--?
YOU?! *YOU* GAVE US UP, TO SAVE YOUR OWN SKIN, KATHERINE--
WHAT ARE YOU TALKING ABOUT? HOW--?!
WE CAN EDIT THE FIGHT, MARTINEZ. *CUT OUT* THE BOY-SCOUT ACT.
AND BE READY FOR *PRIME TIME.*
MOM! MOM, IT'S--

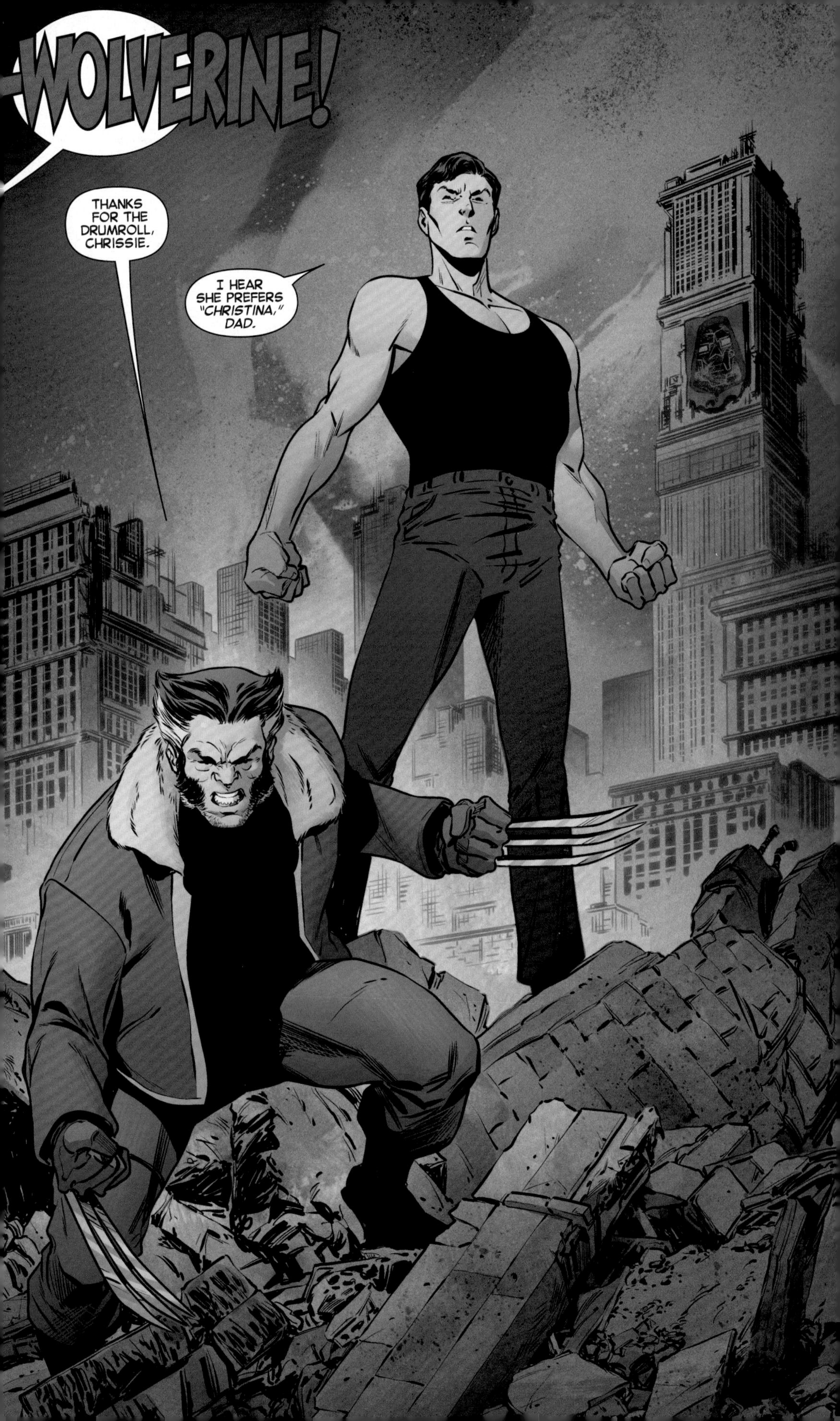
-WOLVERINE!
THANKS FOR THE DRUMROLL, CHRISSIE.
I HEAR SHE PREFERS "CHRISTINA," DAD.

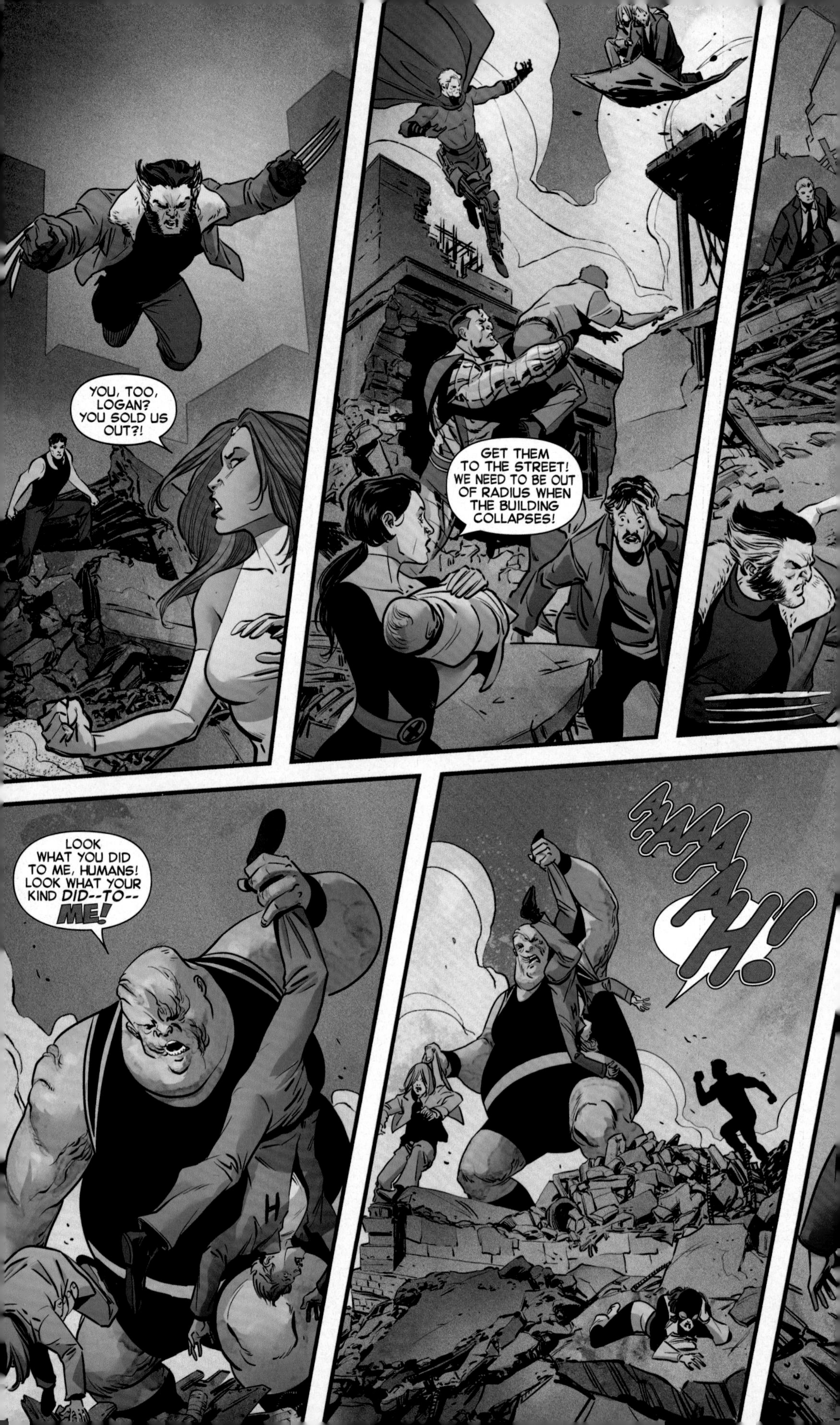
YOU, TOO, LOGAN? YOU SOLD US OUT?!
GET THEM TO THE STREET! WE NEED TO BE OUT OF RADIUS WHEN THE BUILDING COLLAPSES!
LOOK WHAT YOU DID TO ME, HUMANS! LOOK WHAT YOUR KIND DID--TO--ME!
AAAAAH!!

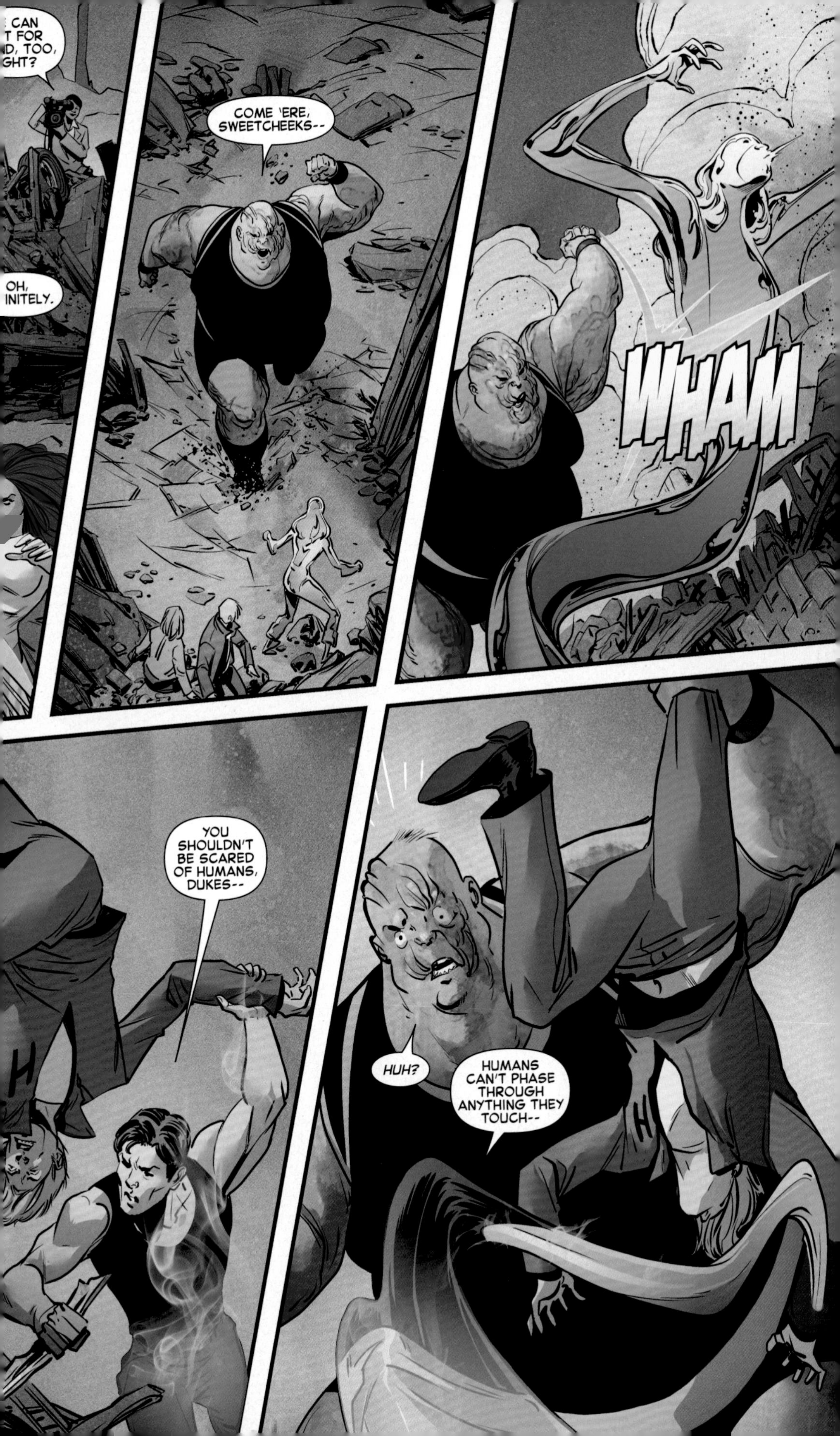

COME 'ERE, SWEETCHEEKS--
WHAM
YOU SHOULDN'T BE SCARED OF HUMANS, DUKES--
HUH?
HUMANS CAN'T PHASE THROUGH ANYTHING THEY TOUCH--

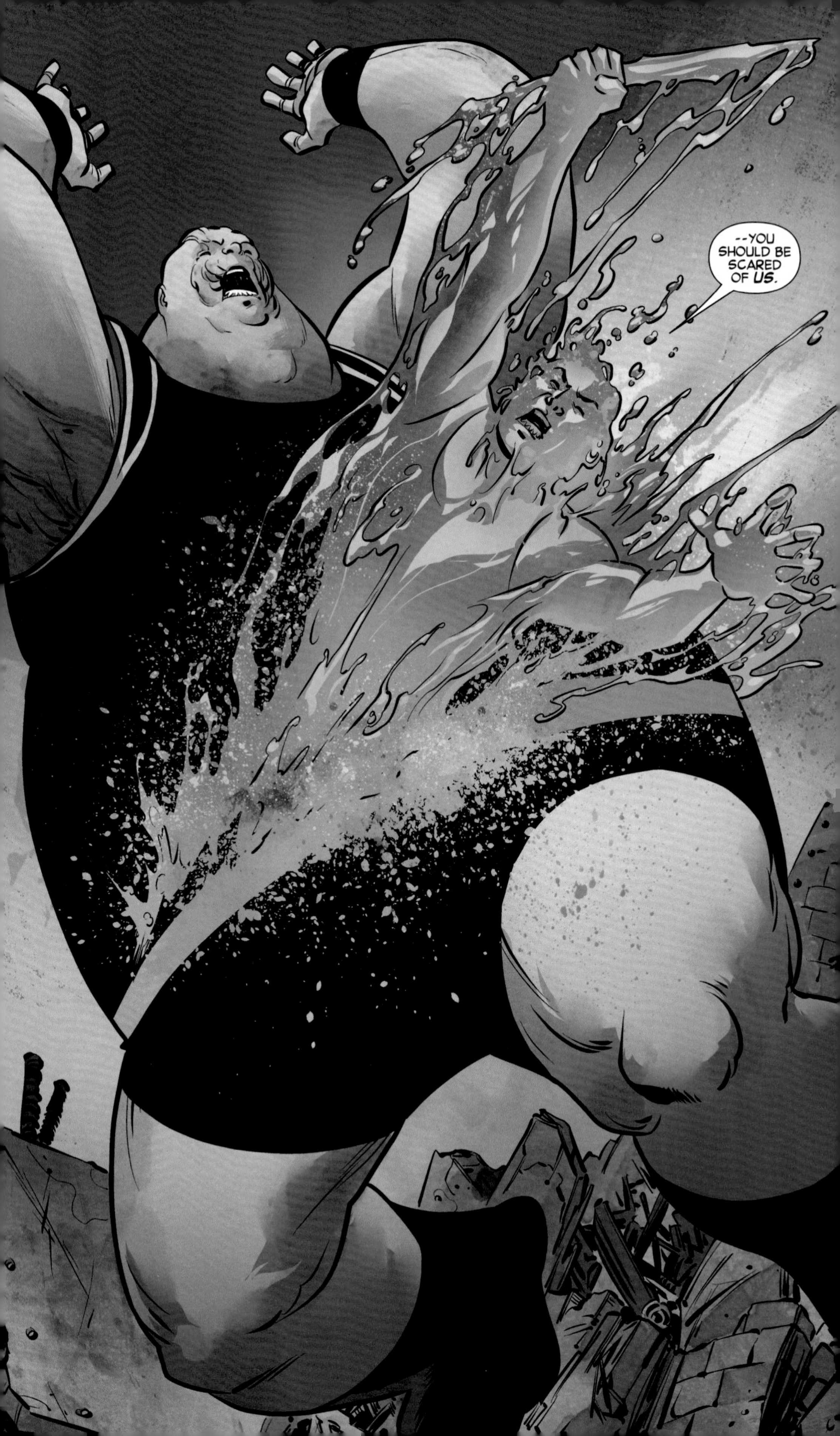
--YOU SHOULD BE SCARED OF US.

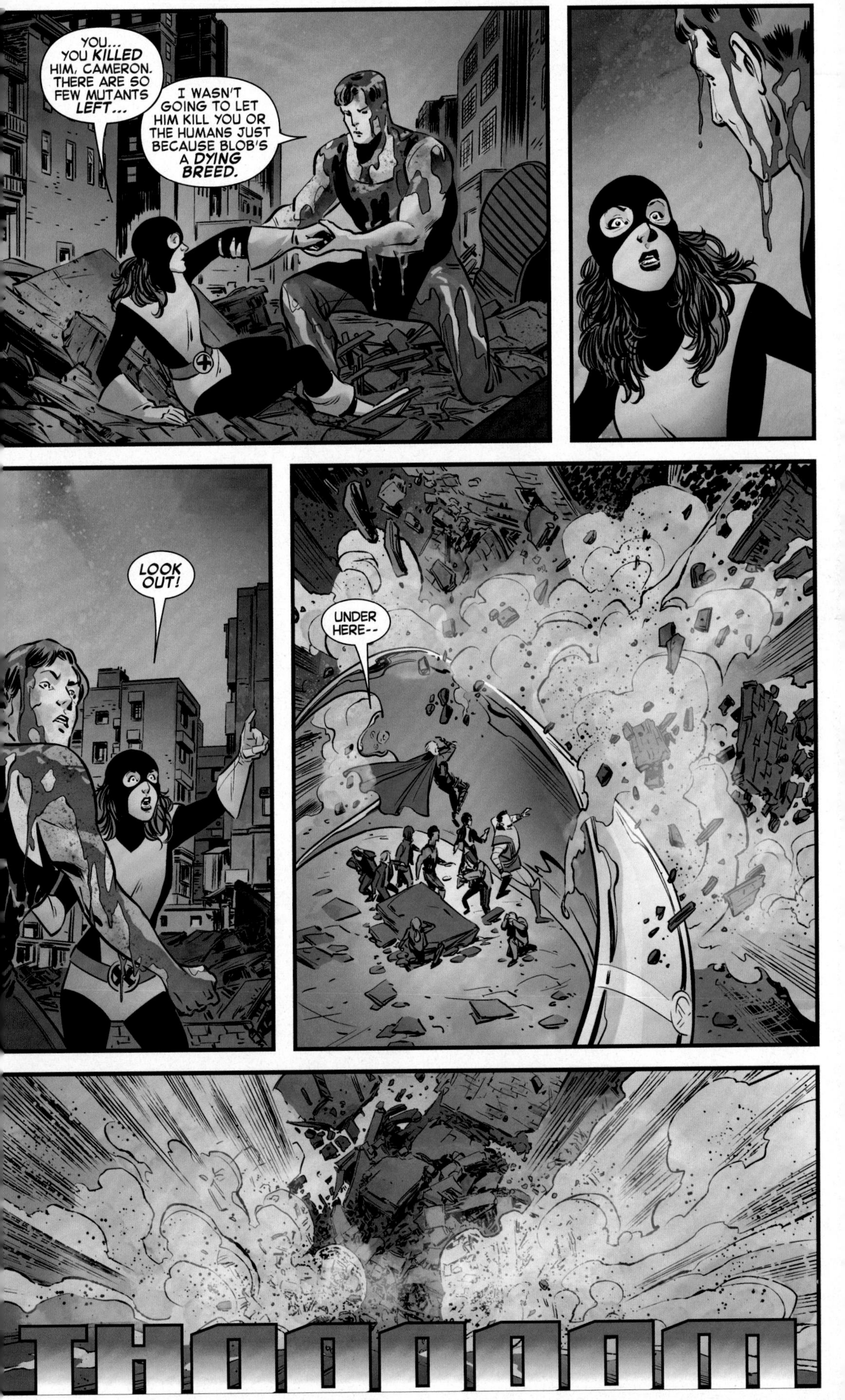

YOU... YOU KILLED HIM, CAMERON. THERE ARE SO FEW MUTANTS LEFT...
I WASN'T GOING TO LET HIM KILL YOU OR THE HUMANS JUST BECAUSE BLOB'S A DYING BREED.
LOOK OUT!
UNDER HERE--
THOOOOOM

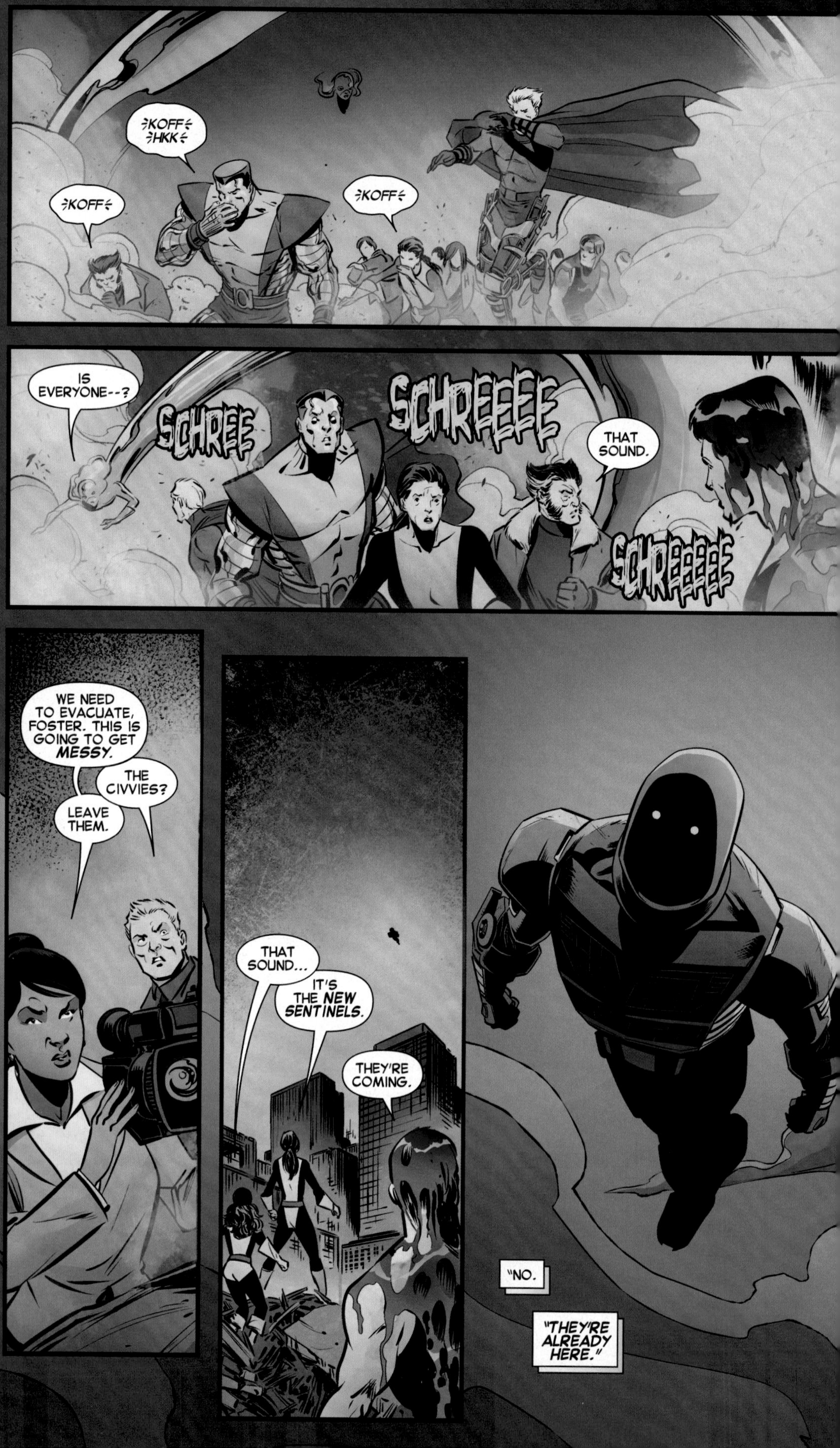

KOFF HKK
KOFF
KOFF
IS EVERYONE--?
SCHREE
SCHREEEE
THAT SOUND.
SCHREEEEE
WE NEED TO EVACUATE, FOSTER. THIS IS GOING TO GET MESSY.
THE CIVVIES?
LEAVE THEM.
THAT SOUND...
IT'S THE NEW SENTINELS.
THEY'RE COMING.
"NO.
"THEY'RE ALREADY HERE."

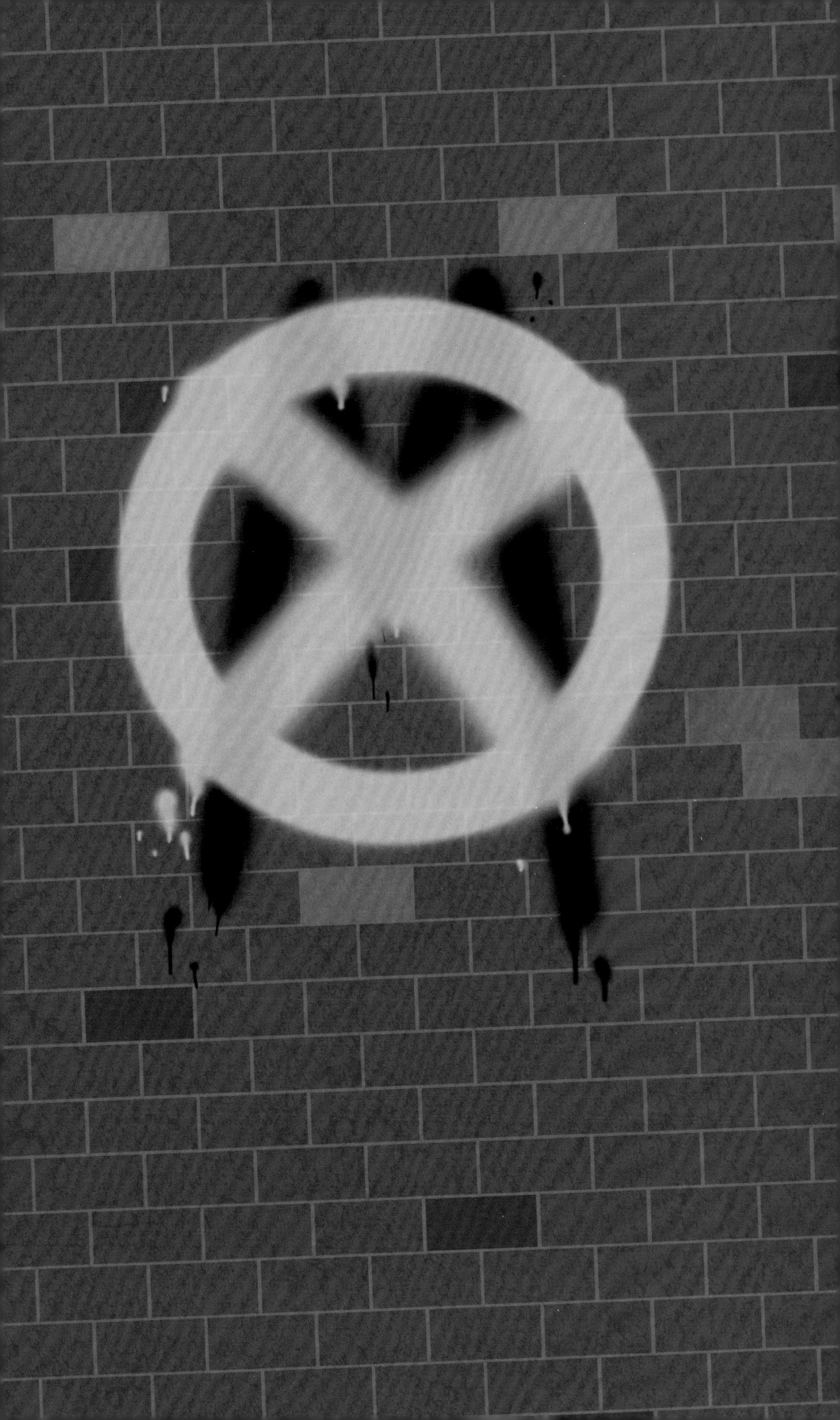

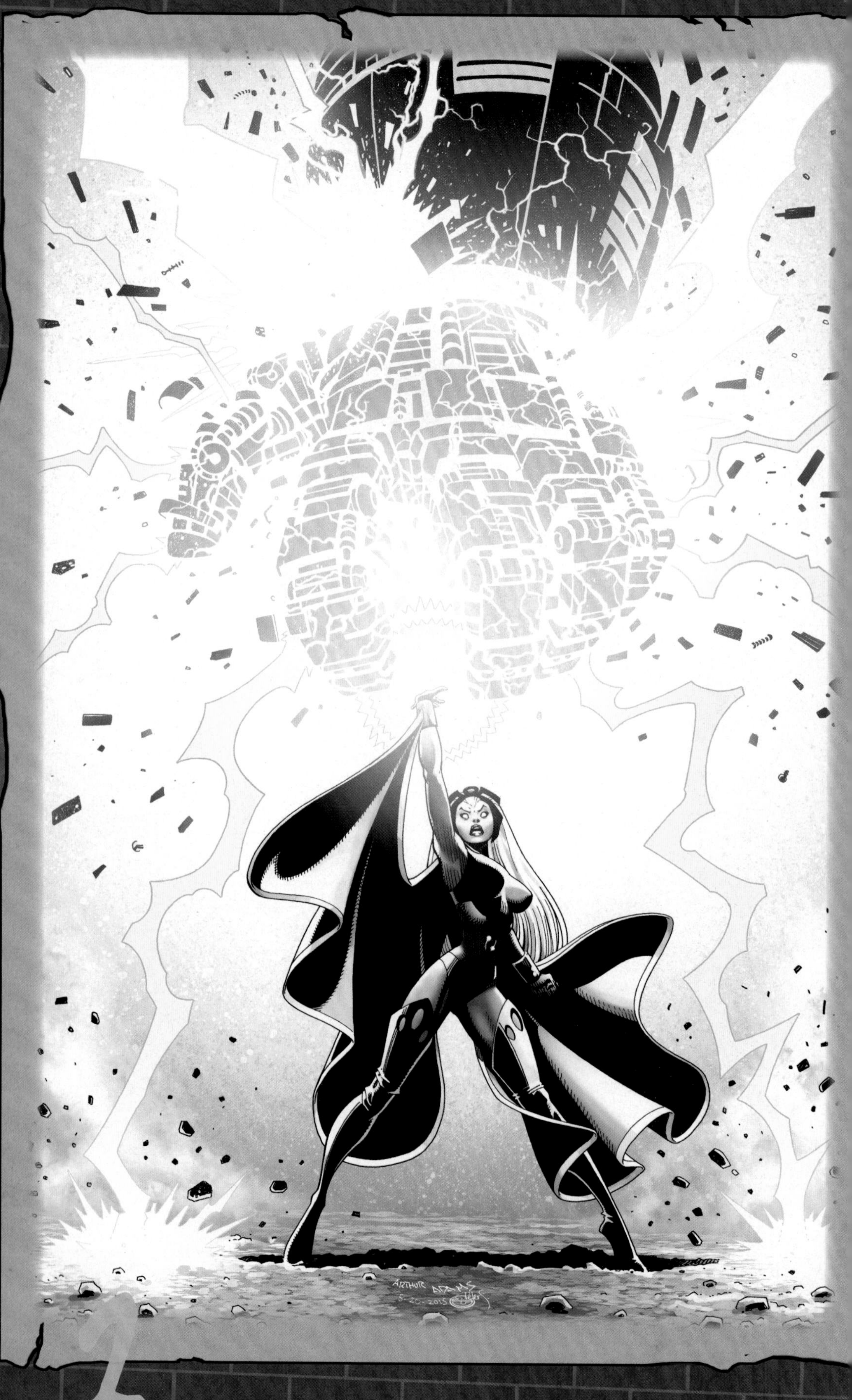
ARTHUR ADAMS
5-20-2015

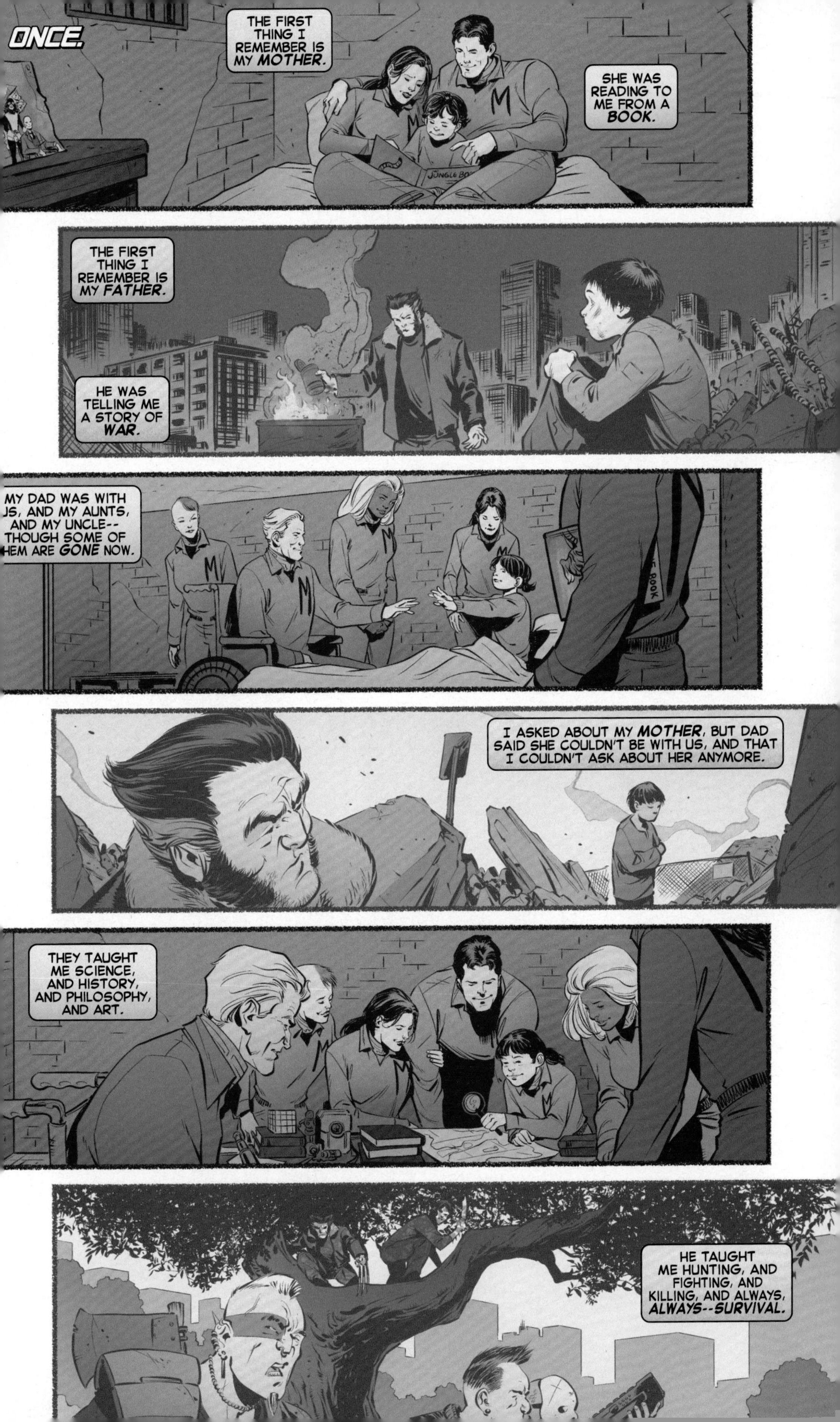

ONCE.
THE FIRST THING I REMEMBER IS MY MOTHER.
SHE WAS READING TO ME FROM A BOOK.
THE FIRST THING I REMEMBER IS MY FATHER.
HE WAS TELLING ME A STORY OF WAR.
MY DAD WAS WITH S, AND MY AUNTS, AND MY UNCLE-- THOUGH SOME OF HEM ARE GONE NOW.
I ASKED ABOUT MY MOTHER, BUT DAD SAID SHE COULDN'T BE WITH US, AND THAT I COULDN'T ASK ABOUT HER ANYMORE.
THEY TAUGHT ME SCIENCE, AND HISTORY, AND PHILOSOPHY, AND ART.
HE TAUGHT ME HUNTING, AND FIGHTING, AND KILLING, AND ALWAYS, ALWAYS--SURVIVAL.

HOME WAS THE *BASE*, AND ITS WALLS WERE CHAIN-LINK.

HOME WAS THE *STREET*, AND ITS WALLS WERE THIN AIR.

I WAS SAFE, BUT I WAS NEVER *FREE*.

I WAS F[ ] BUT I W[ ] NEVER S[ ]

I WAS ON A FETCH MISSION FOR THE MILITARY BASE.

I WAS SCOUTING FOR FOOD TO TRADE IN CENTRUM.

AND THE MOMENT I MET *HIM*, I KNEW HE WAS LIKE *ME*.

AND THE MOMENT I SAW *HER*, I KNEW SHE WAS *DIFFERENT*.

LOGAN WAS ANGRY.

DAD TOLD ME TO FORGET HER.

ARE YOU... REAL?

I-I-I... LIKE *TUPAC* BETTER THAN *BIGGIE*, IF THAT'S WHAT YOU MEAN.

I...DON'T GET THAT REFERENCE.

YOU'RE ONLY, LIKE, A YEAR OR TWO OLDER THAN ME--I'VE--I'VE NEVER MET ANOTHER MUTANT AS *YOUNG* AS YOU.

AND I DON'T MEET A WIDE RANGE OF FIFTEEN-YEAR-OLDS WITH *CROSS-BOWS*.

CLEARLY, WE SHOULD BOTH GET OUT MORE.

IT'S NOT A LOVE STORY.

IT'S NOT A MEET CUTE.

BUT I MET HIM WHEN I COULD, AND FOR THE FIRST TIME SINCE I CAN REMEMBER...

I THOUGHT MAYBE THINGS COUL[ ] *CHANGE*.

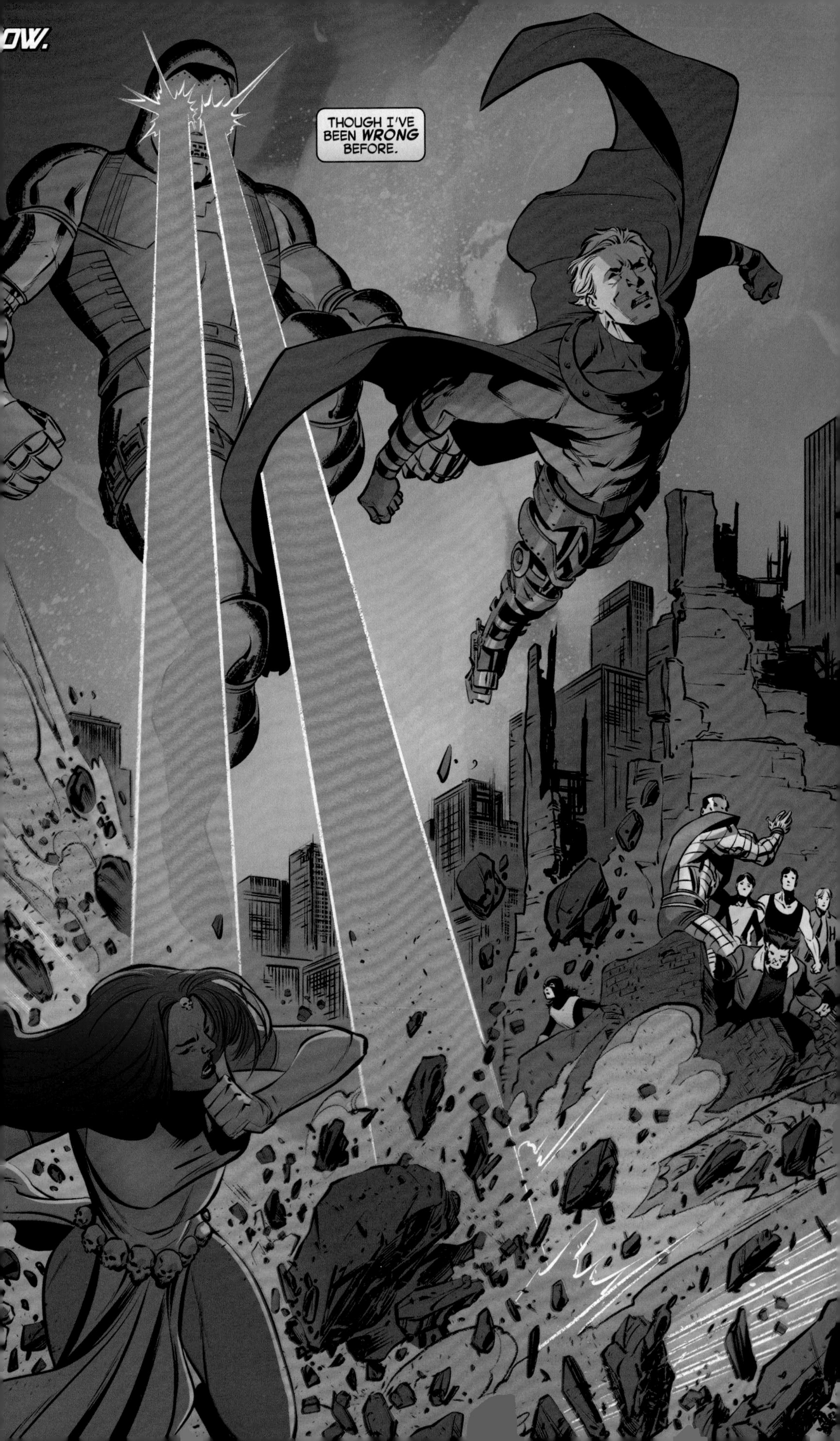
OW.
THOUGH I'VE BEEN WRONG BEFORE.

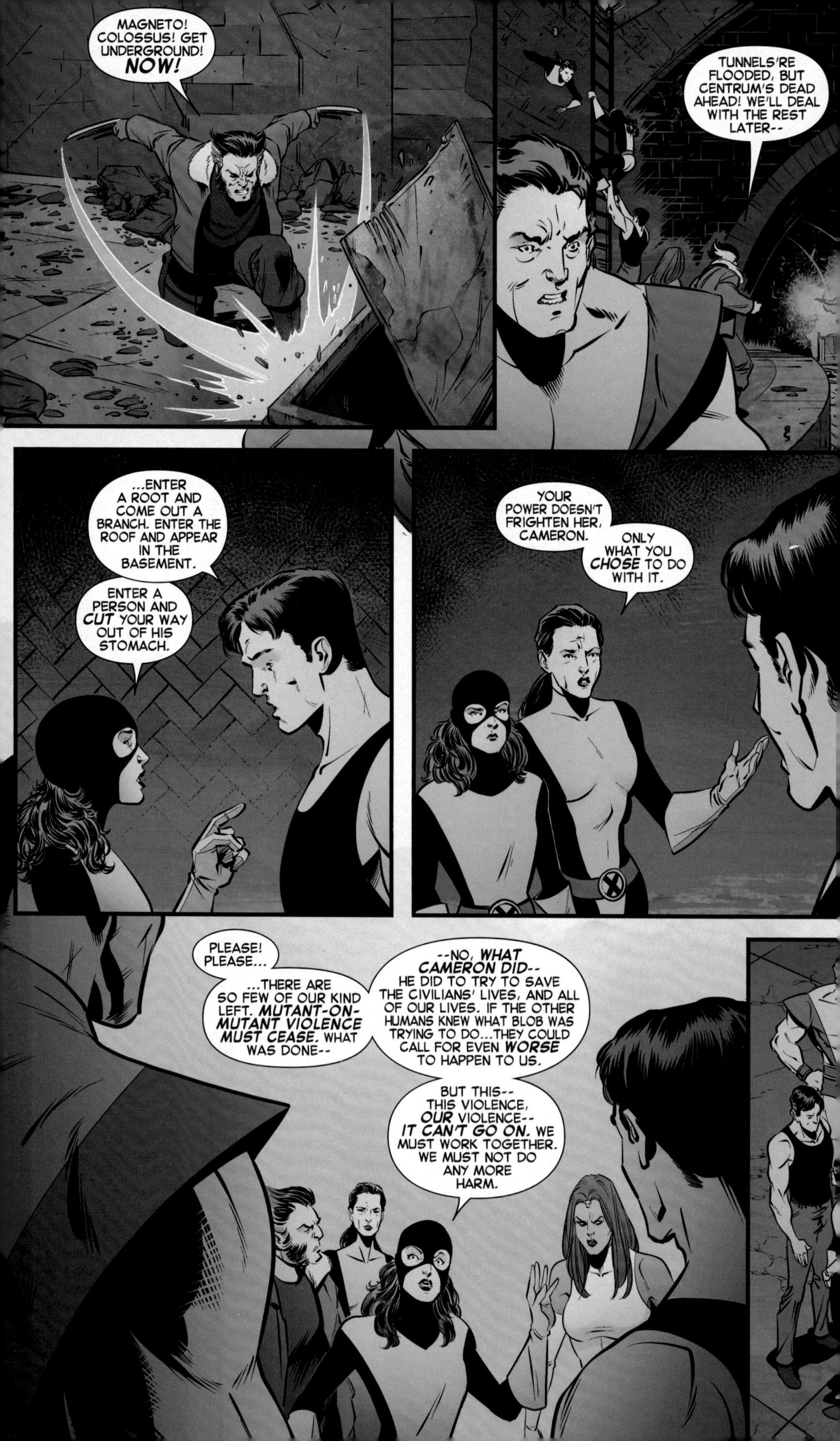

MAGNETO! COLOSSUS! GET UNDERGROUND! **NOW!**
TUNNELS'RE FLOODED, BUT CENTRUM'S DEAD AHEAD! WE'LL DEAL WITH THE REST LATER--
...ENTER A ROOT AND COME OUT A BRANCH. ENTER THE ROOF AND APPEAR IN THE BASEMENT.
ENTER A PERSON AND **CUT** YOUR WAY OUT OF HIS STOMACH.
YOUR POWER DOESN'T FRIGHTEN HER, CAMERON.
ONLY WHAT YOU **CHOSE** TO DO WITH IT.
PLEASE! PLEASE...
...THERE ARE SO FEW OF OUR KIND LEFT. ***MUTANT-ON-MUTANT VIOLENCE MUST CEASE.*** WHAT WAS DONE--
--NO, ***WHAT CAMERON DID***-- HE DID TO TRY TO SAVE THE CIVILIANS' LIVES, AND ALL OF OUR LIVES. IF THE OTHER HUMANS KNEW WHAT BLOB WAS TRYING TO DO...THEY COULD CALL FOR EVEN ***WORSE*** TO HAPPEN TO US.
BUT THIS-- THIS VIOLENCE, ***OUR*** VIOLENCE-- ***IT CAN'T GO ON.*** WE MUST WORK TOGETHER. WE MUST NOT DO ANY MORE HARM.

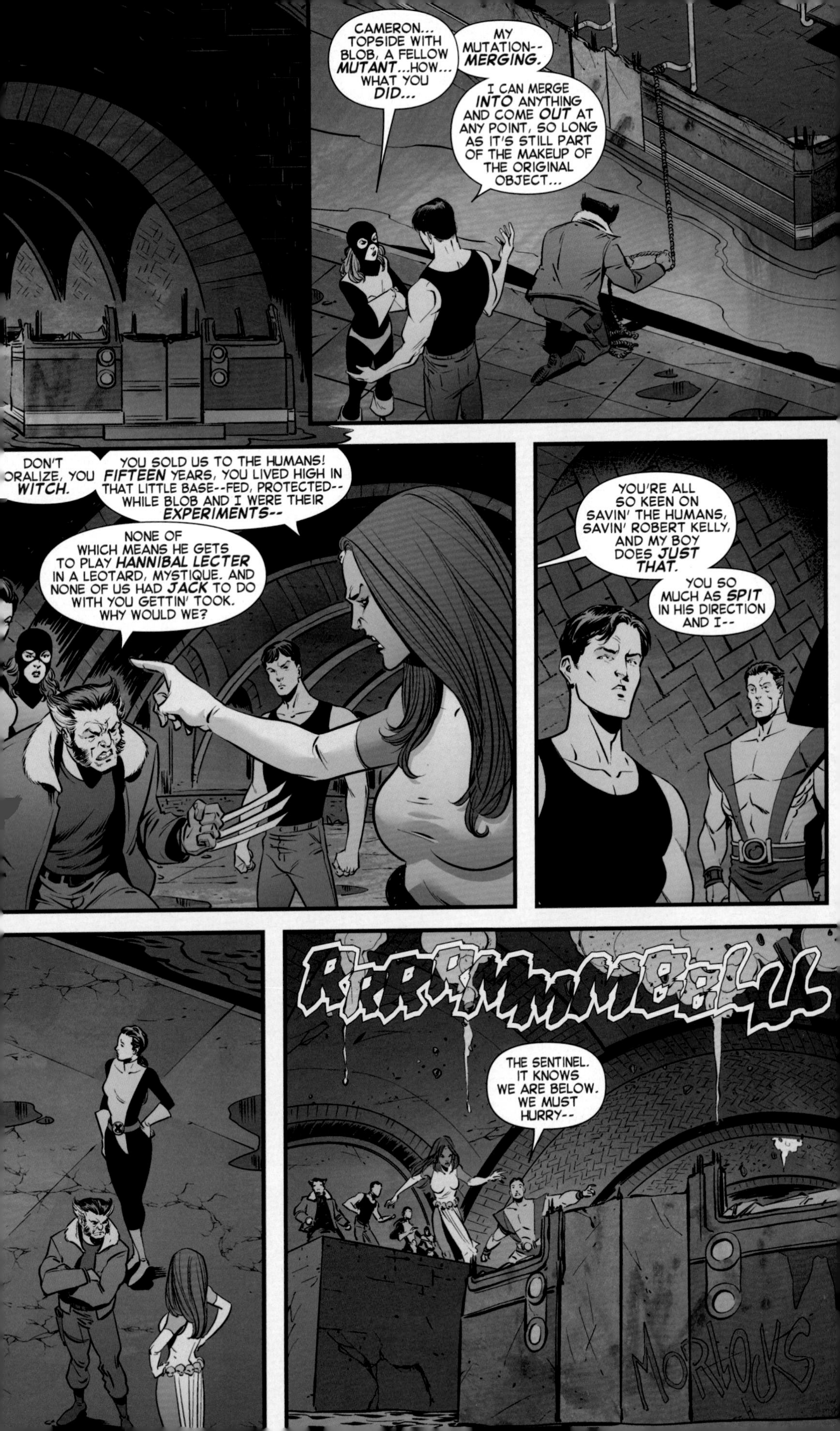
CAMERON... TOPSIDE WITH BLOB, A FELLOW MUTANT...HOW... WHAT YOU DID...
MY MUTATION-- MERGING.
I CAN MERGE INTO ANYTHING AND COME OUT AT ANY POINT, SO LONG AS IT'S STILL PART OF THE MAKEUP OF THE ORIGINAL OBJECT...
DON'T ORALIZE, YOU WITCH.
YOU SOLD US TO THE HUMANS! FIFTEEN YEARS, YOU LIVED HIGH IN THAT LITTLE BASE--FED, PROTECTED-- WHILE BLOB AND I WERE THEIR EXPERIMENTS--
NONE OF WHICH MEANS HE GETS TO PLAY HANNIBAL LECTER IN A LEOTARD, MYSTIQUE. AND NONE OF US HAD JACK TO DO WITH YOU GETTIN' TOOK. WHY WOULD WE?
YOU'RE ALL SO KEEN ON SAVIN' THE HUMANS, SAVIN' ROBERT KELLY, AND MY BOY DOES JUST THAT.
YOU SO MUCH AS SPIT IN HIS DIRECTION AND I--
RRRMMMBBLL
THE SENTINEL. IT KNOWS WE ARE BELOW. WE MUST HURRY--
MORLOCKS

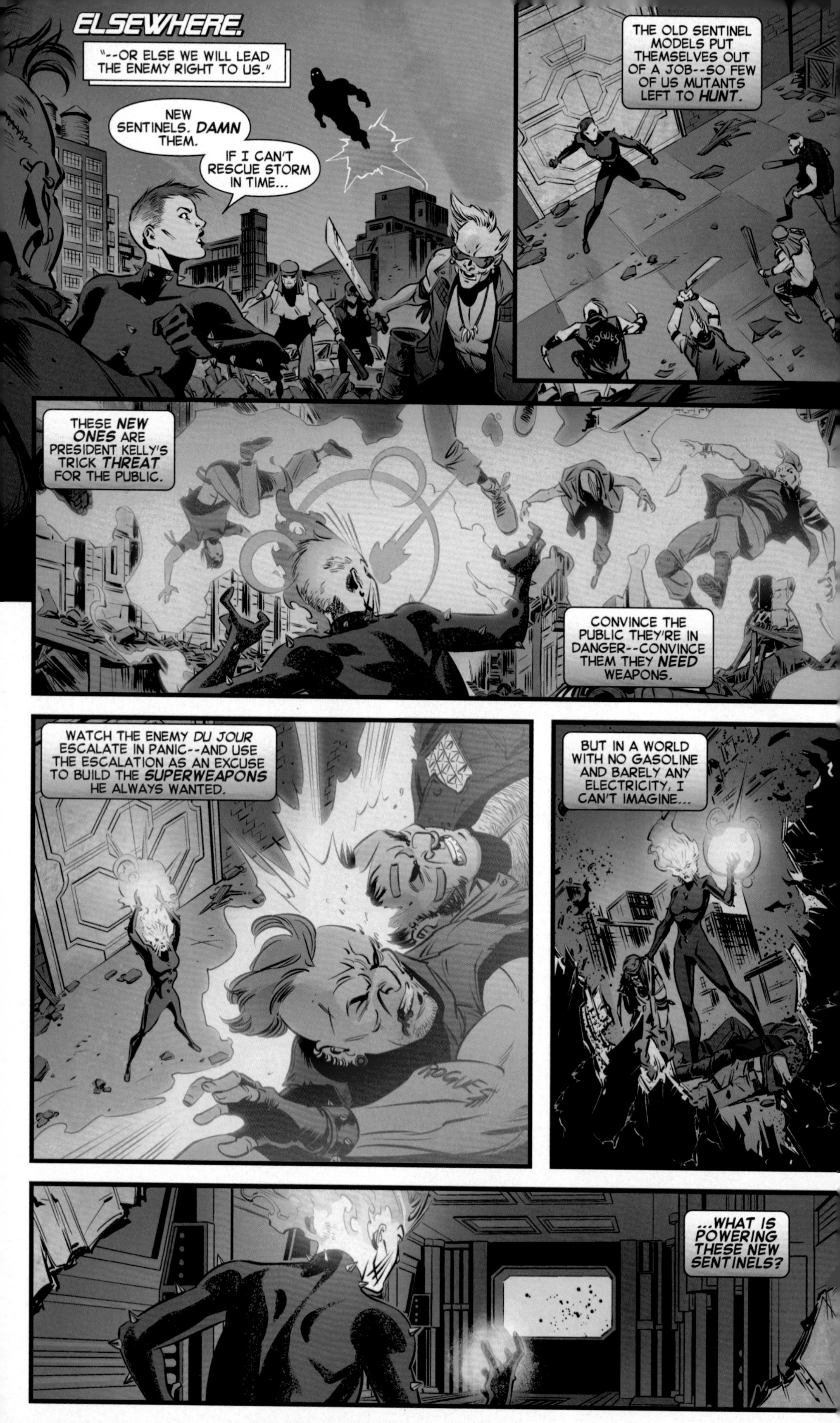
ELSEWHERE.
"--OR ELSE WE WILL LEAD THE ENEMY RIGHT TO US."
NEW SENTINELS. DAMN THEM.
IF I CAN'T RESCUE STORM IN TIME...
THE OLD SENTINEL MODELS PUT THEMSELVES OUT OF A JOB--SO FEW OF US MUTANTS LEFT TO HUNT.
ROGUES
THESE NEW ONES ARE PRESIDENT KELLY'S TRICK THREAT FOR THE PUBLIC.
CONVINCE THE PUBLIC THEY'RE IN DANGER--CONVINCE THEM THEY NEED WEAPONS.
WATCH THE ENEMY DU JOUR ESCALATE IN PANIC--AND USE THE ESCALATION AS AN EXCUSE TO BUILD THE SUPERWEAPONS HE ALWAYS WANTED.
ROGUES
BUT IN A WORLD WITH NO GASOLINE AND BARELY ANY ELECTRICITY, I CAN'T IMAGINE...
...WHAT IS POWERING THESE NEW SENTINELS?

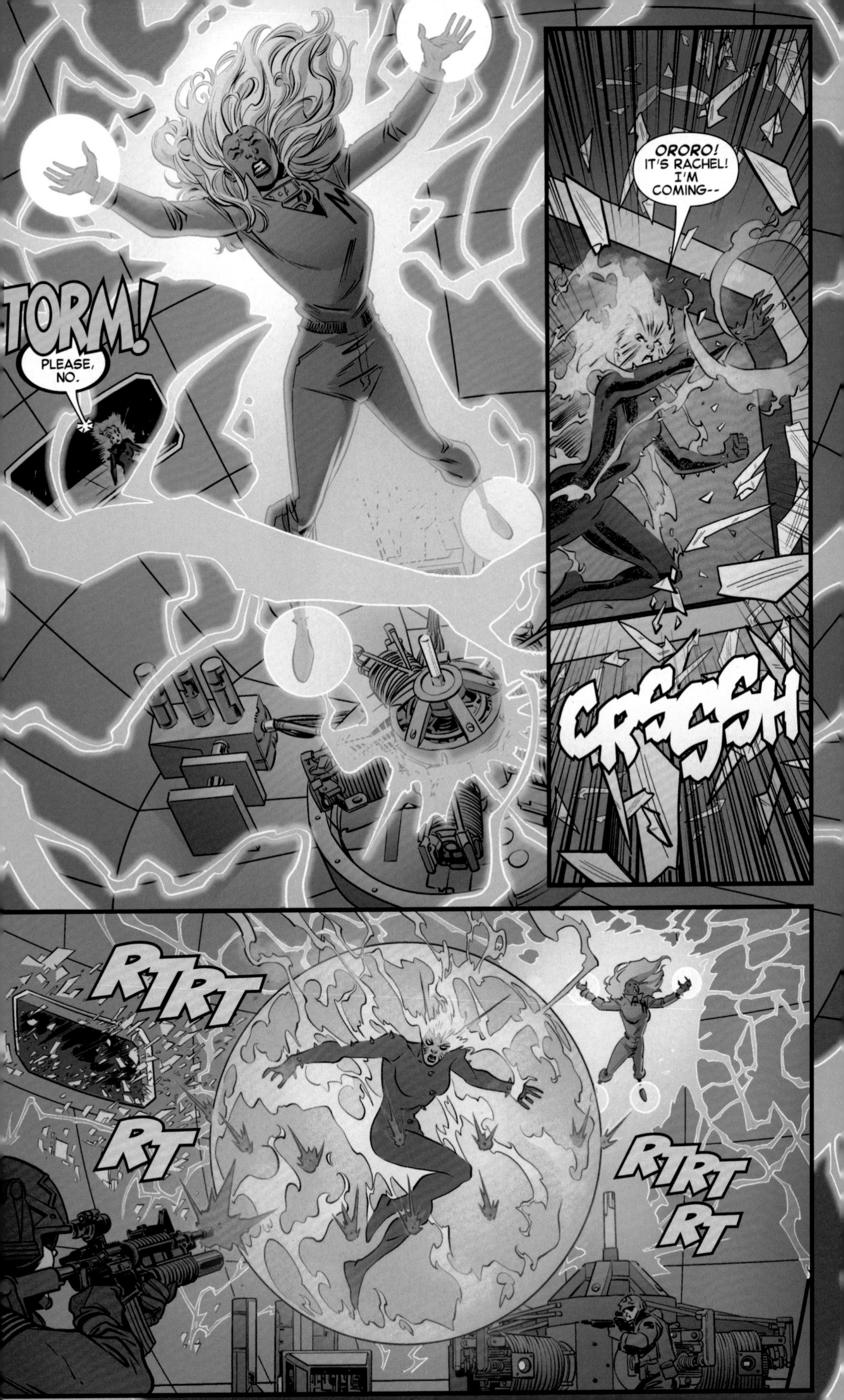
TORM!
PLEASE, NO.
ORORO! IT'S RACHEL! I'M COMING--
CRSSSH
RTRT
RT
RTRT RT

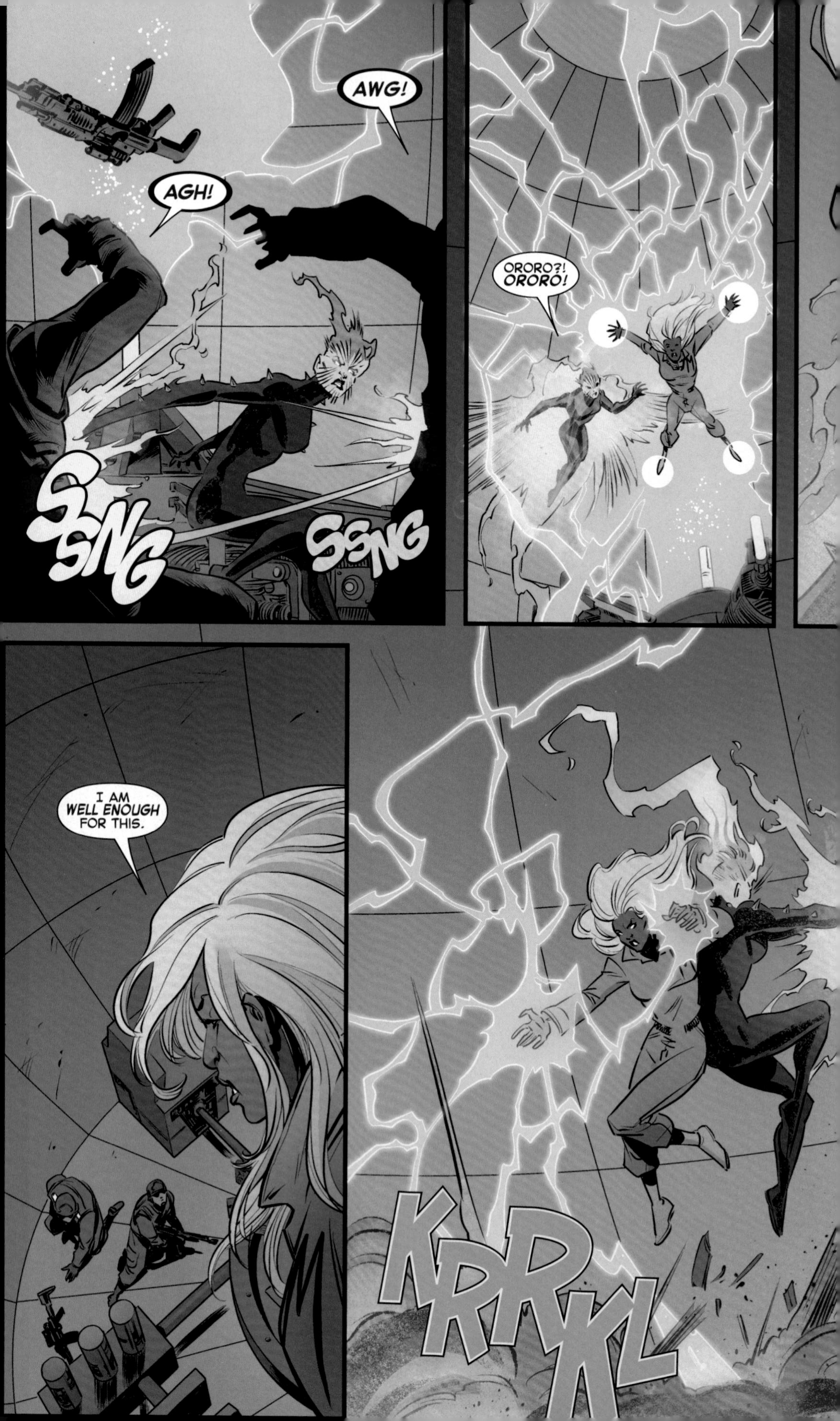
AWG!
AGH!
SSNG
SSNG
ORORO?! ORORO!
I AM WELL ENOUGH FOR THIS.
KRRKL

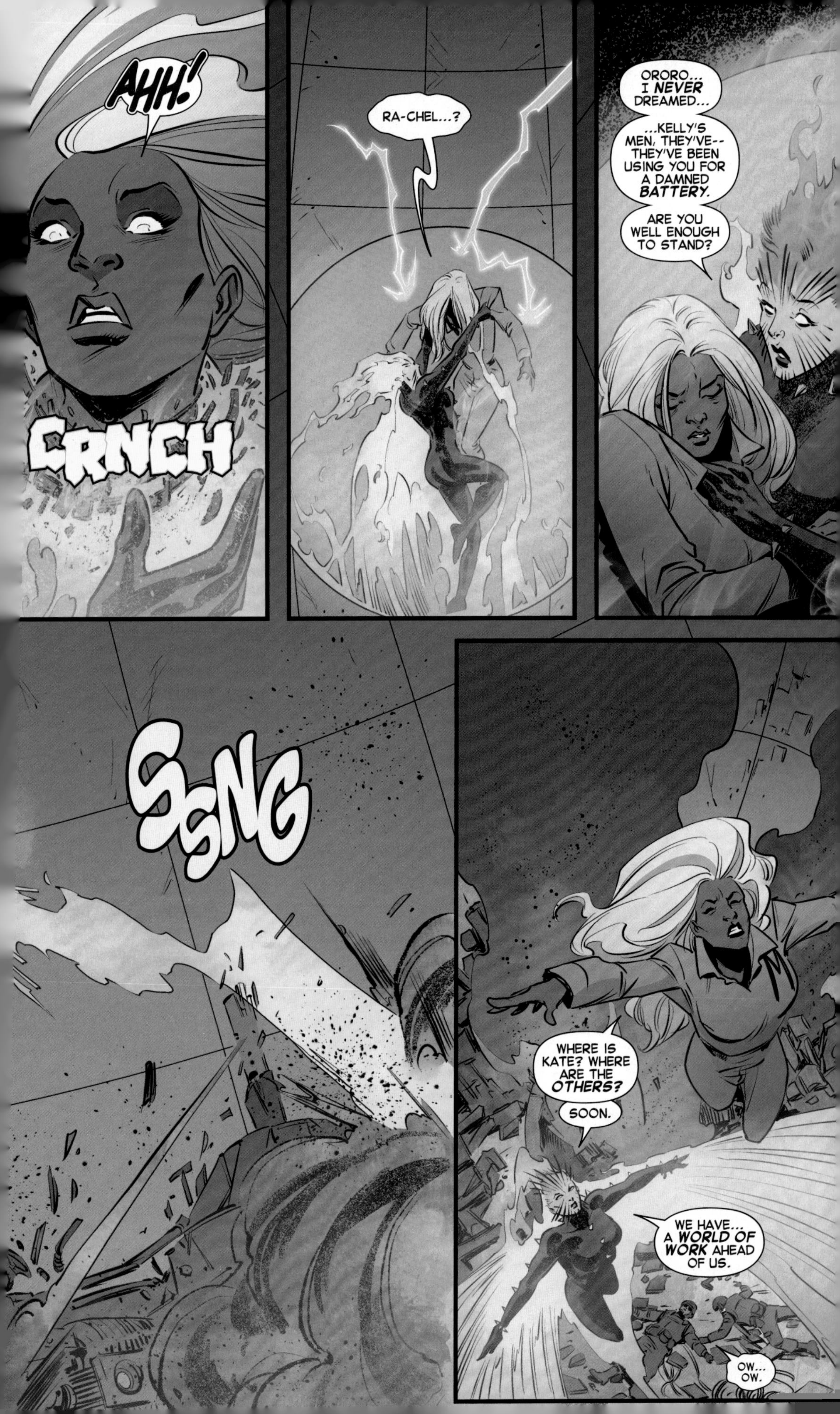
AHH!
CRNCH
RA-CHEL...?
ORORO... I NEVER DREAMED...
...KELLY'S MEN, THEY'VE-- THEY'VE BEEN USING YOU FOR A DAMNED BATTERY.
ARE YOU WELL ENOUGH TO STAND?
SSNG
WHERE IS KATE? WHERE ARE THE OTHERS?
SOON.
WE HAVE... A WORLD OF WORK AHEAD OF US.
OW... OW.

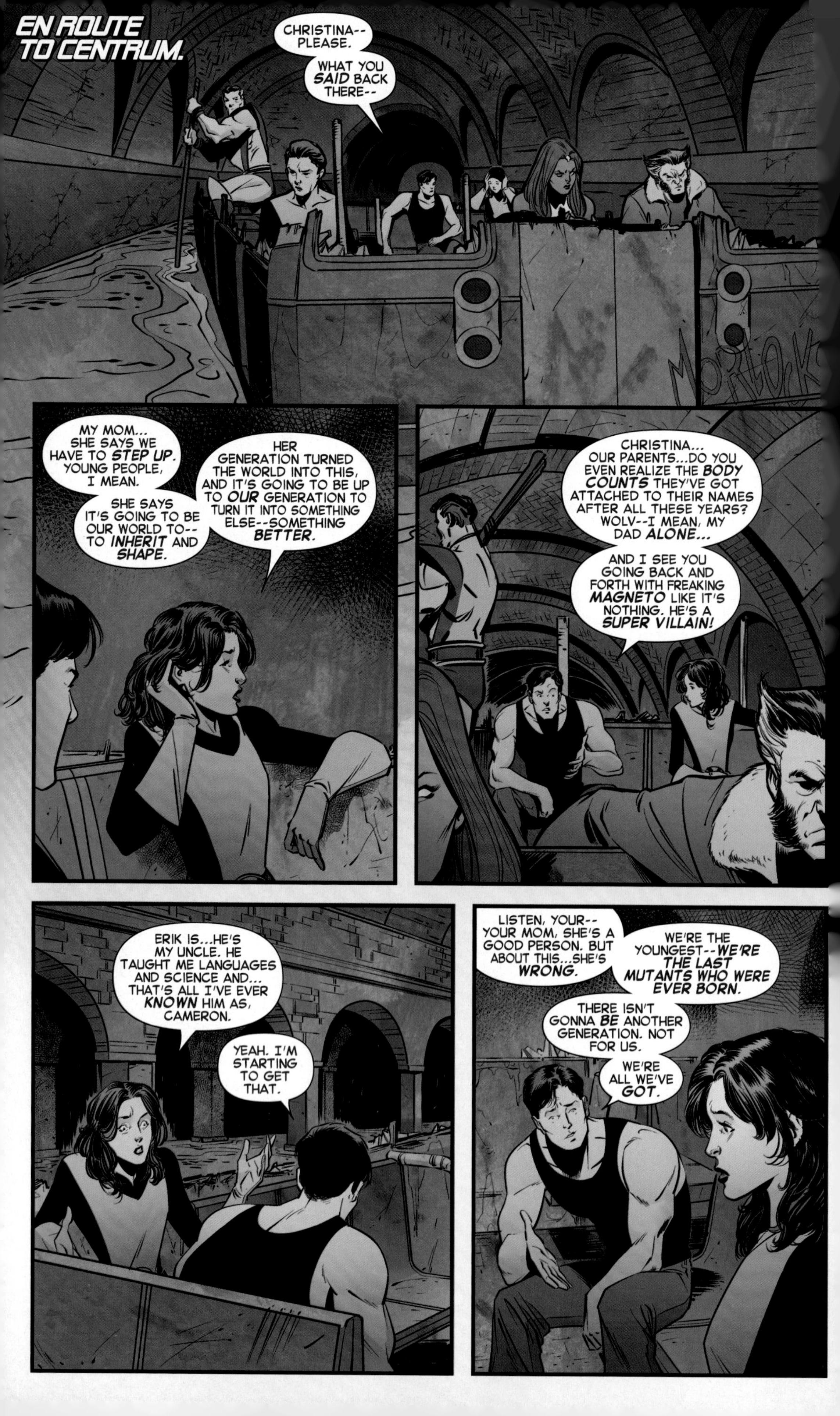
EN ROUTE TO CENTRUM.
CHRISTINA-- PLEASE.
WHAT YOU SAID BACK THERE--
MY MOM... SHE SAYS WE HAVE TO STEP UP. YOUNG PEOPLE, I MEAN.
SHE SAYS IT'S GOING TO BE OUR WORLD TO-- TO INHERIT AND SHAPE.
HER GENERATION TURNED THE WORLD INTO THIS, AND IT'S GOING TO BE UP TO OUR GENERATION TO TURN IT INTO SOMETHING ELSE--SOMETHING BETTER.
CHRISTINA... OUR PARENTS...DO YOU EVEN REALIZE THE BODY COUNTS THEY'VE GOT ATTACHED TO THEIR NAMES AFTER ALL THESE YEARS? WOLV--I MEAN, MY DAD ALONE...
AND I SEE YOU GOING BACK AND FORTH WITH FREAKING MAGNETO LIKE IT'S NOTHING. HE'S A SUPER VILLAIN!
ERIK IS...HE'S MY UNCLE. HE TAUGHT ME LANGUAGES AND SCIENCE AND... THAT'S ALL I'VE EVER KNOWN HIM AS, CAMERON.
YEAH. I'M STARTING TO GET THAT.
LISTEN, YOUR-- YOUR MOM, SHE'S A GOOD PERSON. BUT ABOUT THIS...SHE'S WRONG.
WE'RE THE YOUNGEST--WE'RE THE LAST MUTANTS WHO WERE EVER BORN.
THERE ISN'T GONNA BE ANOTHER GENERATION. NOT FOR US.
WE'RE ALL WE'VE GOT.

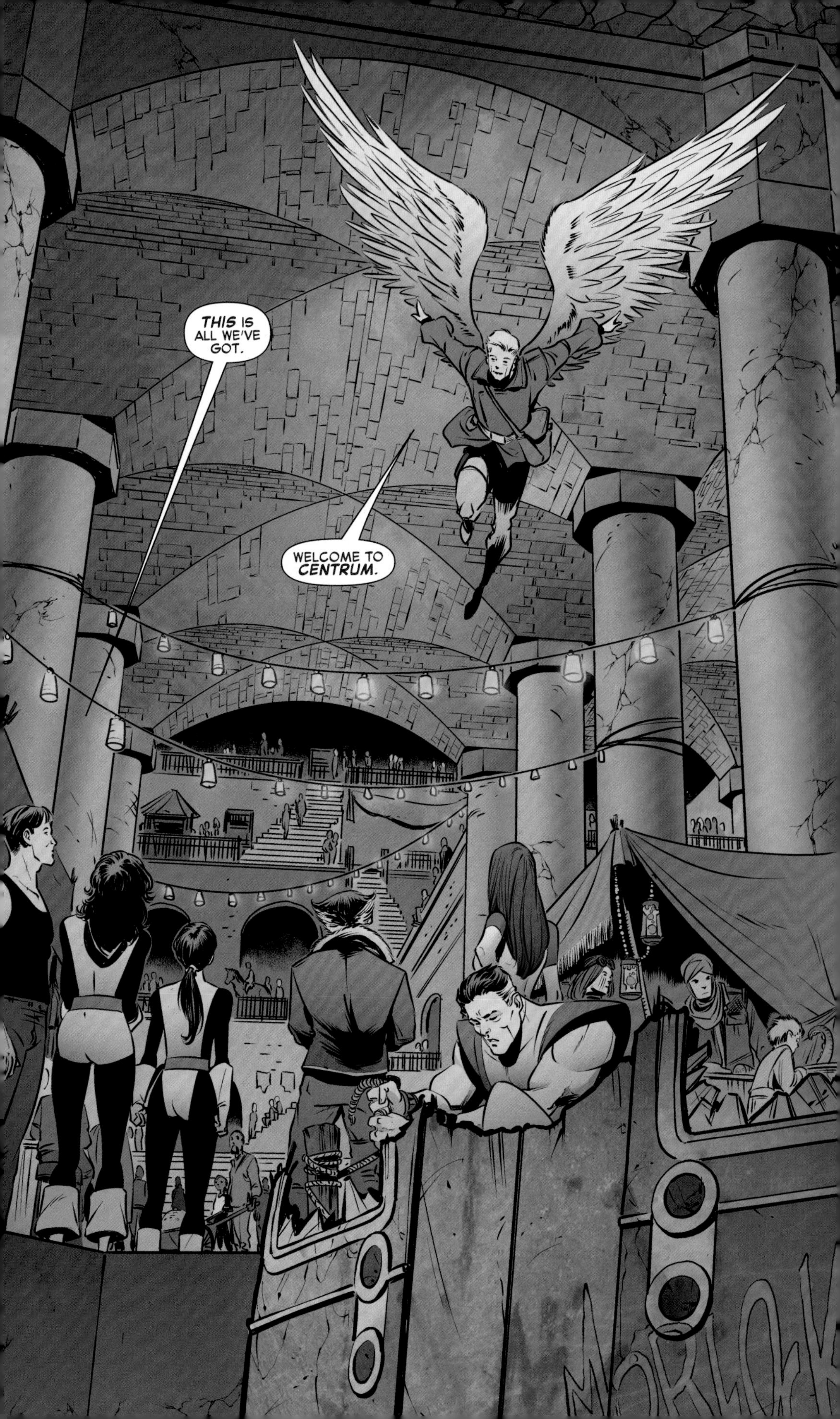
THIS IS ALL WE'VE GOT.
WELCOME TO CENTRUM.

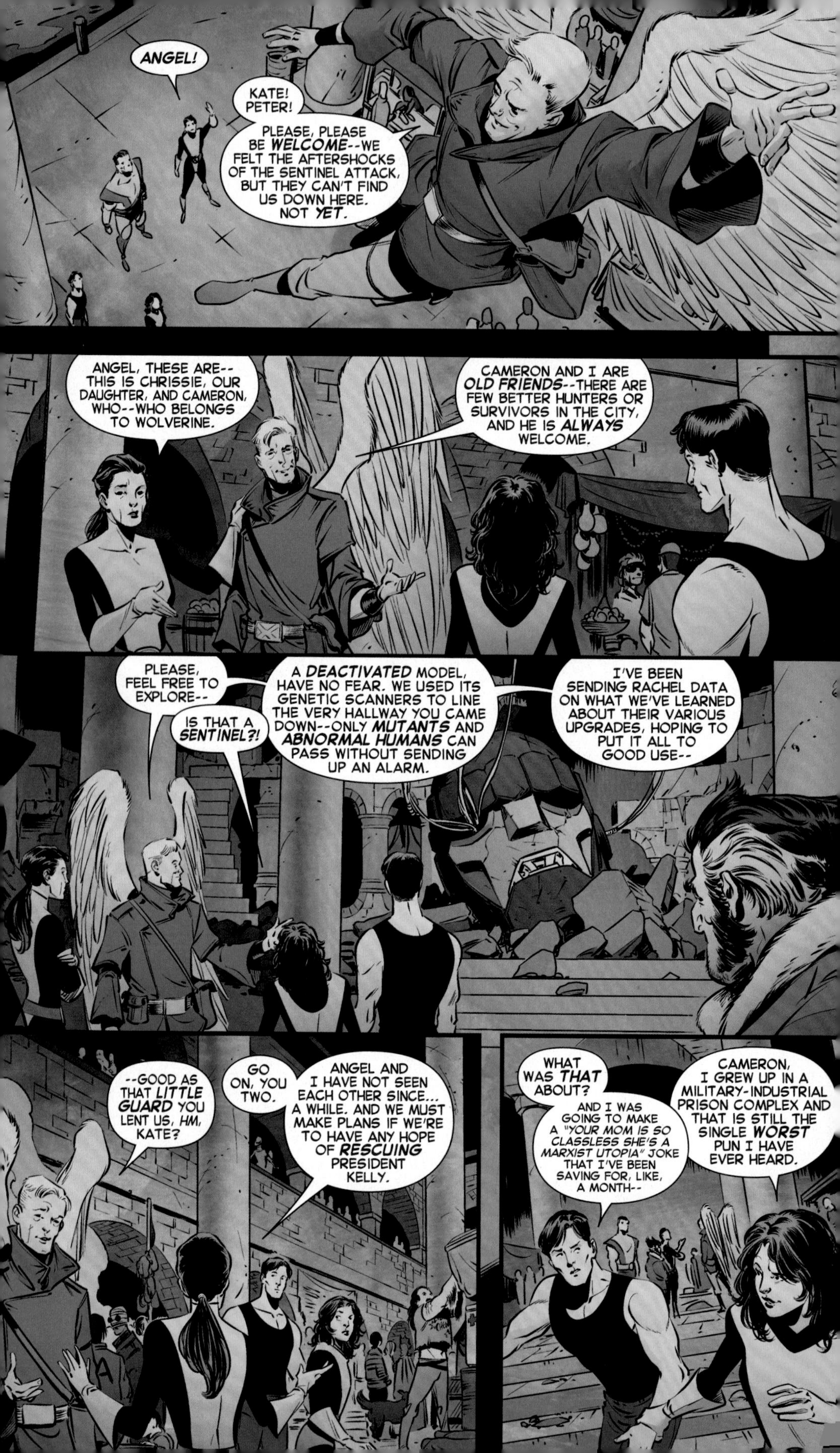
ANGEL!
KATE! PETER!
PLEASE, PLEASE BE WELCOME--WE FELT THE AFTERSHOCKS OF THE SENTINEL ATTACK, BUT THEY CAN'T FIND US DOWN HERE. NOT YET.
ANGEL, THESE ARE-- THIS IS CHRISSIE, OUR DAUGHTER, AND CAMERON, WHO--WHO BELONGS TO WOLVERINE.
CAMERON AND I ARE OLD FRIENDS--THERE ARE FEW BETTER HUNTERS OR SURVIVORS IN THE CITY, AND HE IS ALWAYS WELCOME.
PLEASE, FEEL FREE TO EXPLORE--
IS THAT A SENTINEL?!
A DEACTIVATED MODEL, HAVE NO FEAR. WE USED ITS GENETIC SCANNERS TO LINE THE VERY HALLWAY YOU CAME DOWN--ONLY MUTANTS AND ABNORMAL HUMANS CAN PASS WITHOUT SENDING UP AN ALARM.
I'VE BEEN SENDING RACHEL DATA ON WHAT WE'VE LEARNED ABOUT THEIR VARIOUS UPGRADES, HOPING TO PUT IT ALL TO GOOD USE--
--GOOD AS THAT LITTLE GUARD YOU LENT US, HM, KATE?
GO ON, YOU TWO.
ANGEL AND I HAVE NOT SEEN EACH OTHER SINCE... A WHILE. AND WE MUST MAKE PLANS IF WE'RE TO HAVE ANY HOPE OF RESCUING PRESIDENT KELLY.
WHAT WAS THAT ABOUT?
AND I WAS GOING TO MAKE A "YOUR MOM IS SO CLASSLESS SHE'S A MARXIST UTOPIA" JOKE THAT I'VE BEEN SAVING FOR, LIKE, A MONTH--
CAMERON, I GREW UP IN A MILITARY-INDUSTRIAL PRISON COMPLEX AND THAT IS STILL THE SINGLE WORST PUN I HAVE EVER HEARD.

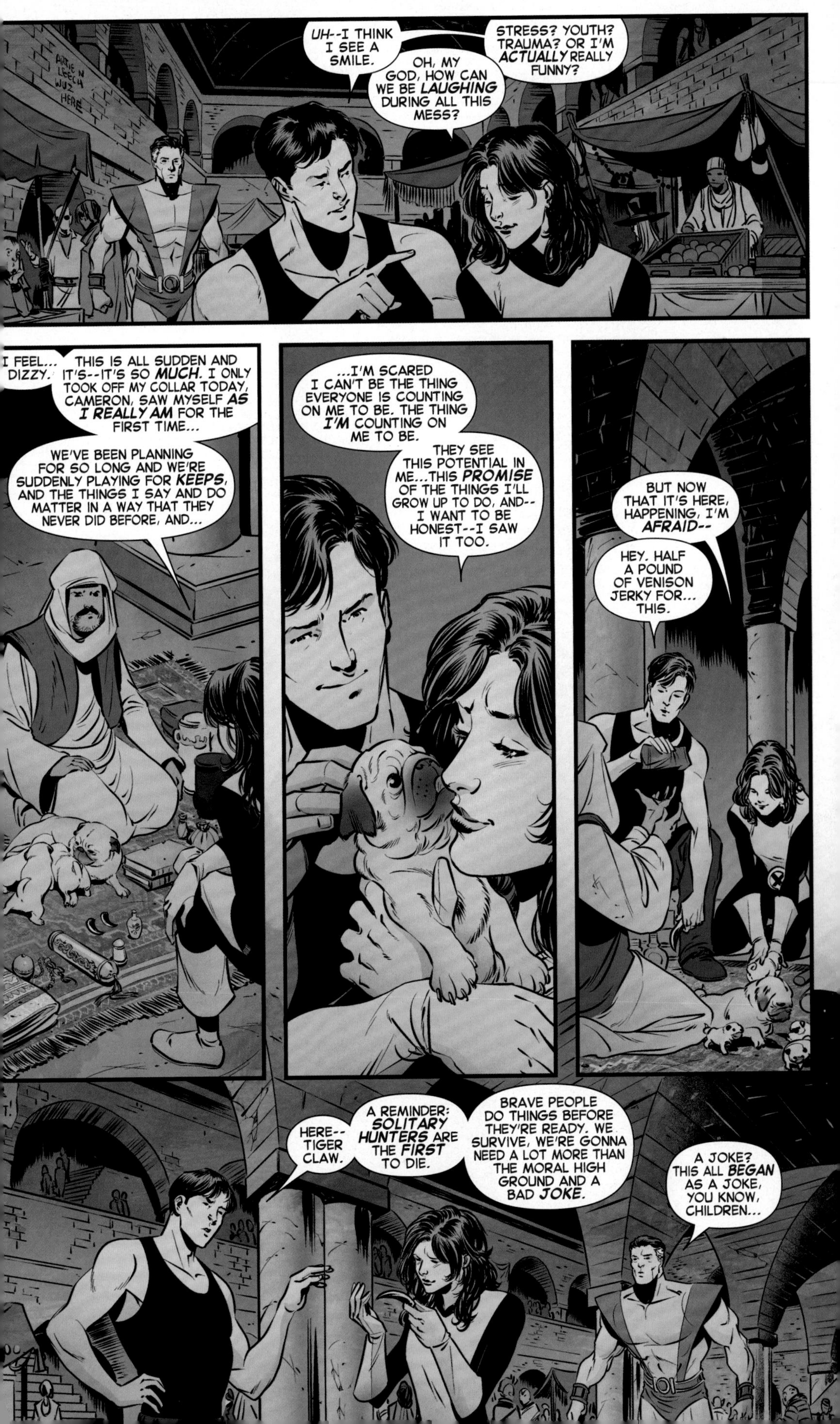
ARTIE N LEECH WUZ HERE
UH--I THINK I SEE A SMILE.
STRESS? YOUTH? TRAUMA? OR I'M ACTUALLY REALLY FUNNY?
OH, MY GOD, HOW CAN WE BE LAUGHING DURING ALL THIS MESS?
I FEEL... DIZZY.
THIS IS ALL SUDDEN AND IT'S--IT'S SO MUCH. I ONLY TOOK OFF MY COLLAR TODAY, CAMERON, SAW MYSELF AS I REALLY AM FOR THE FIRST TIME...
WE'VE BEEN PLANNING FOR SO LONG AND WE'RE SUDDENLY PLAYING FOR KEEPS, AND THE THINGS I SAY AND DO MATTER IN A WAY THAT THEY NEVER DID BEFORE, AND...
...I'M SCARED I CAN'T BE THE THING EVERYONE IS COUNTING ON ME TO BE. THE THING I'M COUNTING ON ME TO BE.
THEY SEE THIS POTENTIAL IN ME...THIS PROMISE OF THE THINGS I'LL GROW UP TO DO, AND--I WANT TO BE HONEST--I SAW IT TOO.
BUT NOW THAT IT'S HERE, HAPPENING, I'M AFRAID--
HEY. HALF A POUND OF VENISON JERKY FOR... THIS.
HERE--TIGER CLAW.
A REMINDER: SOLITARY HUNTERS ARE THE FIRST TO DIE.
BRAVE PEOPLE DO THINGS BEFORE THEY'RE READY. WE SURVIVE, WE'RE GONNA NEED A LOT MORE THAN THE MORAL HIGH GROUND AND A BAD JOKE.
A JOKE? THIS ALL BEGAN AS A JOKE, YOU KNOW, CHILDREN...

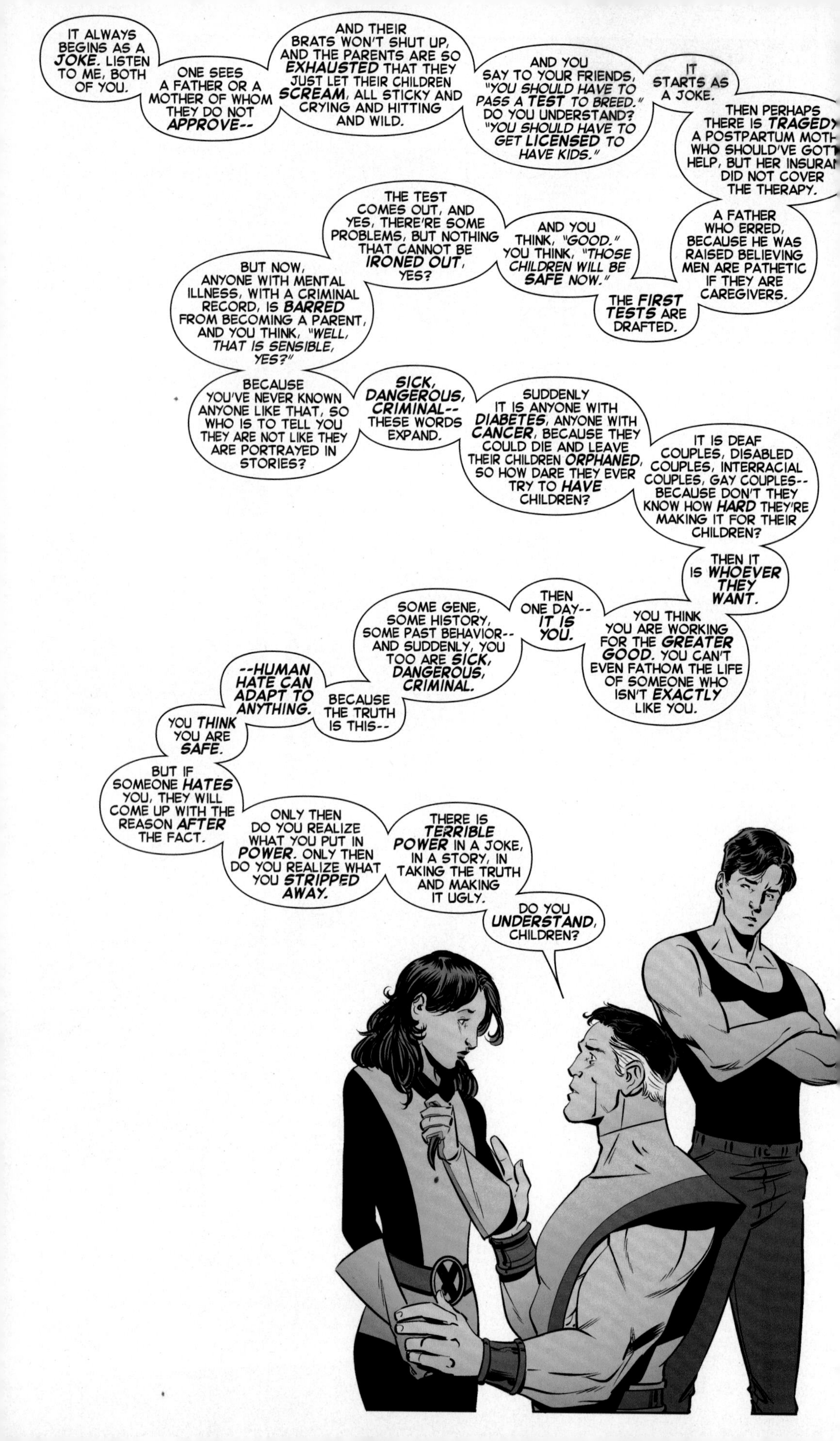

IT ALWAYS BEGINS AS A JOKE. LISTEN TO ME, BOTH OF YOU.
ONE SEES A FATHER OR A MOTHER OF WHOM THEY DO NOT APPROVE--
AND THEIR BRATS WON'T SHUT UP, AND THE PARENTS ARE SO EXHAUSTED THAT THEY JUST LET THEIR CHILDREN SCREAM, ALL STICKY AND CRYING AND HITTING AND WILD.
AND YOU SAY TO YOUR FRIENDS, "YOU SHOULD HAVE TO PASS A TEST TO BREED." DO YOU UNDERSTAND? "YOU SHOULD HAVE TO GET LICENSED TO HAVE KIDS."
IT STARTS AS A JOKE.
THEN PERHAPS THERE IS TRAGED A POSTPARTUM MOTH WHO SHOULD'VE GOT HELP, BUT HER INSURA DID NOT COVER THE THERAPY.
A FATHER WHO ERRED, BECAUSE HE WAS RAISED BELIEVING MEN ARE PATHETIC IF THEY ARE CAREGIVERS.
THE FIRST TESTS ARE DRAFTED.
AND YOU THINK, "GOOD." YOU THINK, "THOSE CHILDREN WILL BE SAFE NOW."
THE TEST COMES OUT, AND YES, THERE'RE SOME PROBLEMS, BUT NOTHING THAT CANNOT BE IRONED OUT, YES?
BUT NOW, ANYONE WITH MENTAL ILLNESS, WITH A CRIMINAL RECORD, IS BARRED FROM BECOMING A PARENT, AND YOU THINK, "WELL, THAT IS SENSIBLE, YES?"
BECAUSE YOU'VE NEVER KNOWN ANYONE LIKE THAT, SO WHO IS TO TELL YOU THEY ARE NOT LIKE THEY ARE PORTRAYED IN STORIES?
SICK, DANGEROUS, CRIMINAL-- THESE WORDS EXPAND.
SUDDENLY IT IS ANYONE WITH DIABETES, ANYONE WITH CANCER, BECAUSE THEY COULD DIE AND LEAVE THEIR CHILDREN ORPHANED, SO HOW DARE THEY EVER TRY TO HAVE CHILDREN?
IT IS DEAF COUPLES, DISABLED COUPLES, INTERRACIAL COUPLES, GAY COUPLES-- BECAUSE DON'T THEY KNOW HOW HARD THEY'RE MAKING IT FOR THEIR CHILDREN?
THEN IT IS WHOEVER THEY WANT.
YOU THINK YOU ARE WORKING FOR THE GREATER GOOD. YOU CAN'T EVEN FATHOM THE LIFE OF SOMEONE WHO ISN'T EXACTLY LIKE YOU.
THEN ONE DAY-- IT IS YOU.
SOME GENE, SOME HISTORY, SOME PAST BEHAVIOR-- AND SUDDENLY, YOU TOO ARE SICK, DANGEROUS, CRIMINAL.
BECAUSE THE TRUTH IS THIS--
--HUMAN HATE CAN ADAPT TO ANYTHING.
YOU THINK YOU ARE SAFE.
BUT IF SOMEONE HATES YOU, THEY WILL COME UP WITH THE REASON AFTER THE FACT.
ONLY THEN DO YOU REALIZE WHAT YOU PUT IN POWER. ONLY THEN DO YOU REALIZE WHAT YOU STRIPPED AWAY.
THERE IS TERRIBLE POWER IN A JOKE, IN A STORY, IN TAKING THE TRUTH AND MAKING IT UGLY.
DO YOU UNDERSTAND, CHILDREN?

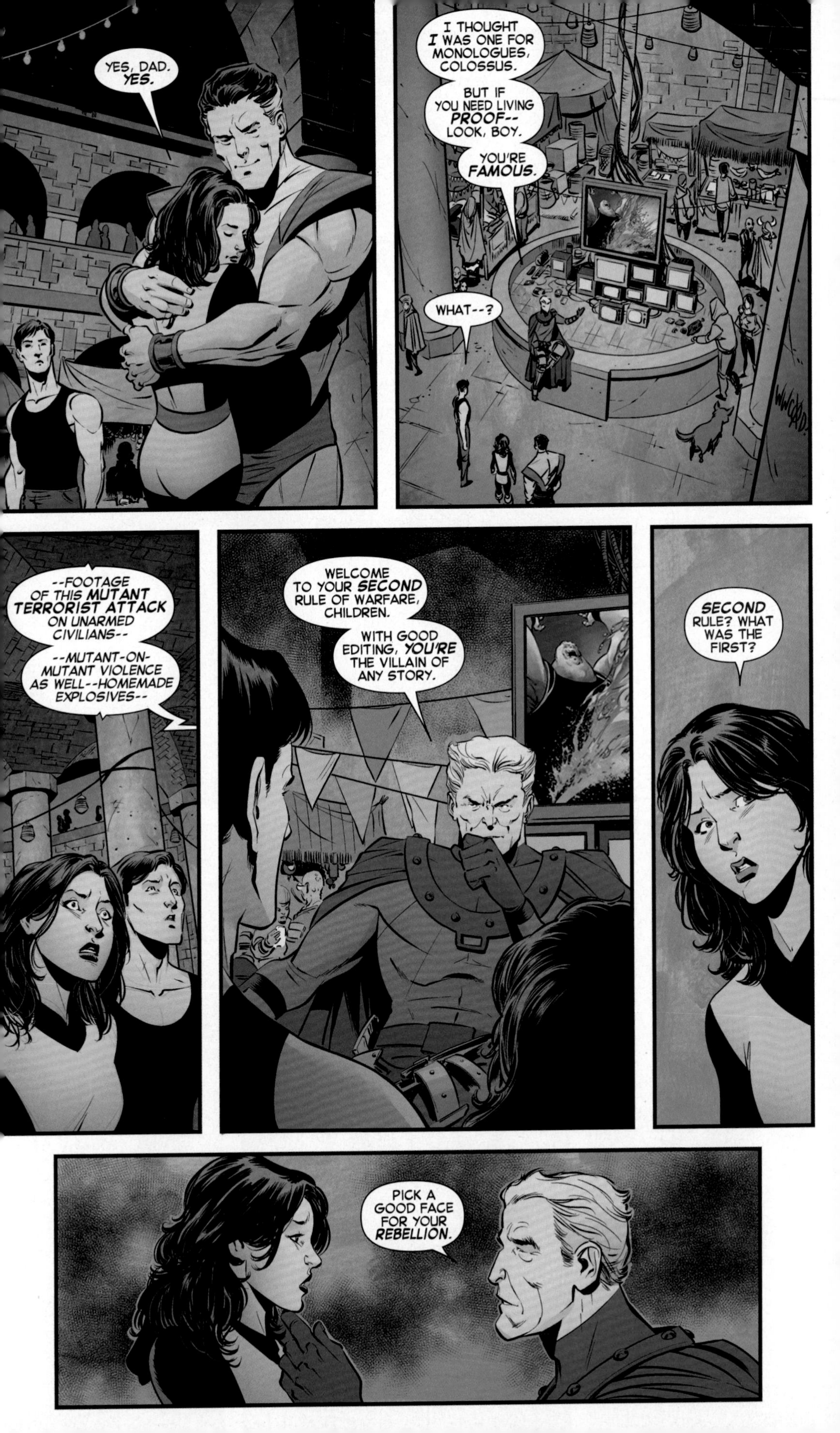
YES, DAD. **YES.**
I THOUGHT *I* WAS ONE FOR MONOLOGUES, COLOSSUS.
BUT IF YOU NEED LIVING *PROOF--* LOOK, BOY.
YOU'RE *FAMOUS.*
WHAT--?
--FOOTAGE OF THIS **MUTANT TERRORIST ATTACK** ON UNARMED CIVILIANS--
--MUTANT-ON-MUTANT VIOLENCE AS WELL--HOMEMADE EXPLOSIVES--
WELCOME TO YOUR ***SECOND*** RULE OF WARFARE, CHILDREN.
WITH GOOD EDITING, ***YOU'RE*** THE VILLAIN OF ANY STORY.
SECOND RULE? WHAT WAS THE FIRST?
PICK A GOOD FACE FOR YOUR ***REBELLION.***

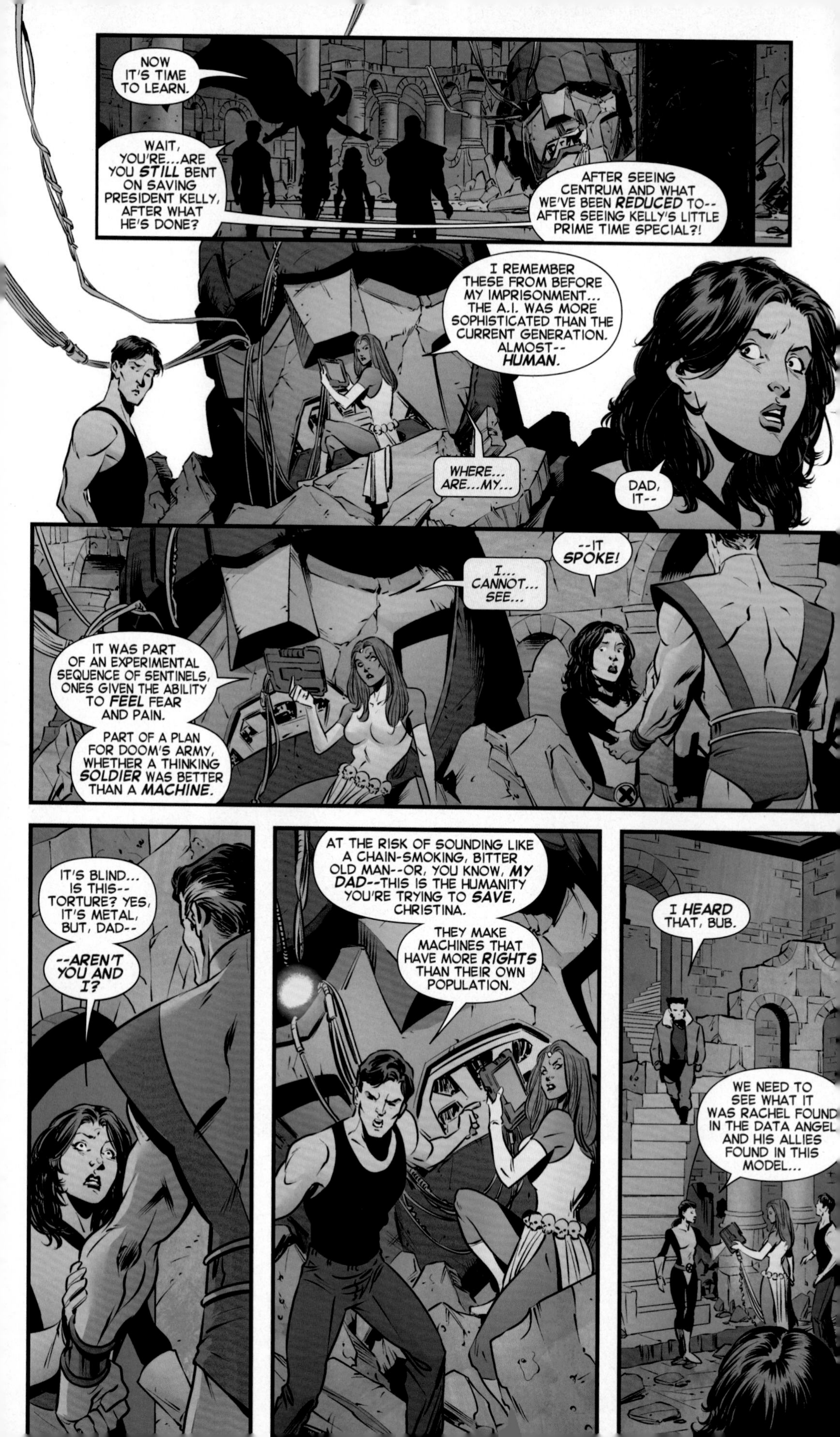
NOW IT'S TIME TO LEARN.
WAIT, YOU'RE...ARE YOU STILL BENT ON SAVING PRESIDENT KELLY, AFTER WHAT HE'S DONE?
AFTER SEEING CENTRUM AND WHAT WE'VE BEEN REDUCED TO--AFTER SEEING KELLY'S LITTLE PRIME TIME SPECIAL?!
I REMEMBER THESE FROM BEFORE MY IMPRISONMENT... THE A.I. WAS MORE SOPHISTICATED THAN THE CURRENT GENERATION. ALMOST--HUMAN.
WHERE... ARE...MY...
DAD, IT--
--IT SPOKE!
I... CANNOT... SEE...
IT WAS PART OF AN EXPERIMENTAL SEQUENCE OF SENTINELS, ONES GIVEN THE ABILITY TO FEEL FEAR AND PAIN.
PART OF A PLAN FOR DOOM'S ARMY, WHETHER A THINKING SOLDIER WAS BETTER THAN A MACHINE.
IT'S BLIND... IS THIS--TORTURE? YES, IT'S METAL, BUT, DAD--
--AREN'T YOU AND I?
AT THE RISK OF SOUNDING LIKE A CHAIN-SMOKING, BITTER OLD MAN--OR, YOU KNOW, MY DAD--THIS IS THE HUMANITY YOU'RE TRYING TO SAVE, CHRISTINA.
THEY MAKE MACHINES THAT HAVE MORE RIGHTS THAN THEIR OWN POPULATION.
I HEARD THAT, BUB.
WE NEED TO SEE WHAT IT WAS RACHEL FOUND IN THE DATA ANGEL AND HIS ALLIES FOUND IN THIS MODEL...

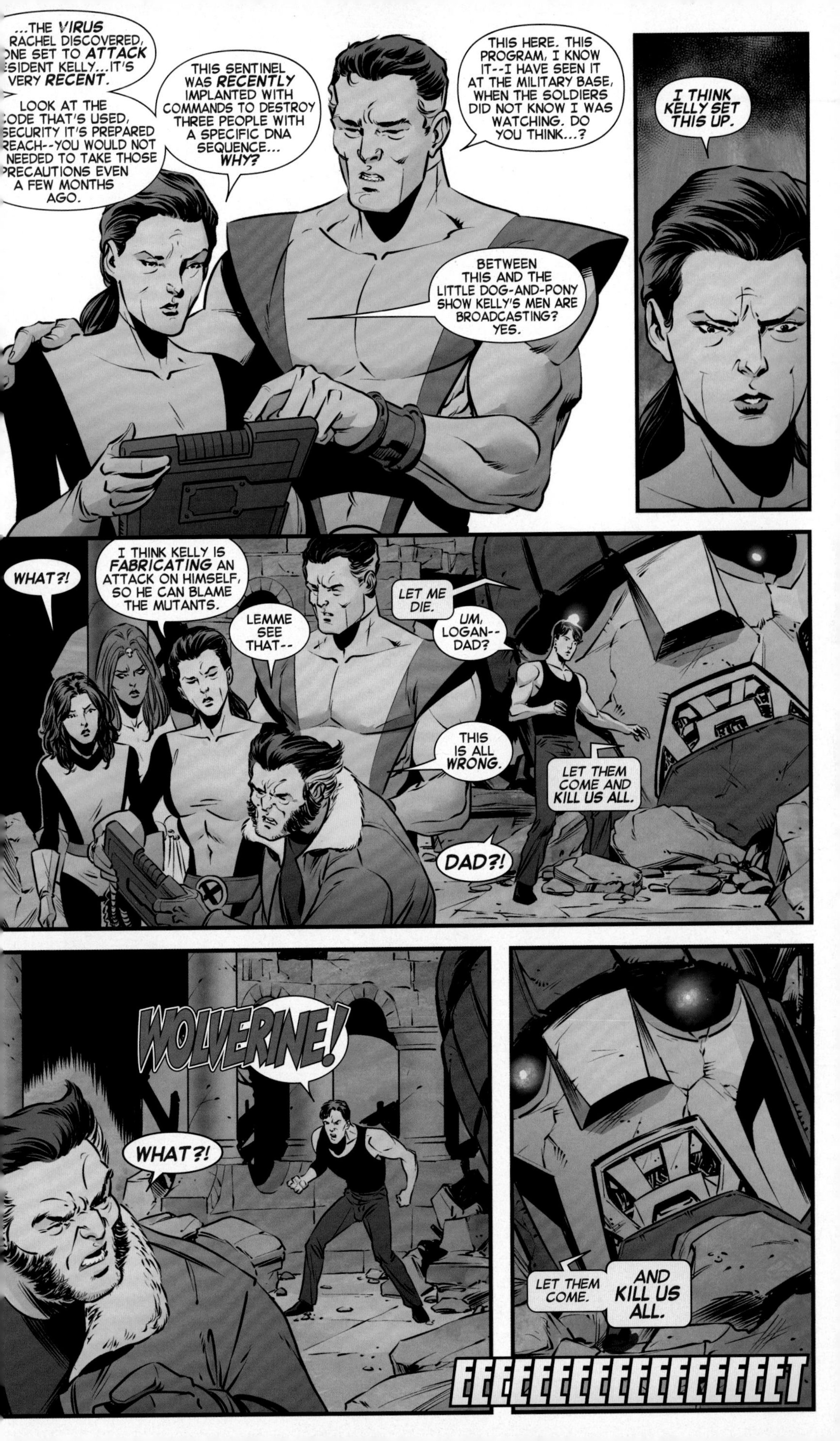
...THE VIRUS RACHEL DISCOVERED, ONE SET TO ATTACK ESIDENT KELLY...IT'S VERY RECENT.
LOOK AT THE CODE THAT'S USED, SECURITY IT'S PREPARED REACH--YOU WOULD NOT NEEDED TO TAKE THOSE PRECAUTIONS EVEN A FEW MONTHS AGO.
THIS SENTINEL WAS RECENTLY IMPLANTED WITH COMMANDS TO DESTROY THREE PEOPLE WITH A SPECIFIC DNA SEQUENCE... WHY?
THIS HERE. THIS PROGRAM, I KNOW IT--I HAVE SEEN IT AT THE MILITARY BASE, WHEN THE SOLDIERS DID NOT KNOW I WAS WATCHING. DO YOU THINK...?
BETWEEN THIS AND THE LITTLE DOG-AND-PONY SHOW KELLY'S MEN ARE BROADCASTING? YES.
I THINK KELLY SET THIS UP.
WHAT?!
I THINK KELLY IS FABRICATING AN ATTACK ON HIMSELF, SO HE CAN BLAME THE MUTANTS.
LEMME SEE THAT--
LET ME DIE.
UM, LOGAN-- DAD?
THIS IS ALL WRONG.
LET THEM COME AND KILL US ALL.
DAD?!
WOLVERINE!
WHAT?!
LET THEM COME.
AND KILL US ALL.
EEEEEEEEEEEEEEEEEET

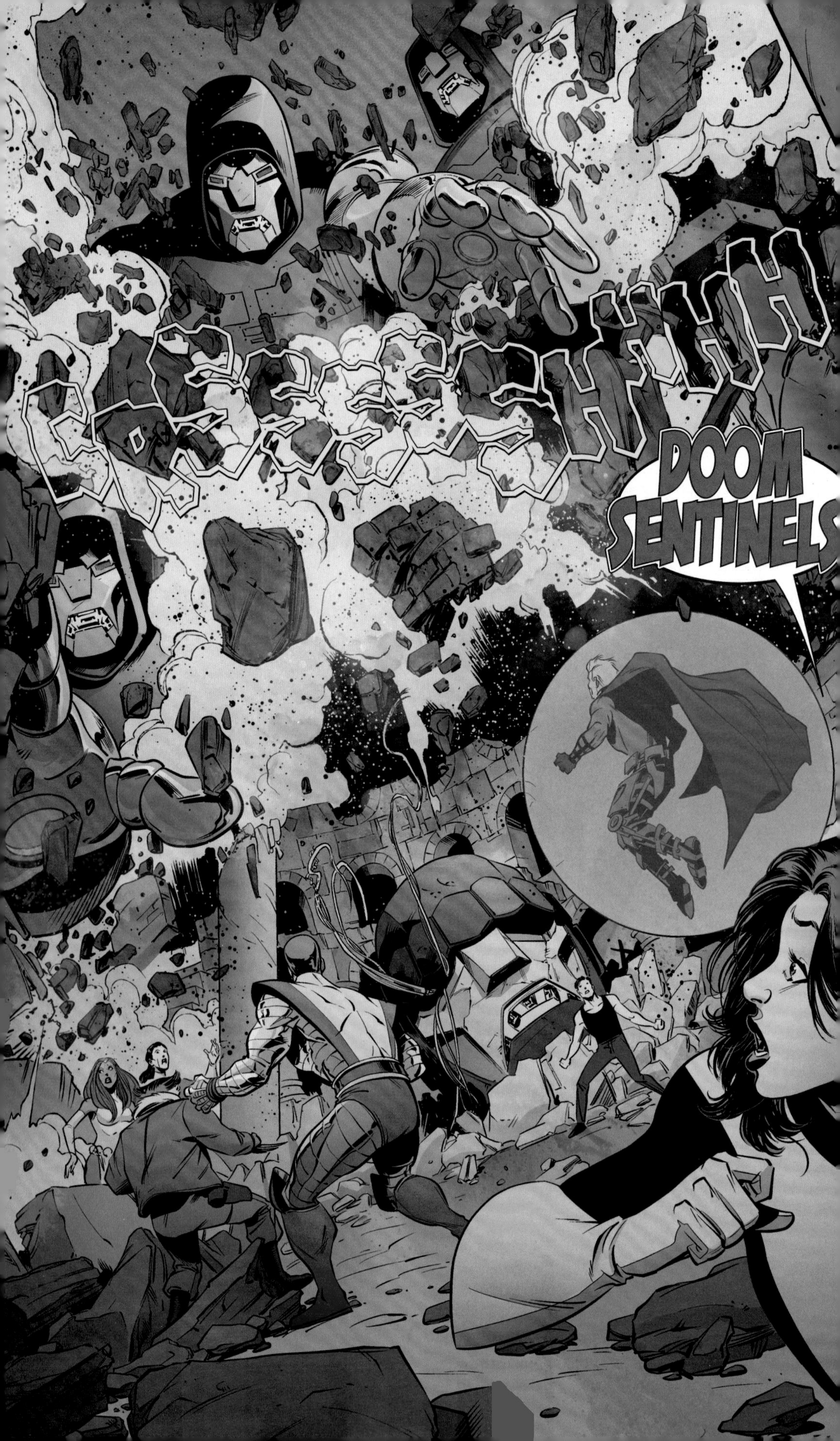
DOOM SENTINELS

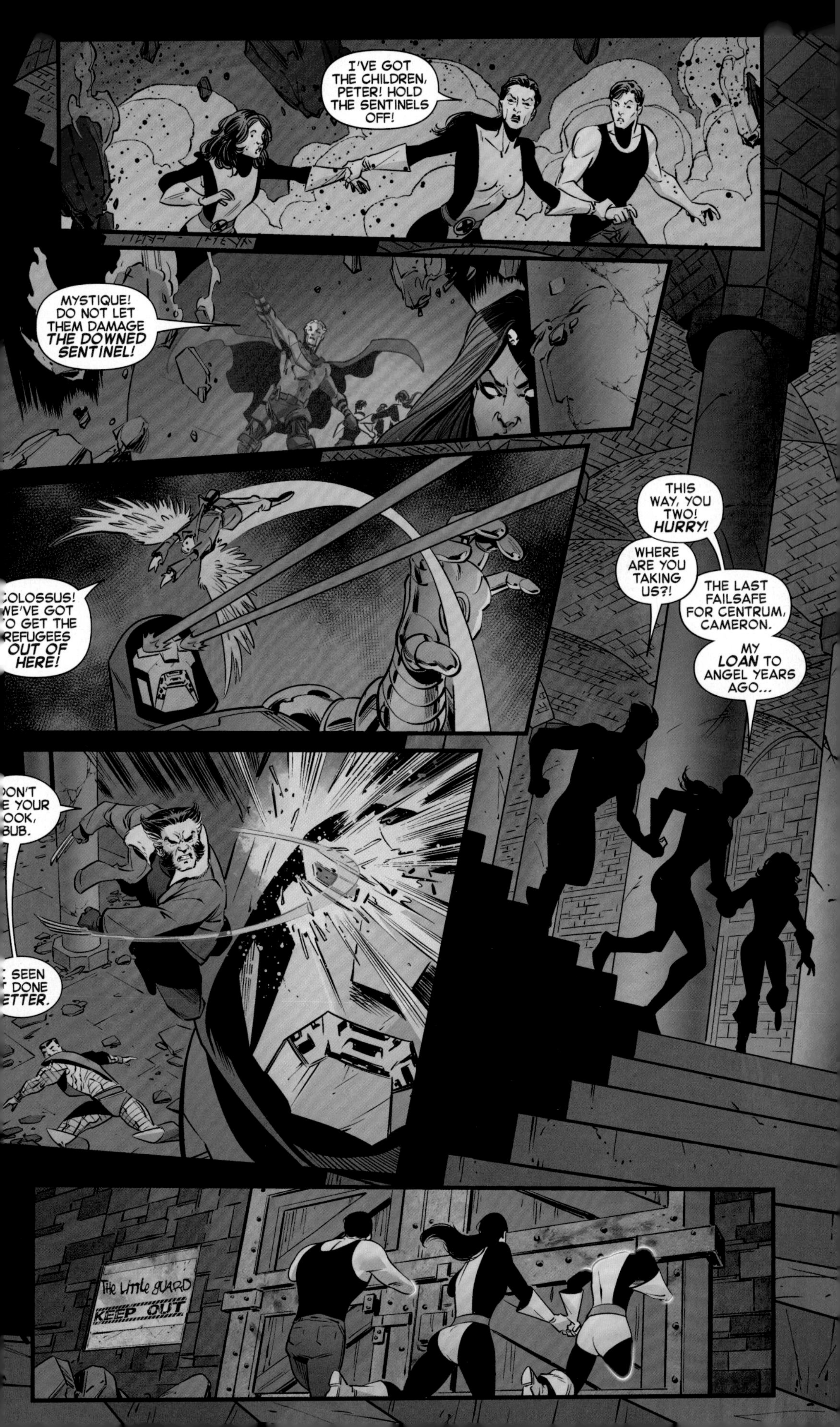
I'VE GOT THE CHILDREN, PETER! HOLD THE SENTINELS OFF!
MYSTIQUE! DO NOT LET THEM DAMAGE THE DOWNED SENTINEL!
COLOSSUS! WE'VE GOT TO GET THE REFUGEES OUT OF HERE!
THIS WAY, YOU TWO! HURRY!
WHERE ARE YOU TAKING US?!
THE LAST FAILSAFE FOR CENTRUM, CAMERON.
MY LOAN TO ANGEL YEARS AGO...
DON'T E YOUR OOK, BUB.
SEEN DONE ETTER.
The Little GUARD
KEEP OUT

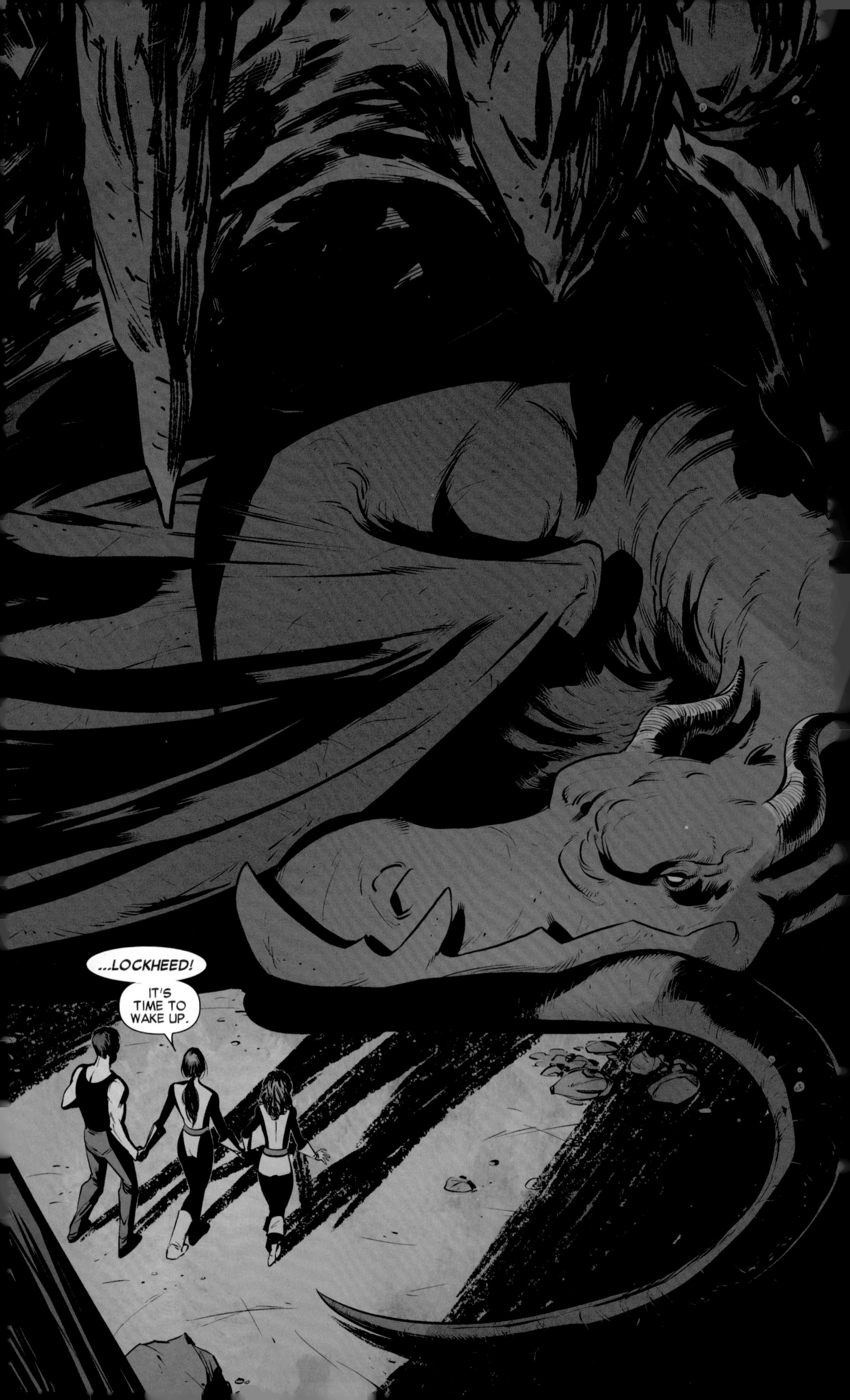
...LOCKHEED!
IT'S TIME TO WAKE UP.

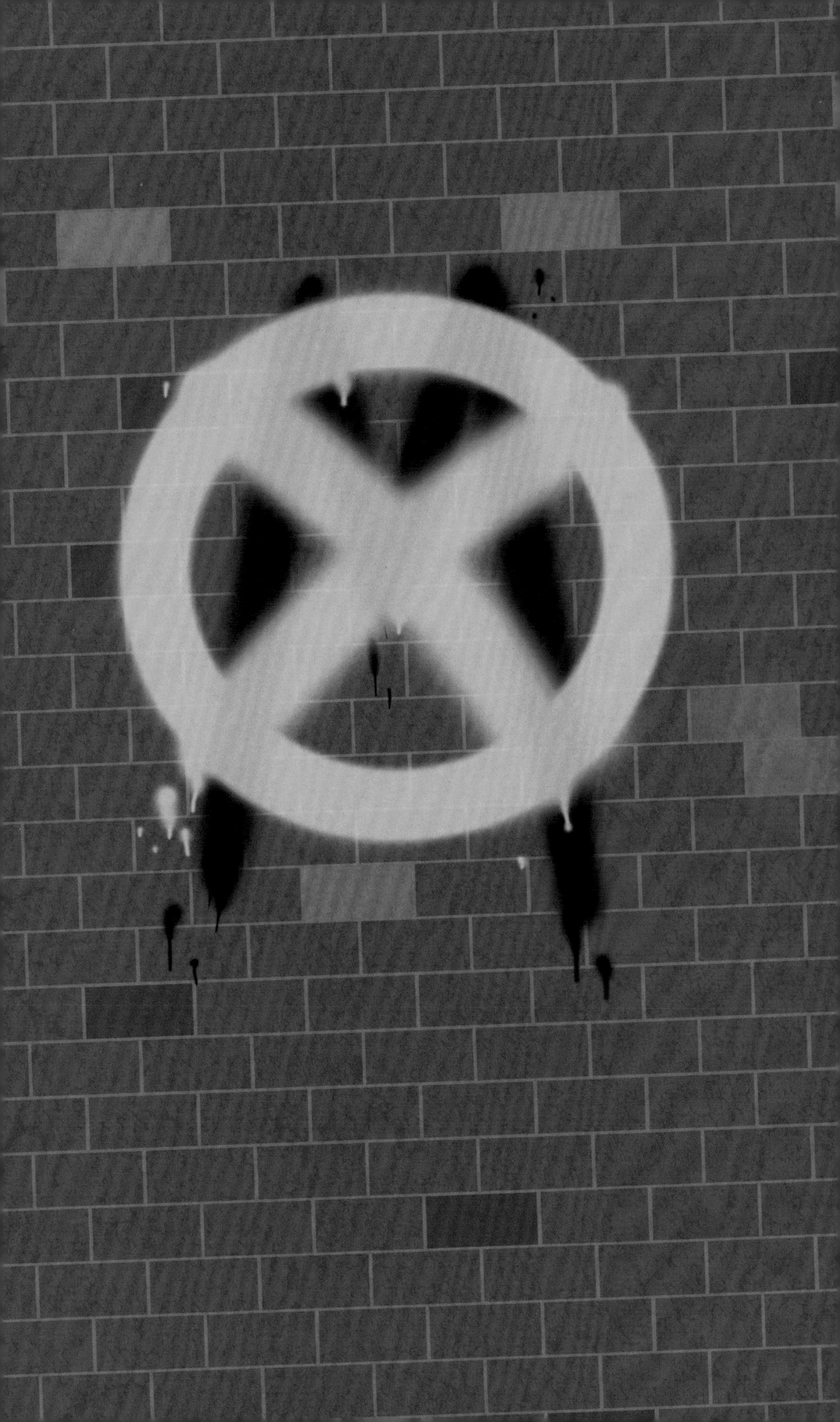

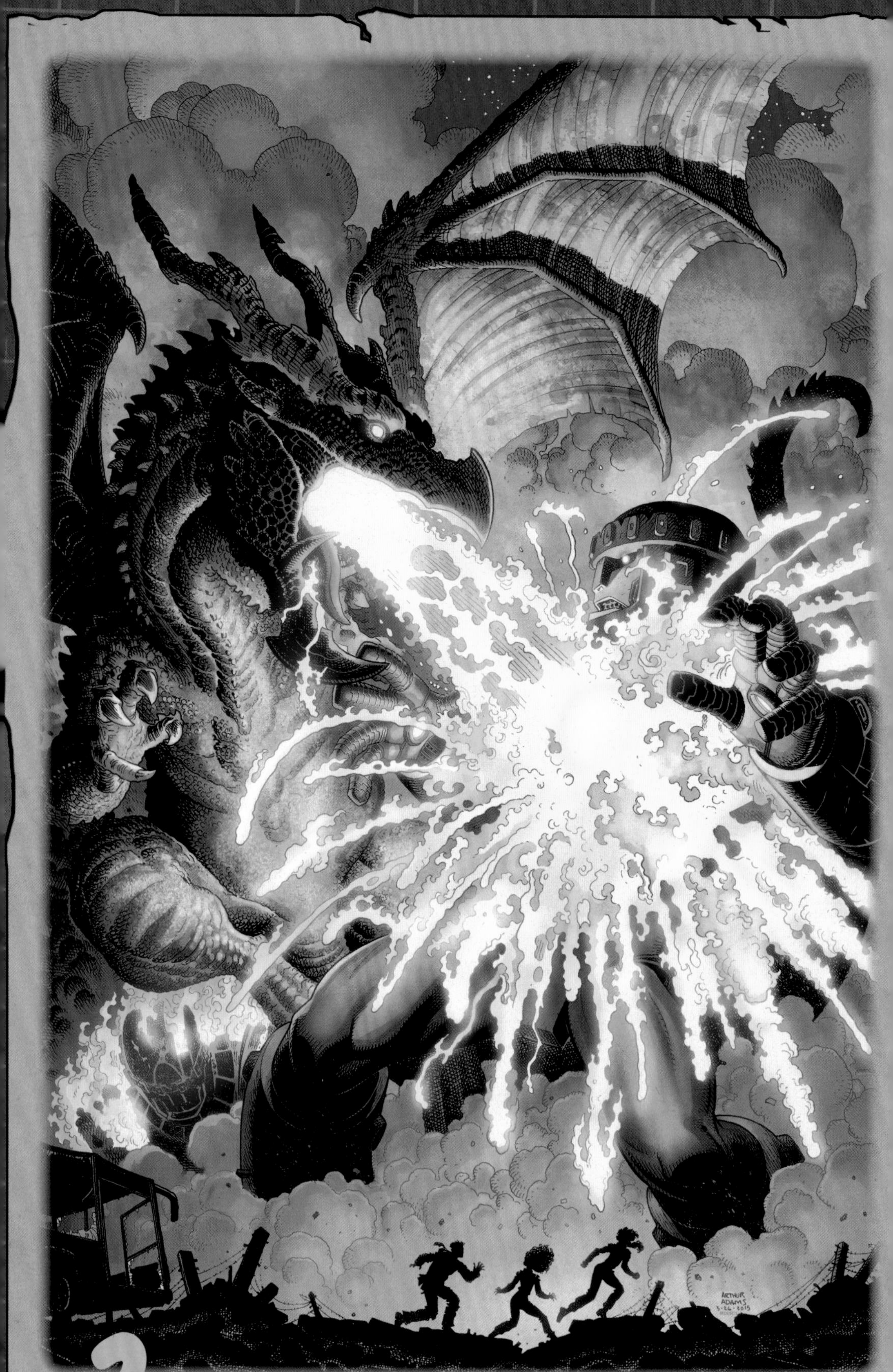
ARTHUR ADAMS 3-26-2015

3

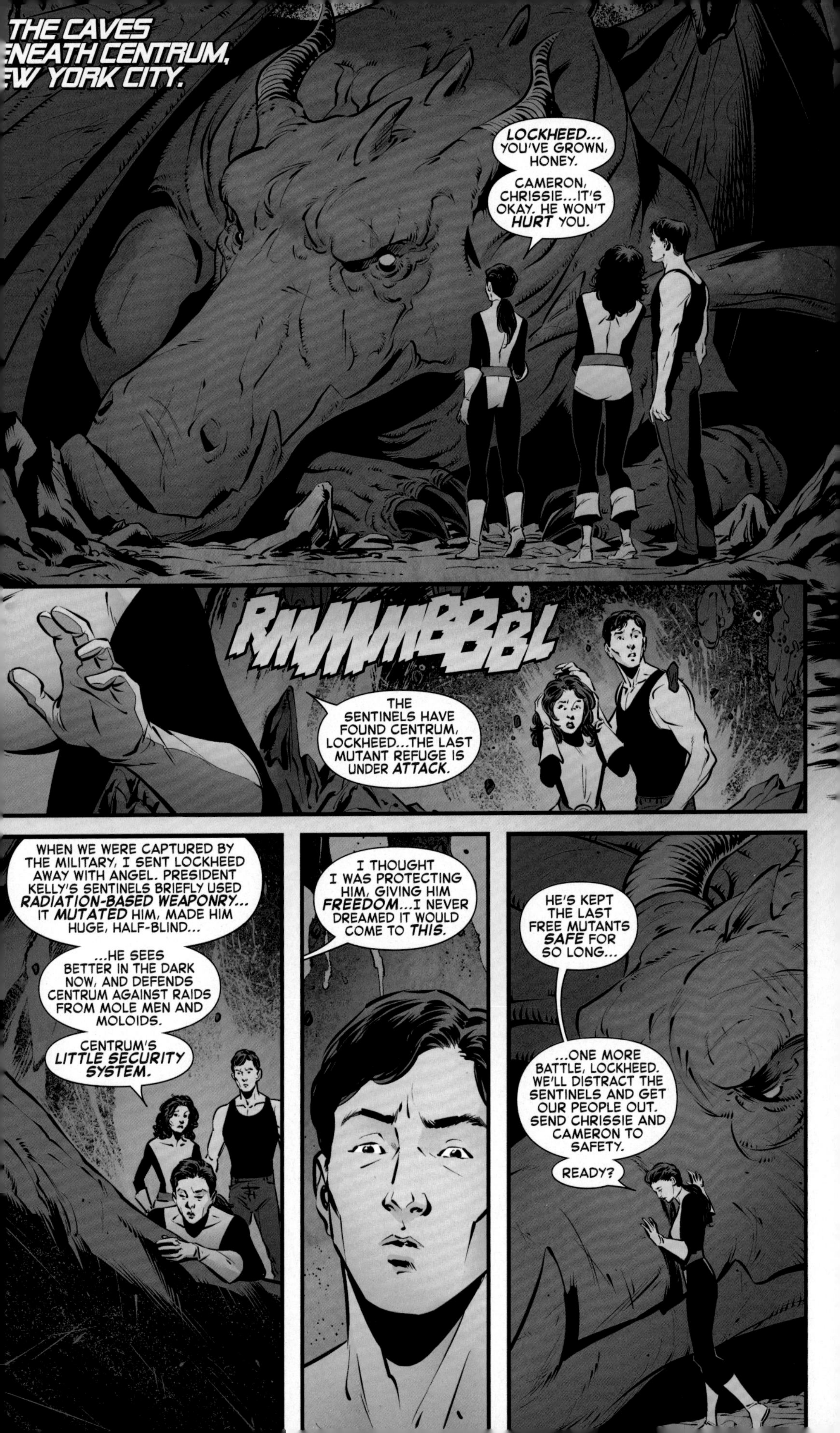
THE CAVES
ENEATH CENTRUM,
EW YORK CITY.
LOCKHEED... YOU'VE GROWN, HONEY.
CAMERON, CHRISSIE...IT'S OKAY. HE WON'T HURT YOU.
RMMMBBBL
THE SENTINELS HAVE FOUND CENTRUM, LOCKHEED...THE LAST MUTANT REFUGE IS UNDER ATTACK.
WHEN WE WERE CAPTURED BY THE MILITARY, I SENT LOCKHEED AWAY WITH ANGEL. PRESIDENT KELLY'S SENTINELS BRIEFLY USED RADIATION-BASED WEAPONRY... IT MUTATED HIM, MADE HIM HUGE, HALF-BLIND...
...HE SEES BETTER IN THE DARK NOW, AND DEFENDS CENTRUM AGAINST RAIDS FROM MOLE MEN AND MOLOIDS.
CENTRUM'S LITTLE SECURITY SYSTEM.
I THOUGHT I WAS PROTECTING HIM, GIVING HIM FREEDOM...I NEVER DREAMED IT WOULD COME TO THIS.
HE'S KEPT THE LAST FREE MUTANTS SAFE FOR SO LONG...
...ONE MORE BATTLE, LOCKHEED. WE'LL DISTRACT THE SENTINELS AND GET OUR PEOPLE OUT. SEND CHRISSIE AND CAMERON TO SAFETY.
READY?

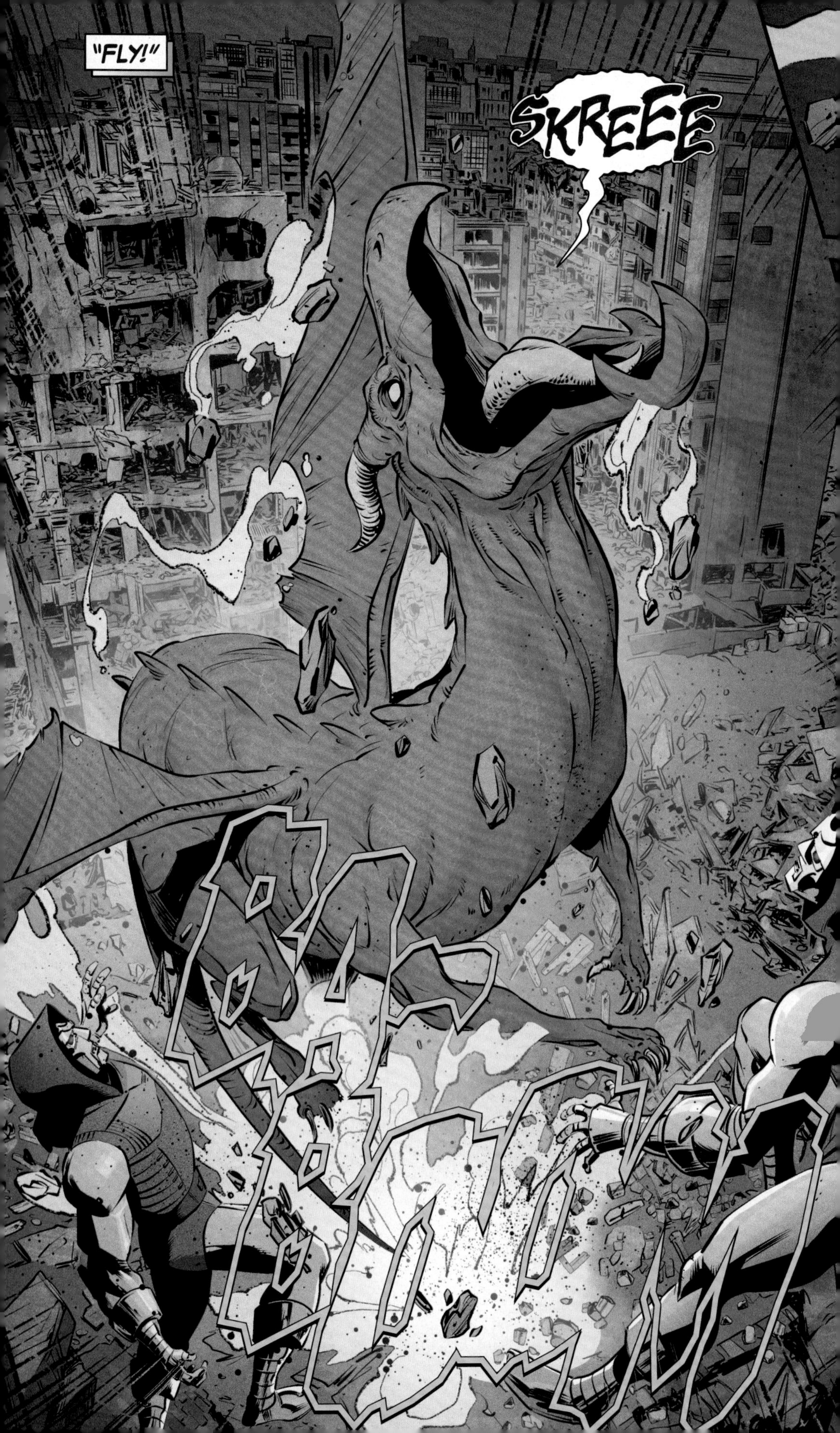
"FLY!"
SKREEE

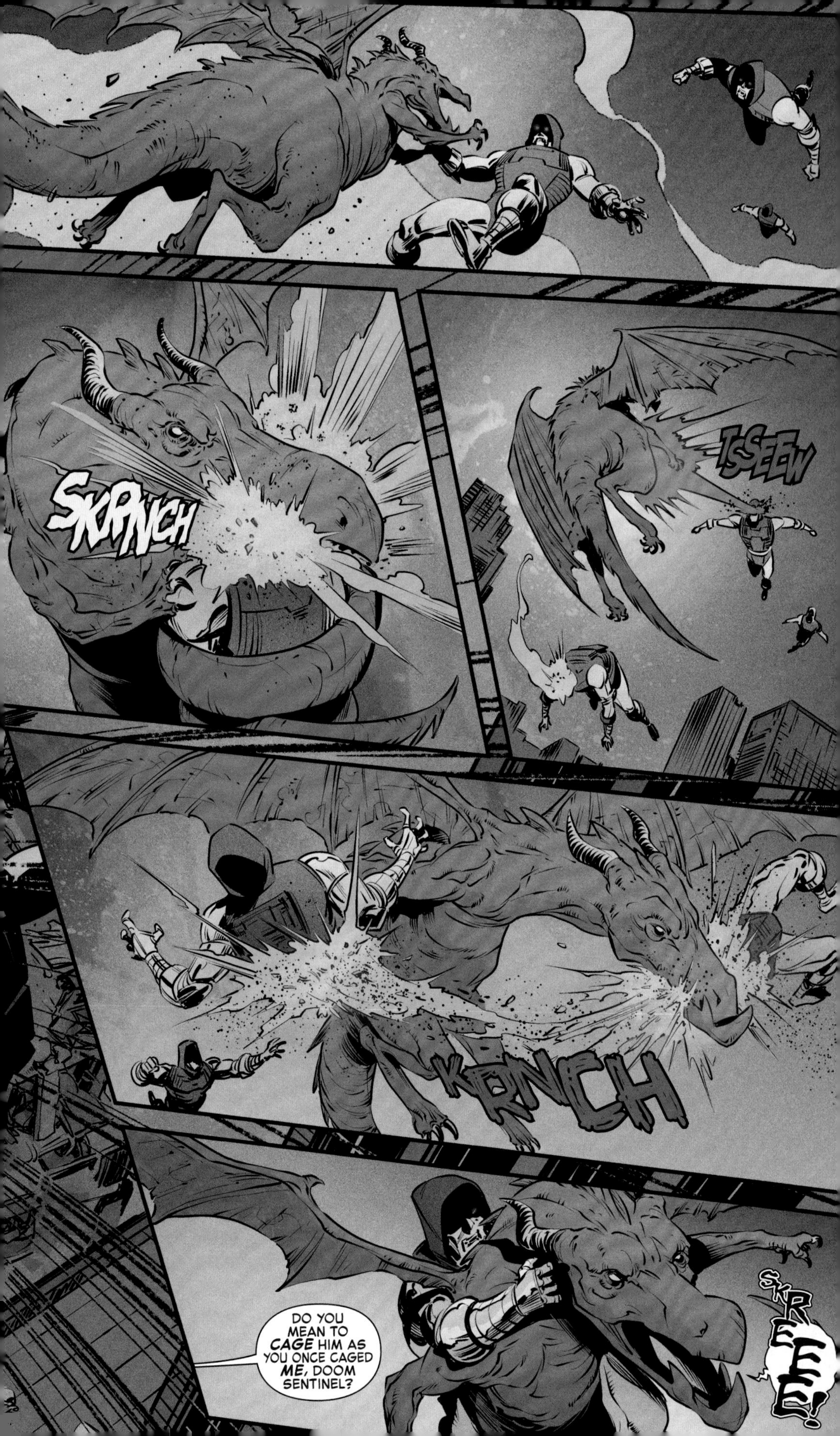
SKRNCH
TSSEEW
KRNCH
DO YOU MEAN TO CAGE HIM AS YOU ONCE CAGED ME, DOOM SENTINEL?
SKREEE!

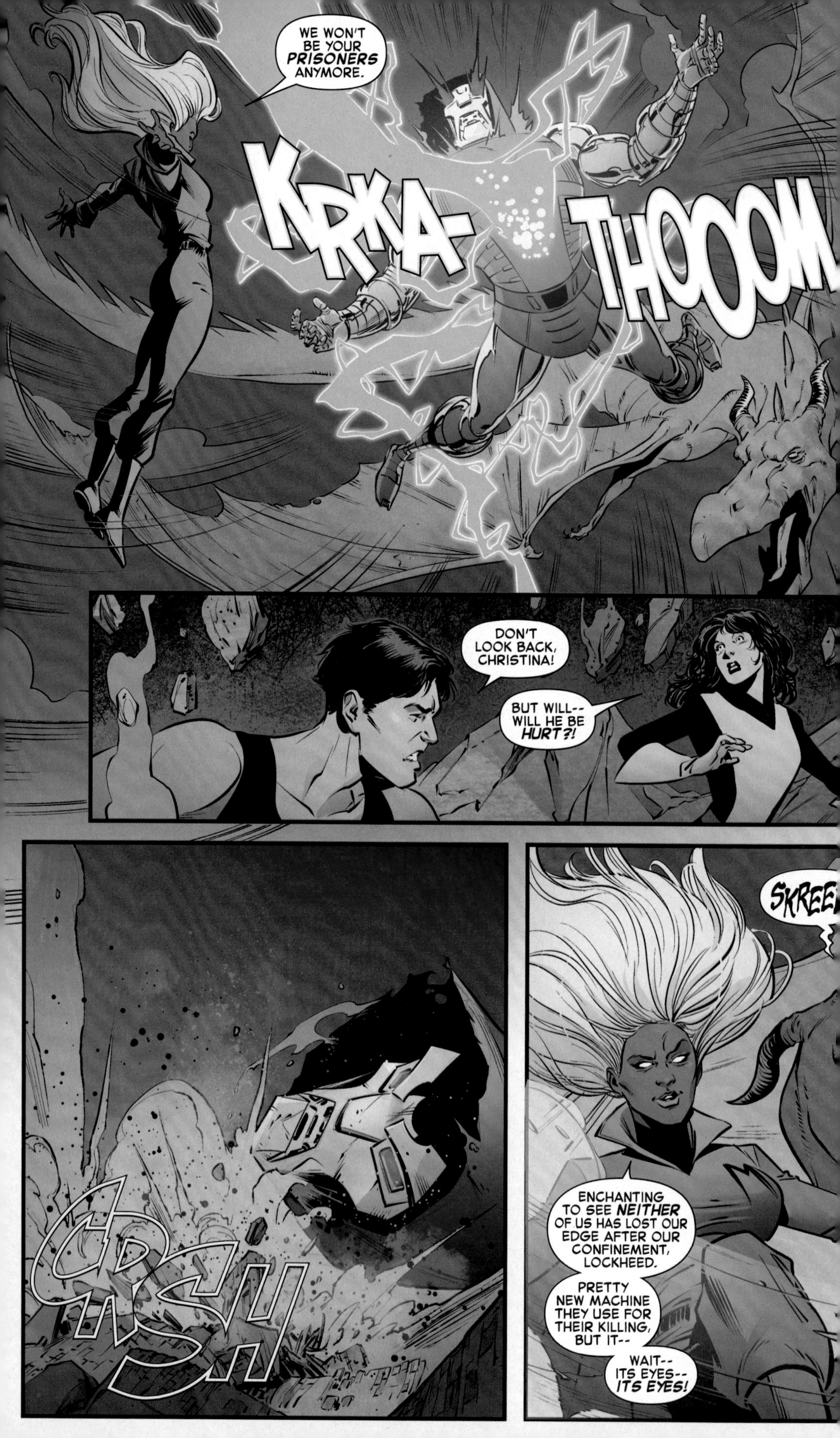
WE WON'T BE YOUR PRISONERS ANYMORE.
KRKA-
THOOOM
DON'T LOOK BACK, CHRISTINA!
BUT WILL-- WILL HE BE HURT?!
CRASH
SKREE
ENCHANTING TO SEE NEITHER OF US HAS LOST OUR EDGE AFTER OUR CONFINEMENT, LOCKHEED.
PRETTY NEW MACHINE THEY USE FOR THEIR KILLING, BUT IT--
WAIT-- ITS EYES-- ITS EYES!

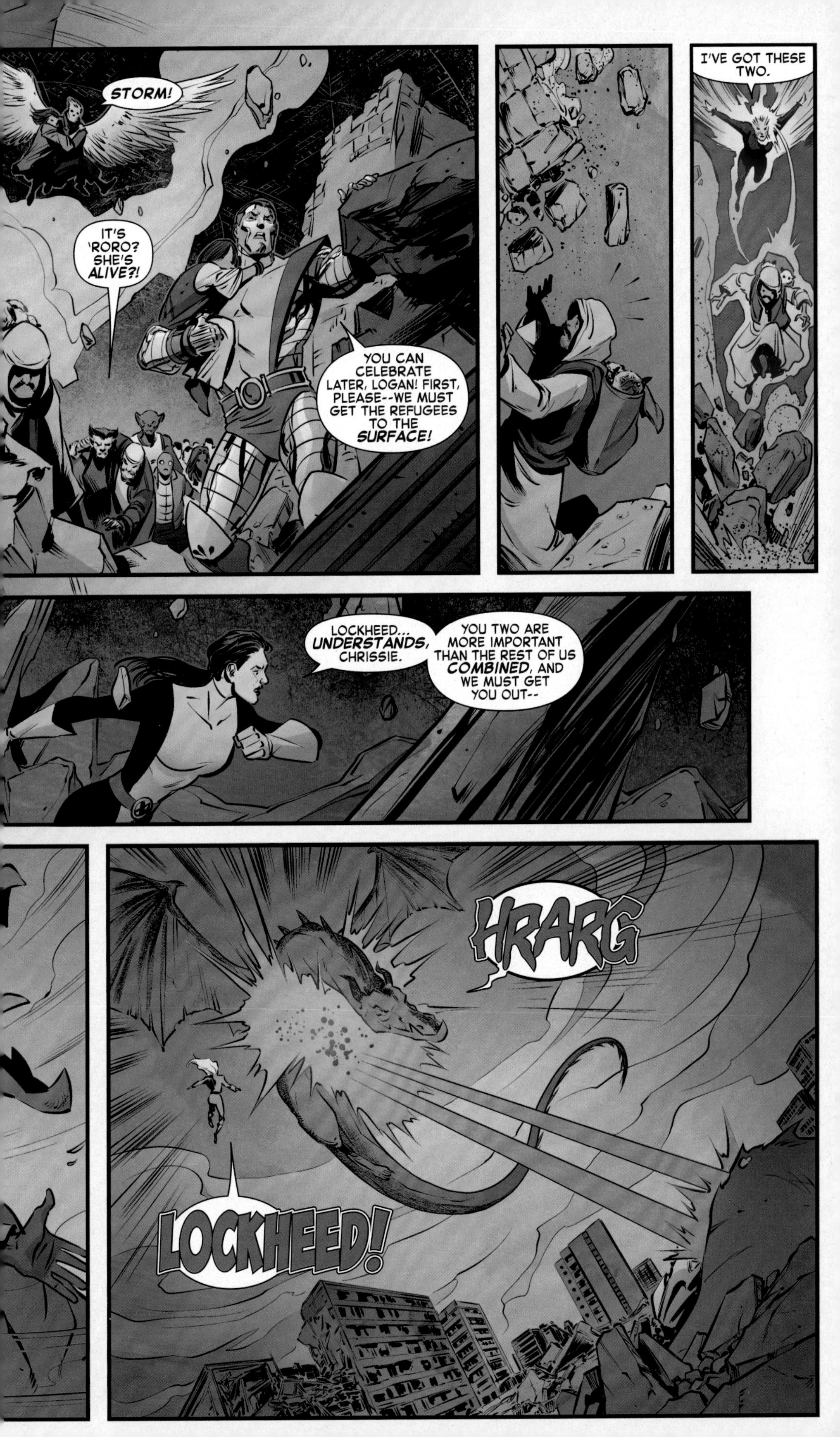
STORM!
IT'S 'RORO? SHE'S ALIVE?!
YOU CAN CELEBRATE LATER, LOGAN! FIRST, PLEASE--WE MUST GET THE REFUGEES TO THE SURFACE!
I'VE GOT THESE TWO.
LOCKHEED... UNDERSTANDS, CHRISSIE.
YOU TWO ARE MORE IMPORTANT THAN THE REST OF US COMBINED, AND WE MUST GET YOU OUT--
HRARG
LOCKHEED!

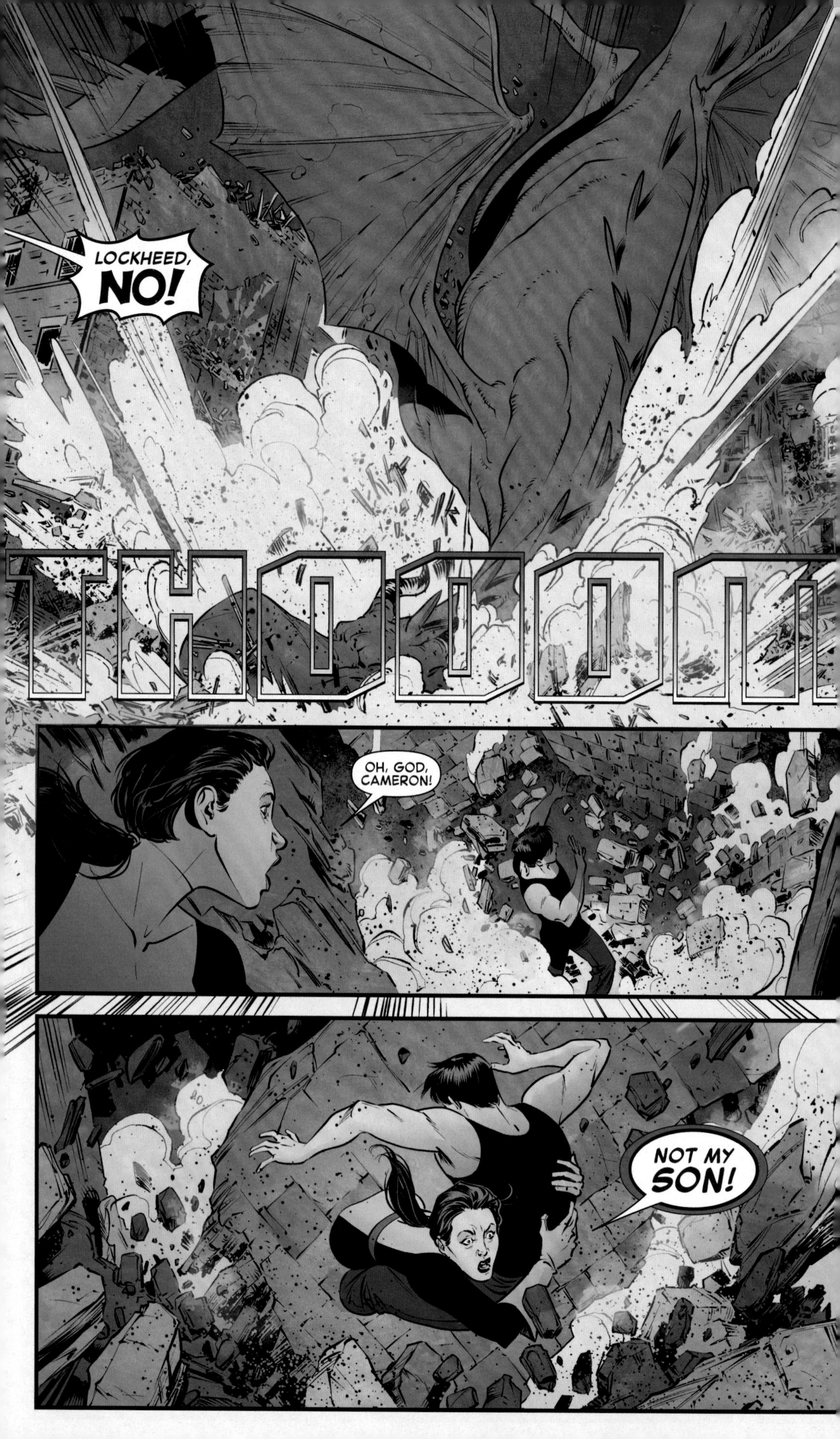
LOCKHEED, NO!
THOOOM
OH, GOD, CAMERON!
NOT MY SON!

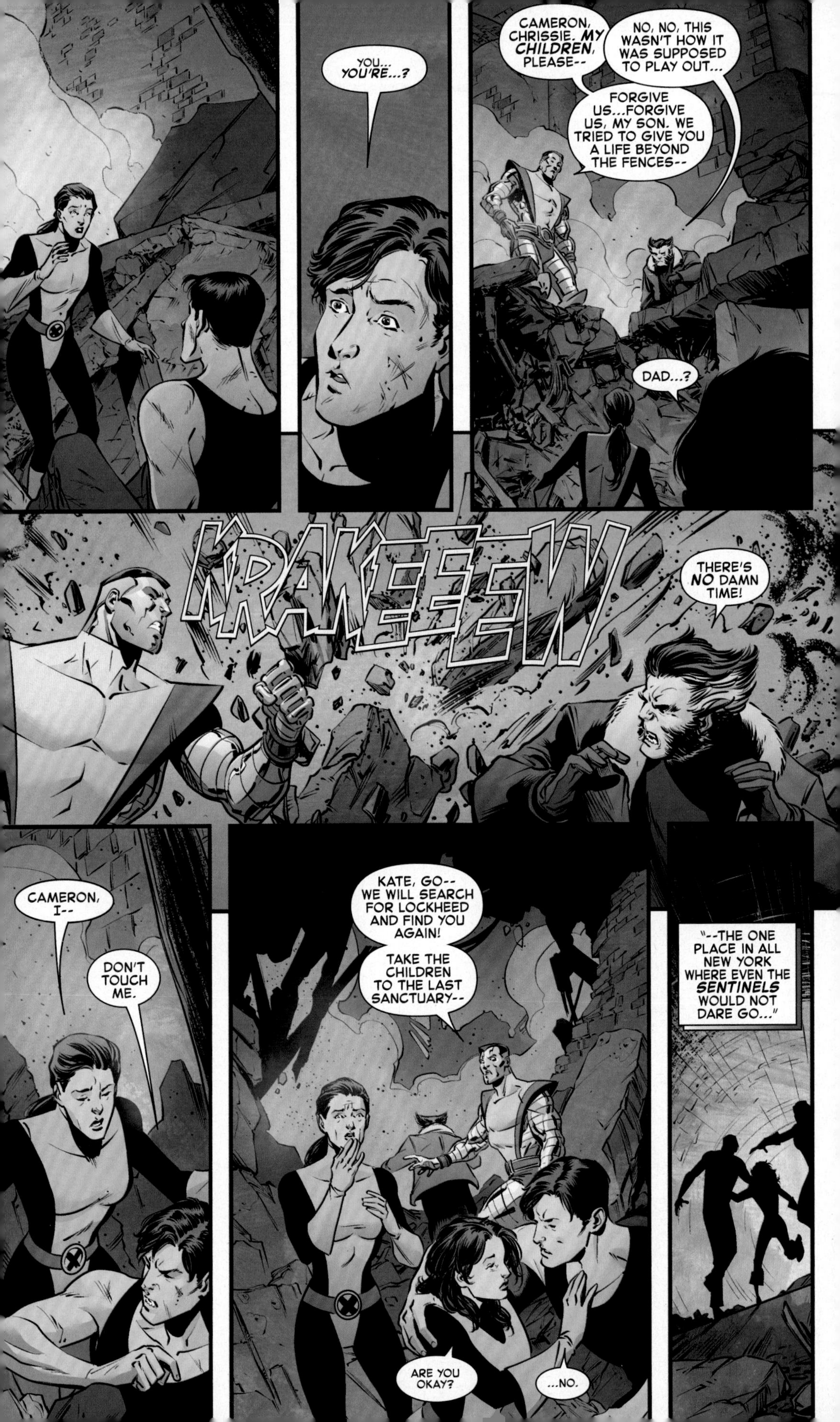
YOU... YOU'RE...?
CAMERON, CHRISSIE. MY CHILDREN, PLEASE--
NO, NO, THIS WASN'T HOW IT WAS SUPPOSED TO PLAY OUT...
FORGIVE US...FORGIVE US, MY SON. WE TRIED TO GIVE YOU A LIFE BEYOND THE FENCES--
DAD...?
KRAKEEEW
THERE'S NO DAMN TIME!
CAMERON, I--
DON'T TOUCH ME.
KATE, GO-- WE WILL SEARCH FOR LOCKHEED AND FIND YOU AGAIN!
TAKE THE CHILDREN TO THE LAST SANCTUARY--
ARE YOU OKAY?
...NO.
"--THE ONE PLACE IN ALL NEW YORK WHERE EVEN THE SENTINELS WOULD NOT DARE GO..."

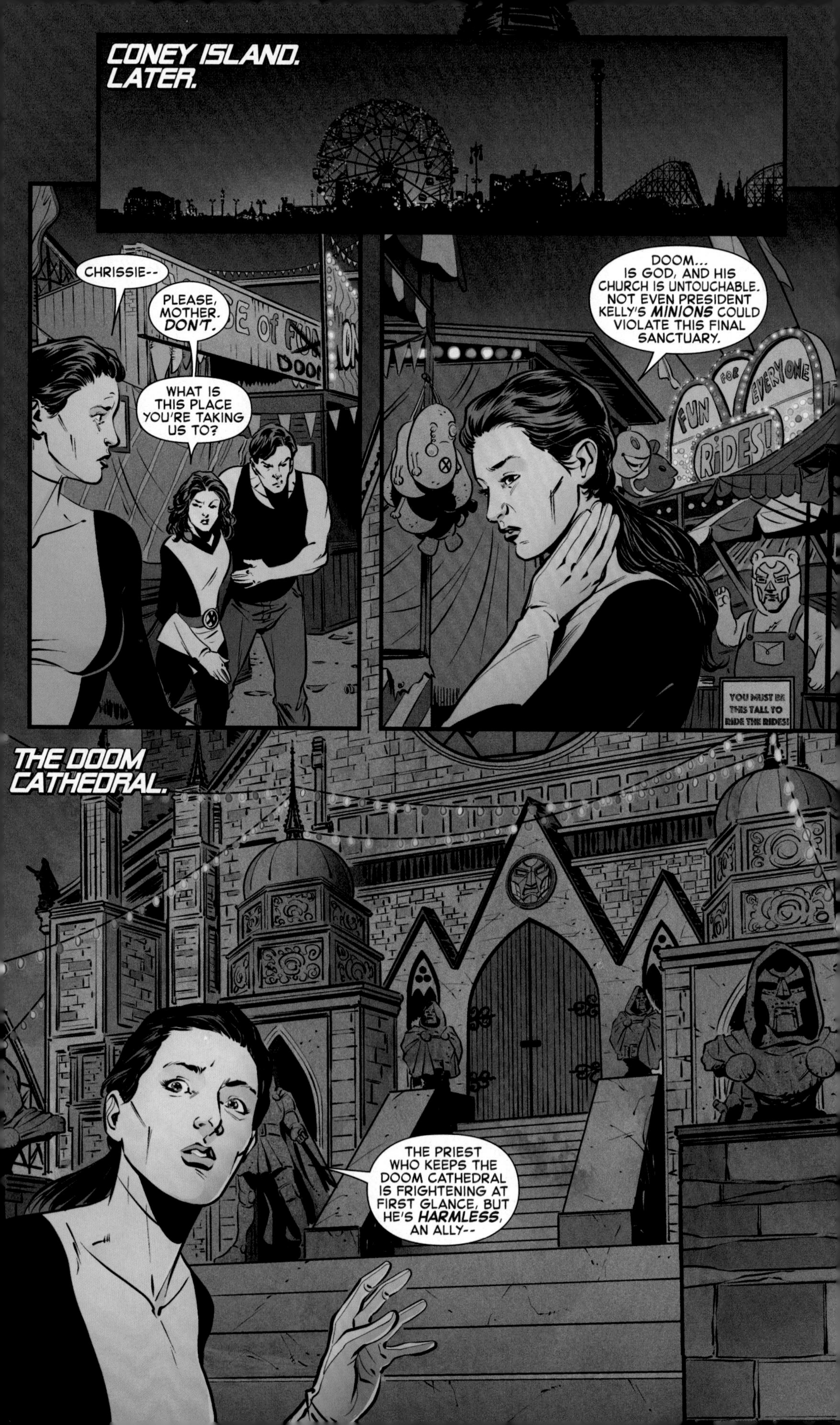
CONEY ISLAND.
LATER.
CHRISSIE--
PLEASE, MOTHER. DON'T.
WHAT IS THIS PLACE YOU'RE TAKING US TO?
DOOM... IS GOD, AND HIS CHURCH IS UNTOUCHABLE. NOT EVEN PRESIDENT KELLY'S MINIONS COULD VIOLATE THIS FINAL SANCTUARY.
FUN FOR EVERYONE
RIDES!
YOU MUST BE THIS TALL TO RIDE THE RIDES!
THE DOOM CATHEDRAL.
THE PRIEST WHO KEEPS THE DOOM CATHEDRAL IS FRIGHTENING AT FIRST GLANCE, BUT HE'S HARMLESS, AN ALLY--

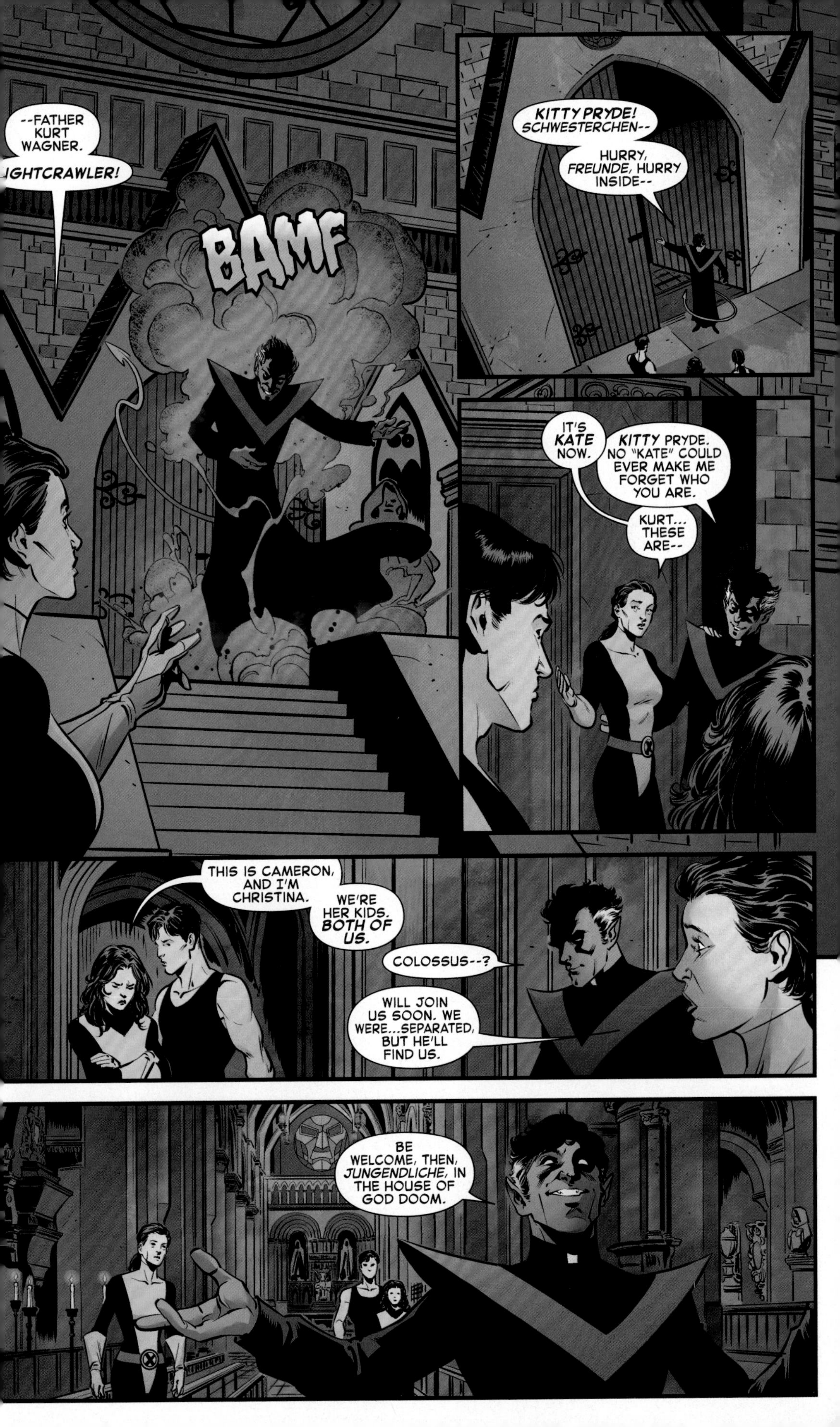
--FATHER KURT WAGNER.
IGHTCRAWLER!
BAMF
KITTY PRYDE! SCHWESTERCHEN--
HURRY, FREUNDE, HURRY INSIDE--
IT'S KATE NOW.
KITTY PRYDE. NO "KATE" COULD EVER MAKE ME FORGET WHO YOU ARE.
KURT... THESE ARE--
THIS IS CAMERON, AND I'M CHRISTINA.
WE'RE HER KIDS. BOTH OF US.
COLOSSUS--?
WILL JOIN US SOON. WE WERE...SEPARATED, BUT HE'LL FIND US.
BE WELCOME, THEN, JUNGENDLICHE, IN THE HOUSE OF GOD DOOM.

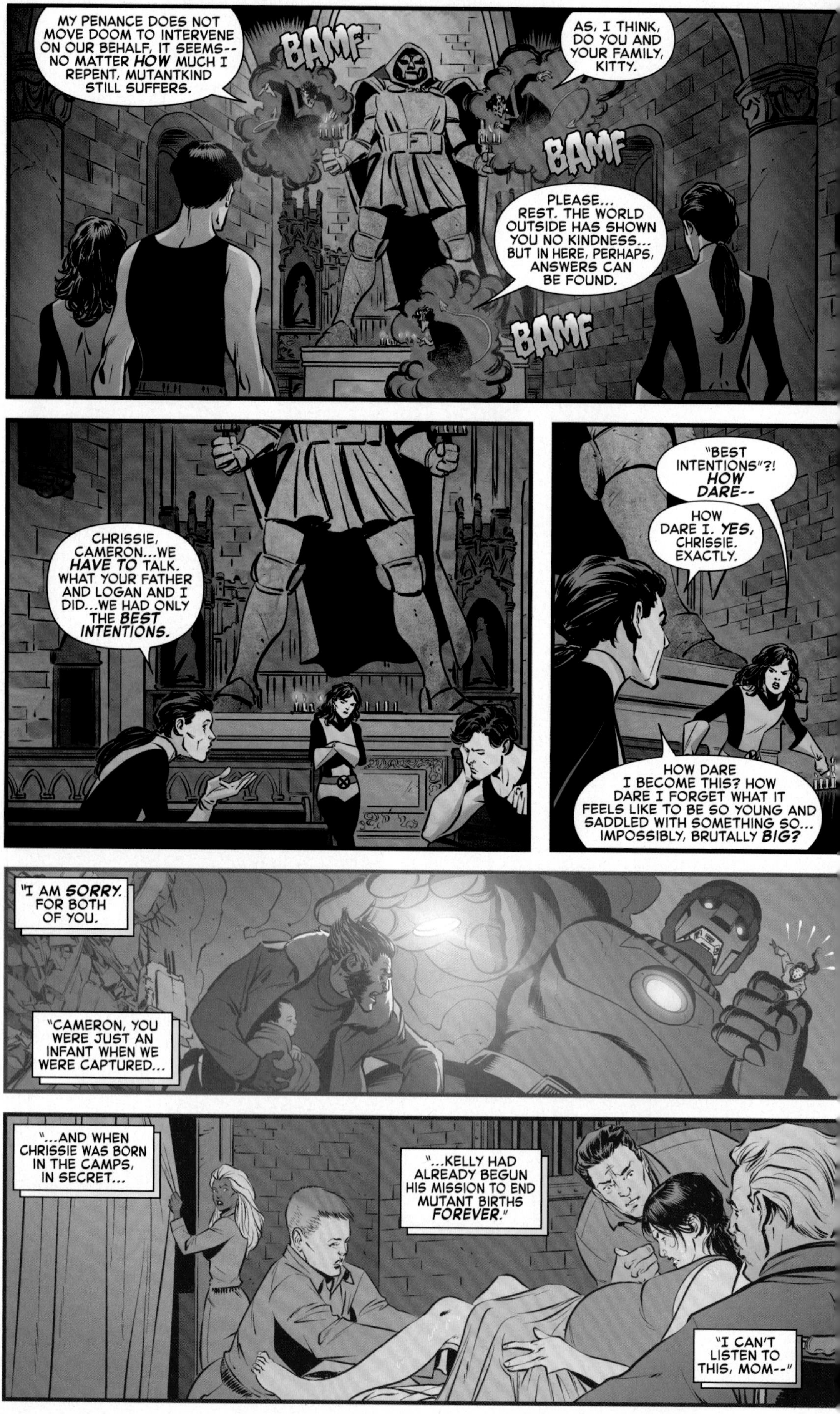
MY PENANCE DOES NOT MOVE DOOM TO INTERVENE ON OUR BEHALF, IT SEEMS-- NO MATTER HOW MUCH I REPENT, MUTANTKIND STILL SUFFERS.
BAMF
AS, I THINK, DO YOU AND YOUR FAMILY, KITTY.
BAMF
PLEASE... REST. THE WORLD OUTSIDE HAS SHOWN YOU NO KINDNESS... BUT IN HERE, PERHAPS, ANSWERS CAN BE FOUND.
BAMF
CHRISSIE, CAMERON...WE HAVE TO TALK. WHAT YOUR FATHER AND LOGAN AND I DID...WE HAD ONLY THE BEST INTENTIONS.
"BEST INTENTIONS"?! HOW DARE--
HOW DARE I. YES, CHRISSIE. EXACTLY.
HOW DARE I BECOME THIS? HOW DARE I FORGET WHAT IT FEELS LIKE TO BE SO YOUNG AND SADDLED WITH SOMETHING SO... IMPOSSIBLY, BRUTALLY BIG?
"I AM SORRY. FOR BOTH OF YOU.
"CAMERON, YOU WERE JUST AN INFANT WHEN WE WERE CAPTURED...
"...AND WHEN CHRISSIE WAS BORN IN THE CAMPS, IN SECRET...
"...KELLY HAD ALREADY BEGUN HIS MISSION TO END MUTANT BIRTHS FOREVER."
"I CAN'T LISTEN TO THIS, MOM--"

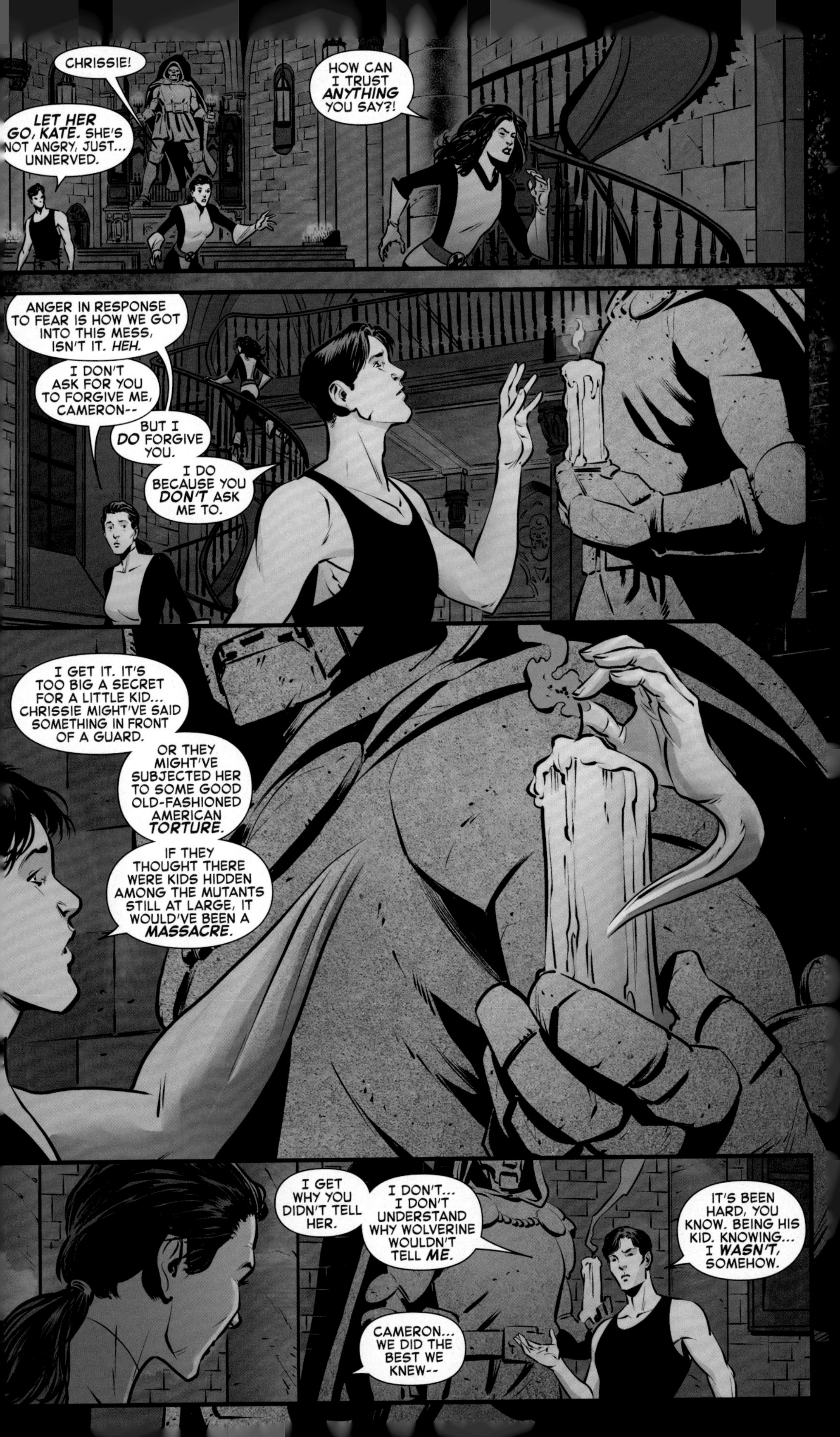
CHRISSIE!
LET HER GO, KATE. SHE'S NOT ANGRY, JUST... UNNERVED.
HOW CAN I TRUST ANYTHING YOU SAY?!
ANGER IN RESPONSE TO FEAR IS HOW WE GOT INTO THIS MESS, ISN'T IT. HEH.
I DON'T ASK FOR YOU TO FORGIVE ME, CAMERON--
BUT I DO FORGIVE YOU.
I DO BECAUSE YOU DON'T ASK ME TO.
I GET IT. IT'S TOO BIG A SECRET FOR A LITTLE KID... CHRISSIE MIGHT'VE SAID SOMETHING IN FRONT OF A GUARD.
OR THEY MIGHT'VE SUBJECTED HER TO SOME GOOD OLD-FASHIONED AMERICAN TORTURE.
IF THEY THOUGHT THERE WERE KIDS HIDDEN AMONG THE MUTANTS STILL AT LARGE, IT WOULD'VE BEEN A MASSACRE.
I GET WHY YOU DIDN'T TELL HER.
I DON'T... I DON'T UNDERSTAND WHY WOLVERINE WOULDN'T TELL ME.
IT'S BEEN HARD, YOU KNOW. BEING HIS KID. KNOWING... I WASN'T, SOMEHOW.
CAMERON... WE DID THE BEST WE KNEW--

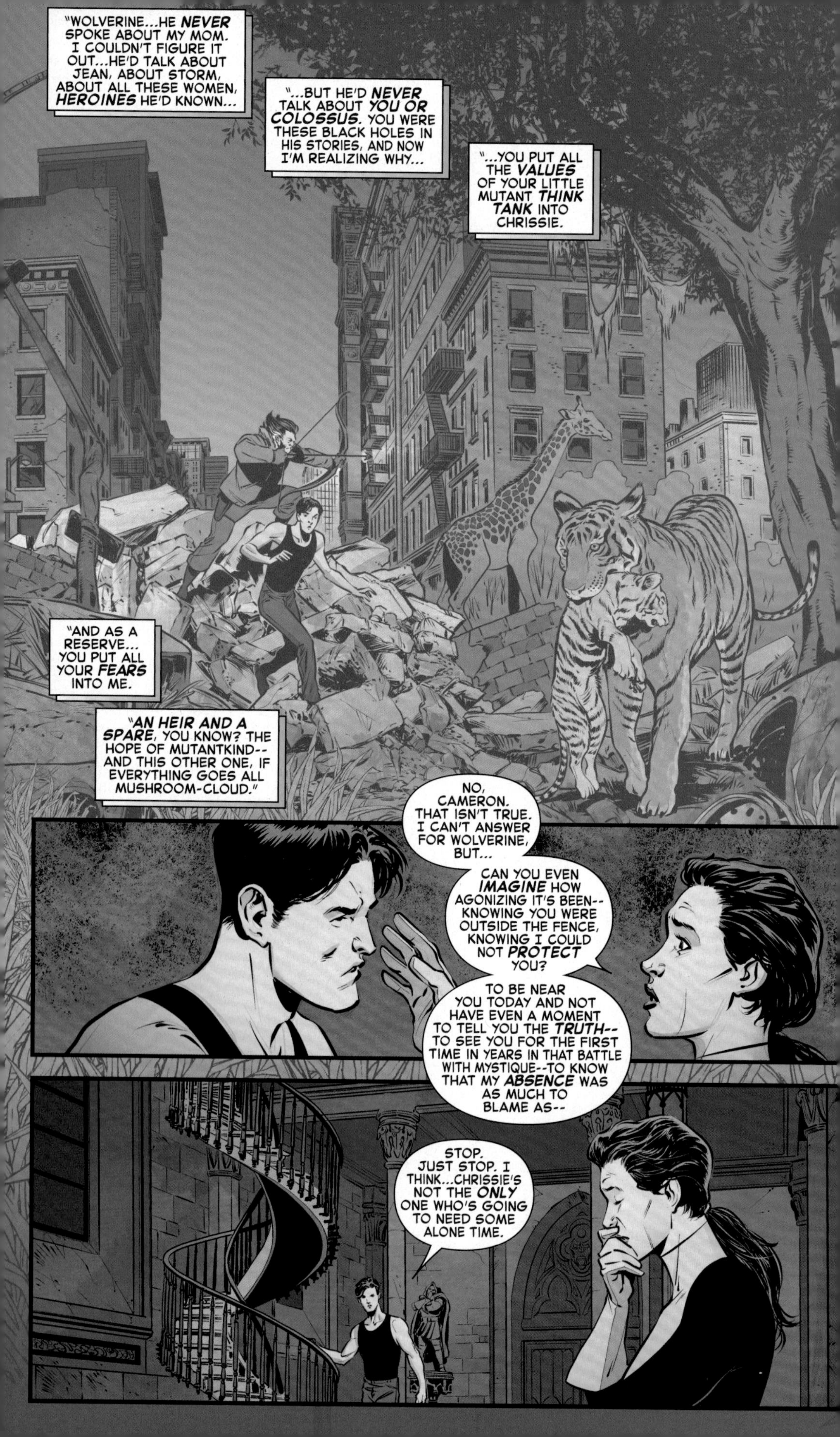
"WOLVERINE...HE NEVER SPOKE ABOUT MY MOM. I COULDN'T FIGURE IT OUT...HE'D TALK ABOUT JEAN, ABOUT STORM, ABOUT ALL THESE WOMEN, HEROINES HE'D KNOWN...
"...BUT HE'D NEVER TALK ABOUT YOU OR COLOSSUS. YOU WERE THESE BLACK HOLES IN HIS STORIES, AND NOW I'M REALIZING WHY...
"...YOU PUT ALL THE VALUES OF YOUR LITTLE MUTANT THINK TANK INTO CHRISSIE.
"AND AS A RESERVE... YOU PUT ALL YOUR FEARS INTO ME.
"AN HEIR AND A SPARE, YOU KNOW? THE HOPE OF MUTANTKIND-- AND THIS OTHER ONE, IF EVERYTHING GOES ALL MUSHROOM-CLOUD."
NO, CAMERON. THAT ISN'T TRUE. I CAN'T ANSWER FOR WOLVERINE, BUT...
CAN YOU EVEN IMAGINE HOW AGONIZING IT'S BEEN-- KNOWING YOU WERE OUTSIDE THE FENCE, KNOWING I COULD NOT PROTECT YOU?
TO BE NEAR YOU TODAY AND NOT HAVE EVEN A MOMENT TO TELL YOU THE TRUTH-- TO SEE YOU FOR THE FIRST TIME IN YEARS IN THAT BATTLE WITH MYSTIQUE--TO KNOW THAT MY ABSENCE WAS AS MUCH TO BLAME AS--
STOP. JUST STOP. I THINK...CHRISSIE'S NOT THE ONLY ONE WHO'S GOING TO NEED SOME ALONE TIME.

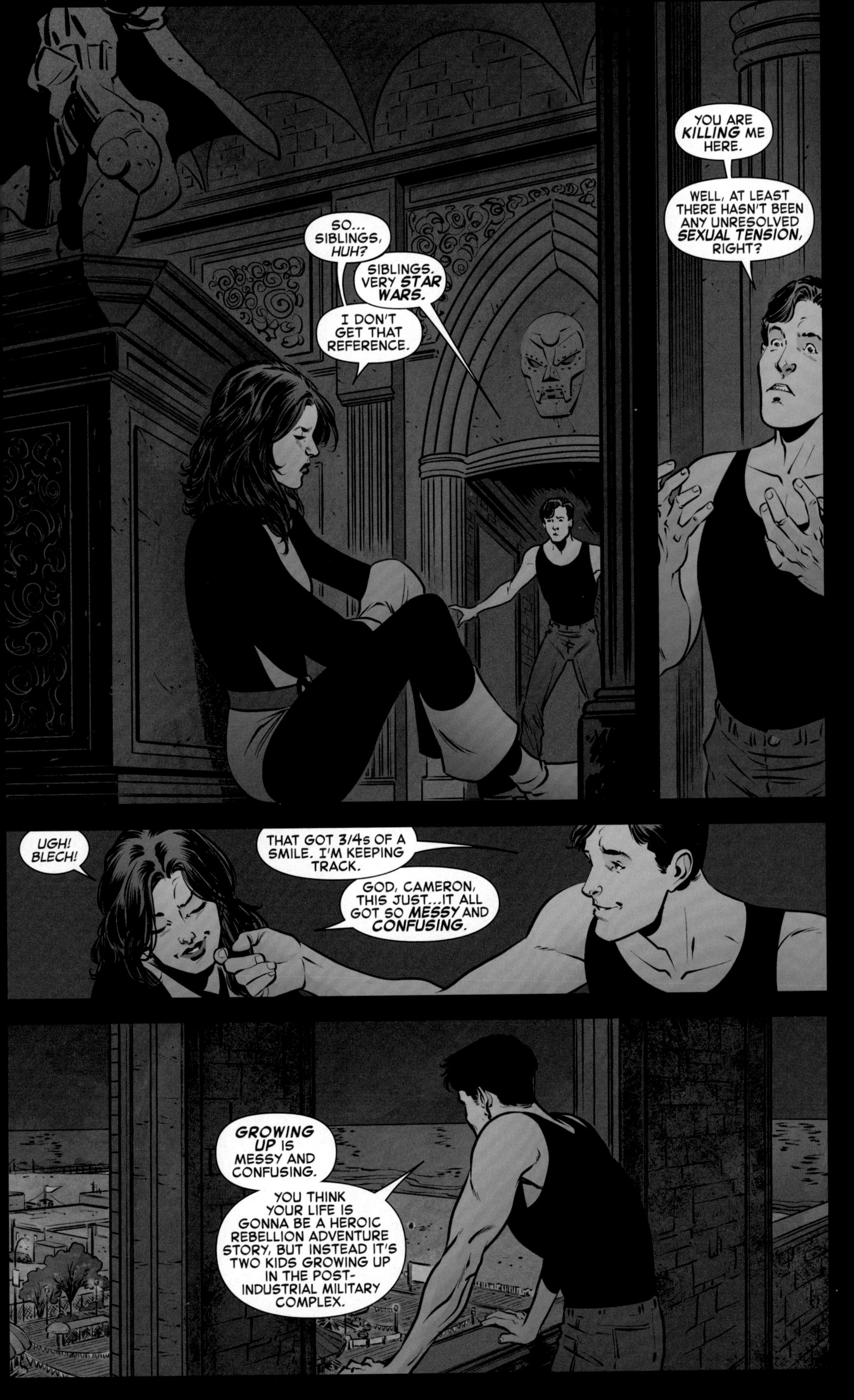
SO... SIBLINGS, HUH?
SIBLINGS. VERY STAR WARS.
I DON'T GET THAT REFERENCE.
YOU ARE KILLING ME HERE.
WELL, AT LEAST THERE HASN'T BEEN ANY UNRESOLVED SEXUAL TENSION, RIGHT?
UGH! BLECH!
THAT GOT 3/4s OF A SMILE. I'M KEEPING TRACK.
GOD, CAMERON, THIS JUST...IT ALL GOT SO MESSY AND CONFUSING.
GROWING UP IS MESSY AND CONFUSING.
YOU THINK YOUR LIFE IS GONNA BE A HEROIC REBELLION ADVENTURE STORY, BUT INSTEAD IT'S TWO KIDS GROWING UP IN THE POST-INDUSTRIAL MILITARY COMPLEX.

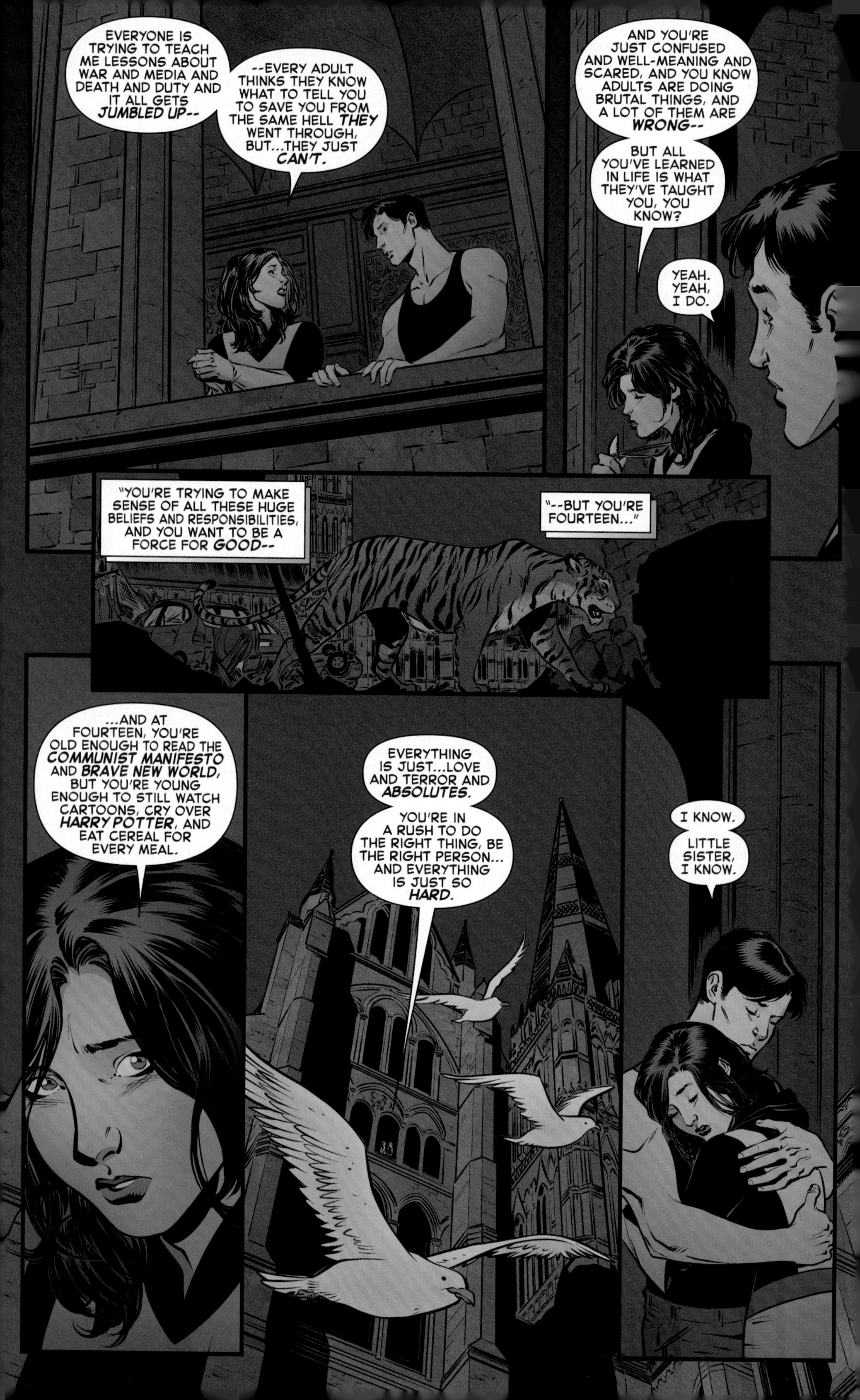
EVERYONE IS TRYING TO TEACH ME LESSONS ABOUT WAR AND MEDIA AND DEATH AND DUTY AND IT ALL GETS *JUMBLED UP--*
--EVERY ADULT THINKS THEY KNOW WHAT TO TELL YOU TO SAVE YOU FROM THE SAME HELL *THEY* WENT THROUGH, BUT...THEY JUST *CAN'T.*
AND YOU'RE JUST CONFUSED AND WELL-MEANING AND SCARED, AND YOU KNOW ADULTS ARE DOING BRUTAL THINGS, AND A LOT OF THEM ARE *WRONG--*
BUT ALL YOU'VE LEARNED IN LIFE IS WHAT THEY'VE TAUGHT YOU, YOU KNOW?
YEAH. YEAH, I DO.
"YOU'RE TRYING TO MAKE SENSE OF ALL THESE HUGE BELIEFS AND RESPONSIBILITIES, AND YOU WANT TO BE A FORCE FOR *GOOD--*
"--BUT YOU'RE FOURTEEN..."
...AND AT FOURTEEN, YOU'RE OLD ENOUGH TO READ THE *COMMUNIST MANIFESTO* AND *BRAVE NEW WORLD,* BUT YOU'RE YOUNG ENOUGH TO STILL WATCH CARTOONS, CRY OVER *HARRY POTTER,* AND EAT CEREAL FOR EVERY MEAL.
EVERYTHING IS JUST...LOVE AND TERROR AND *ABSOLUTES.*
YOU'RE IN A RUSH TO DO THE RIGHT THING, BE THE RIGHT PERSON... AND EVERYTHING IS JUST SO *HARD.*
I KNOW.
LITTLE SISTER, I KNOW.

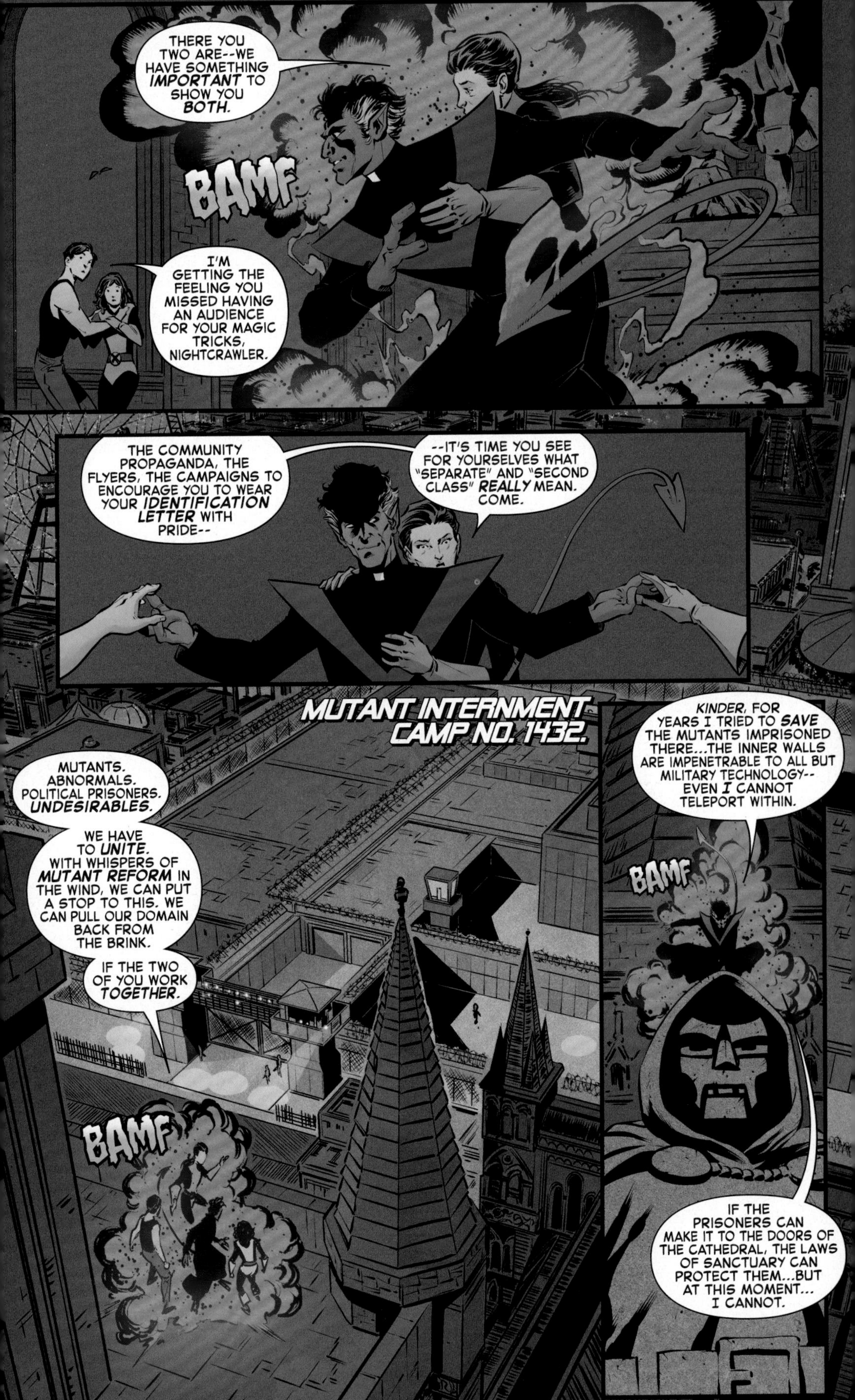

THERE YOU TWO ARE--WE HAVE SOMETHING IMPORTANT TO SHOW YOU BOTH.
BAMF
I'M GETTING THE FEELING YOU MISSED HAVING AN AUDIENCE FOR YOUR MAGIC TRICKS, NIGHTCRAWLER.
THE COMMUNITY PROPAGANDA, THE FLYERS, THE CAMPAIGNS TO ENCOURAGE YOU TO WEAR YOUR IDENTIFICATION LETTER WITH PRIDE--
--IT'S TIME YOU SEE FOR YOURSELVES WHAT "SEPARATE" AND "SECOND CLASS" REALLY MEAN. COME.
MUTANT INTERNMENT CAMP NO. 1432.
MUTANTS. ABNORMALS. POLITICAL PRISONERS. UNDESIRABLES.
WE HAVE TO UNITE. WITH WHISPERS OF MUTANT REFORM IN THE WIND, WE CAN PUT A STOP TO THIS. WE CAN PULL OUR DOMAIN BACK FROM THE BRINK.
IF THE TWO OF YOU WORK TOGETHER.
BAMF
KINDER, FOR YEARS I TRIED TO SAVE THE MUTANTS IMPRISONED THERE...THE INNER WALLS ARE IMPENETRABLE TO ALL BUT MILITARY TECHNOLOGY--EVEN I CANNOT TELEPORT WITHIN.
BAMF
IF THE PRISONERS CAN MAKE IT TO THE DOORS OF THE CATHEDRAL, THE LAWS OF SANCTUARY CAN PROTECT THEM...BUT AT THIS MOMENT... I CANNOT.

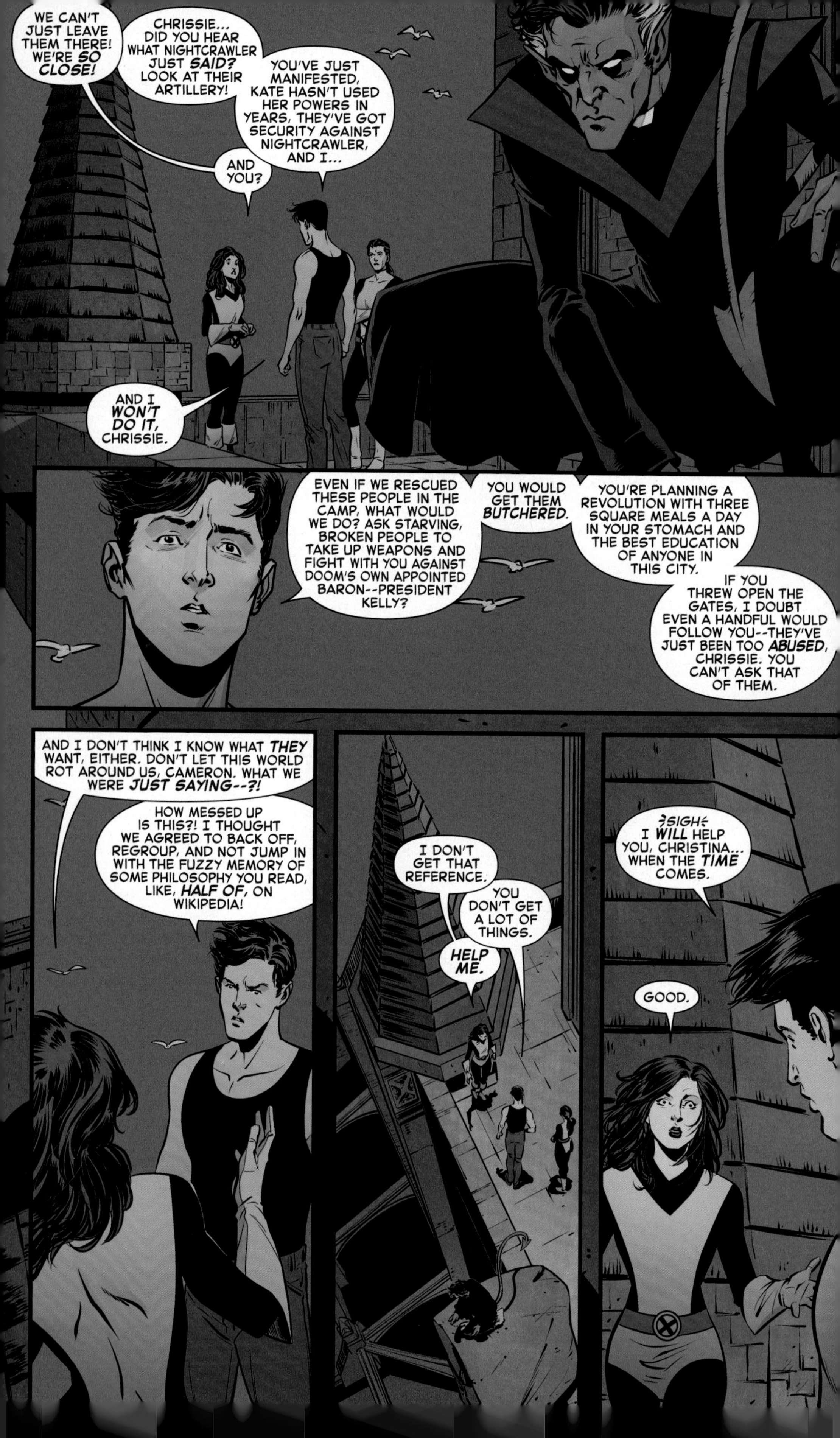

WE CAN'T JUST LEAVE THEM THERE! WE'RE SO CLOSE!
CHRISSIE... DID YOU HEAR WHAT NIGHTCRAWLER JUST SAID? LOOK AT THEIR ARTILLERY!
YOU'VE JUST MANIFESTED, KATE HASN'T USED HER POWERS IN YEARS, THEY'VE GOT SECURITY AGAINST NIGHTCRAWLER, AND I...
AND YOU?
AND I WON'T DO IT, CHRISSIE.
EVEN IF WE RESCUED THESE PEOPLE IN THE CAMP, WHAT WOULD WE DO? ASK STARVING, BROKEN PEOPLE TO TAKE UP WEAPONS AND FIGHT WITH YOU AGAINST DOOM'S OWN APPOINTED BARON--PRESIDENT KELLY?
YOU WOULD GET THEM BUTCHERED.
YOU'RE PLANNING A REVOLUTION WITH THREE SQUARE MEALS A DAY IN YOUR STOMACH AND THE BEST EDUCATION OF ANYONE IN THIS CITY.
IF YOU THREW OPEN THE GATES, I DOUBT EVEN A HANDFUL WOULD FOLLOW YOU--THEY'VE JUST BEEN TOO ABUSED, CHRISSIE. YOU CAN'T ASK THAT OF THEM.
AND I DON'T THINK I KNOW WHAT THEY WANT, EITHER. DON'T LET THIS WORLD ROT AROUND US, CAMERON. WHAT WE WERE JUST SAYING--?!
HOW MESSED UP IS THIS?! I THOUGHT WE AGREED TO BACK OFF, REGROUP, AND NOT JUMP IN WITH THE FUZZY MEMORY OF SOME PHILOSOPHY YOU READ, LIKE, HALF OF, ON WIKIPEDIA!
I DON'T GET THAT REFERENCE.
YOU DON'T GET A LOT OF THINGS.
HELP ME.
⋟SIGH⋞ I WILL HELP YOU, CHRISTINA... WHEN THE TIME COMES.
GOOD.

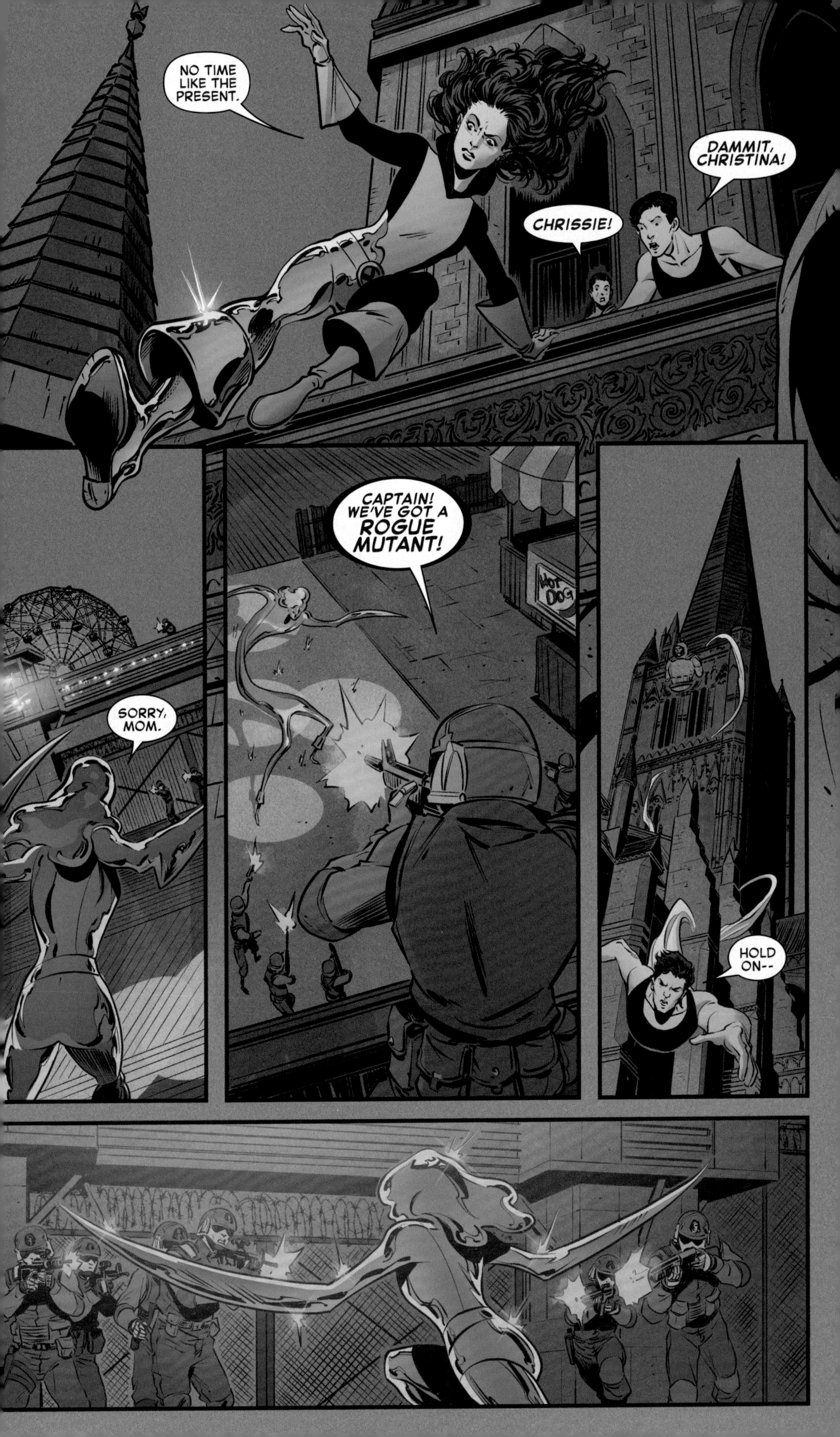
NO TIME LIKE THE PRESENT.
DAMMIT, CHRISTINA!
CHRISSIE!
SORRY, MOM.
CAPTAIN! WE'VE GOT A ROGUE MUTANT!
HOT DOG
HOLD ON--

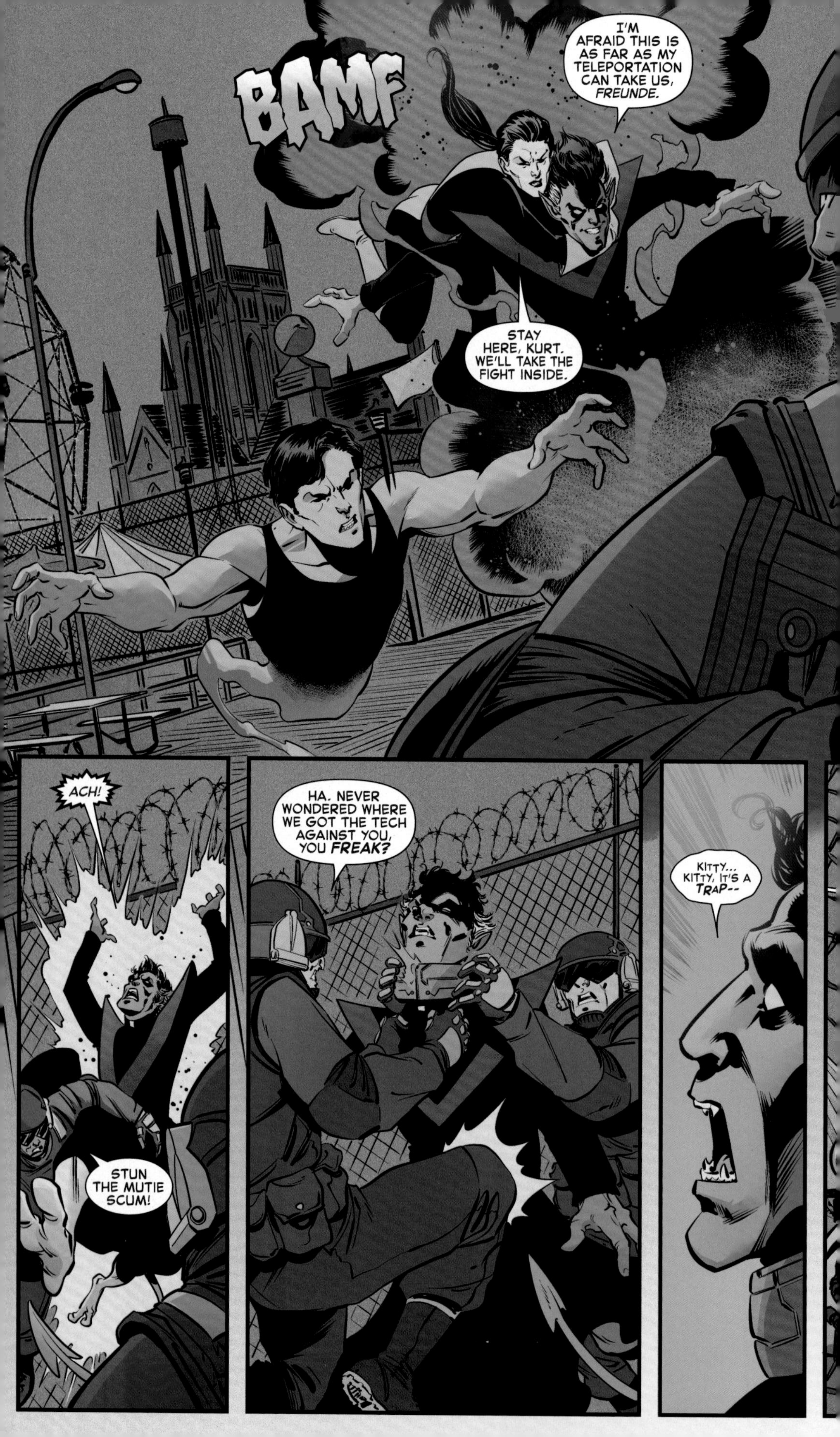
BAMF
I'M AFRAID THIS IS AS FAR AS MY TELEPORTATION CAN TAKE US, *FREUNDE.*
STAY HERE, KURT. WE'LL TAKE THE FIGHT INSIDE.
ACH!
STUN THE MUTIE SCUM!
HA. NEVER WONDERED WHERE WE GOT THE TECH AGAINST YOU, YOU ***FREAK?***
KITTY... KITTY, IT'S A *TRAP--*

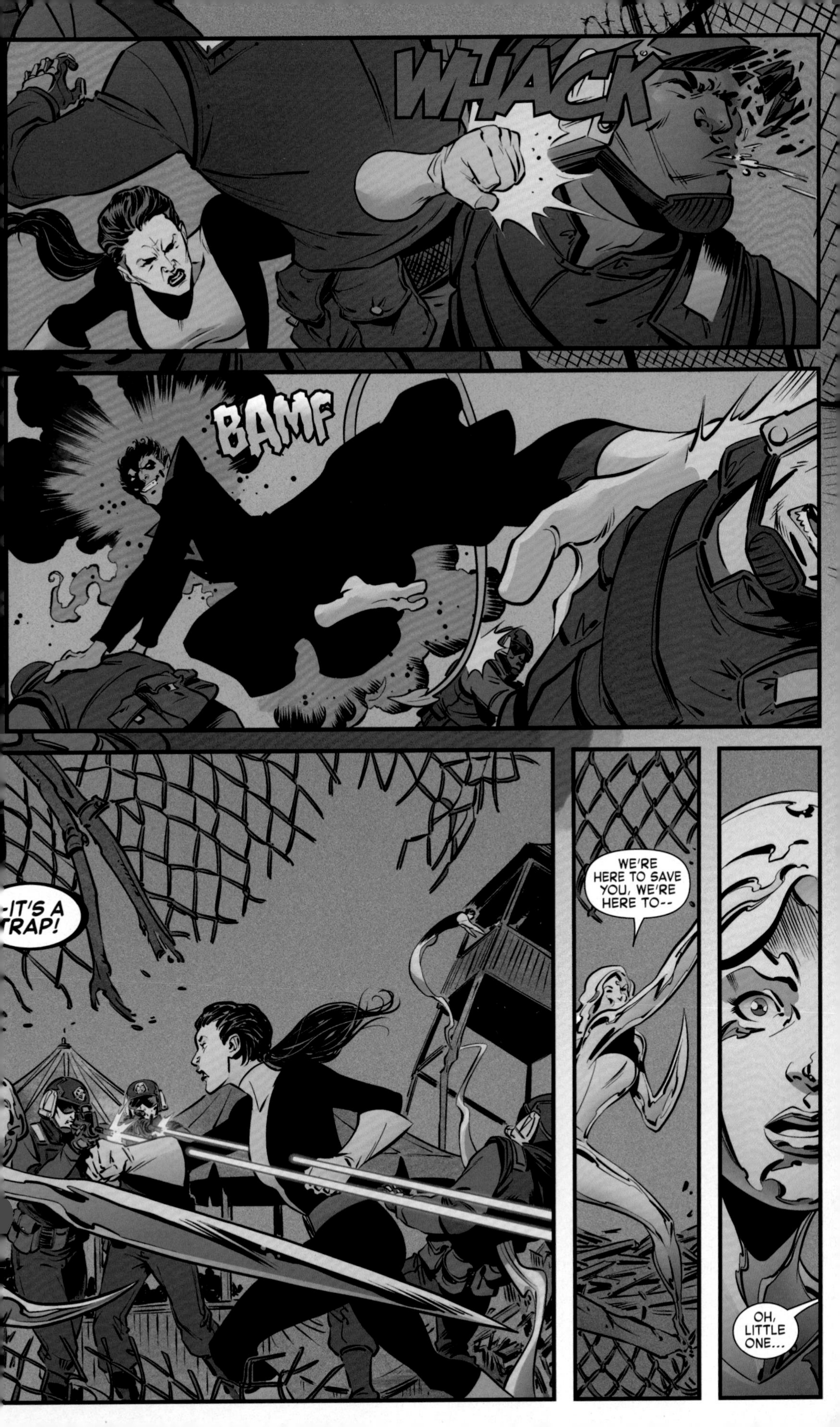
WHACK
BAMF
-IT'S A TRAP!
WE'RE HERE TO SAVE YOU, WE'RE HERE TO--
OH, LITTLE ONE...

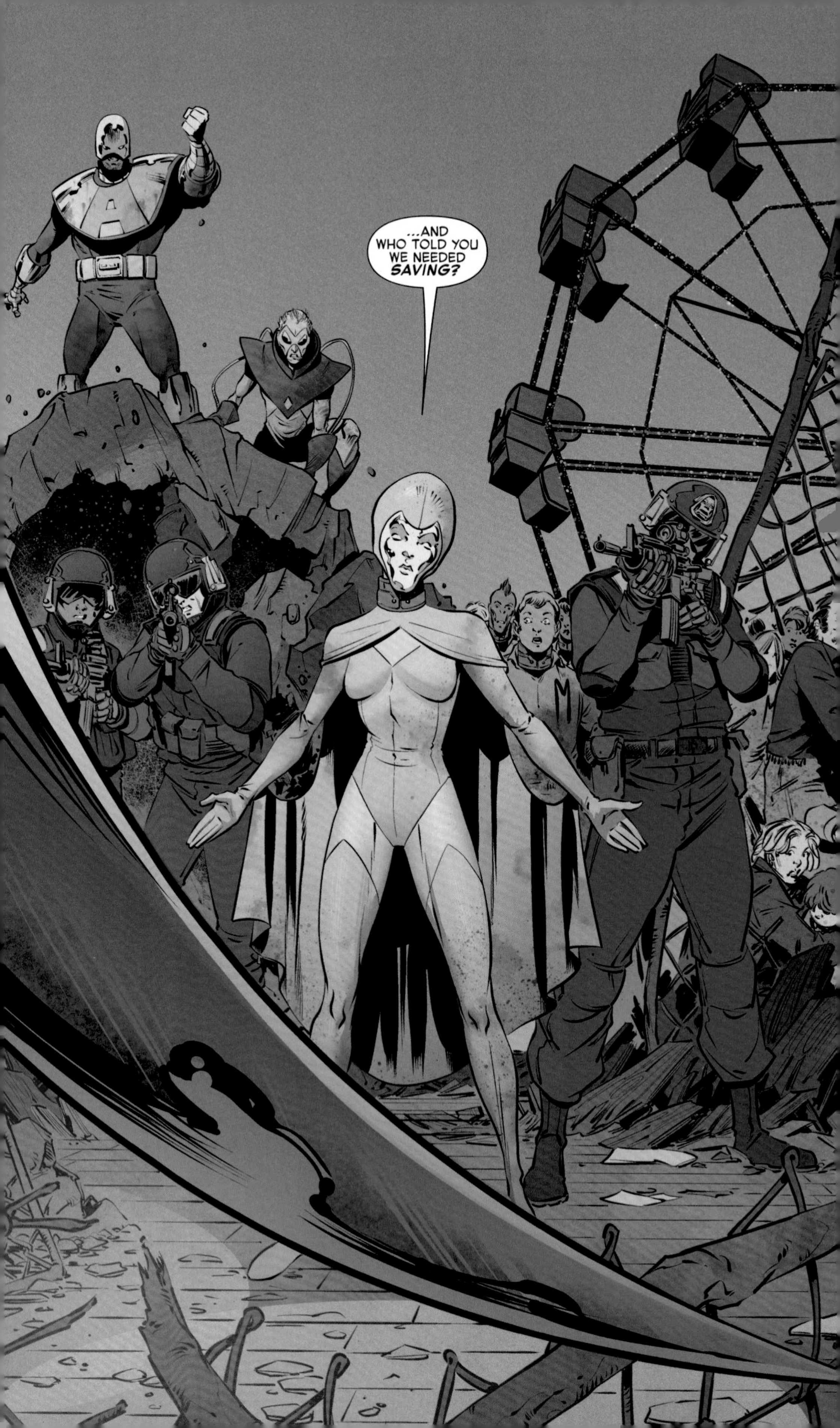
...AND WHO TOLD YOU WE NEEDED SAVING?

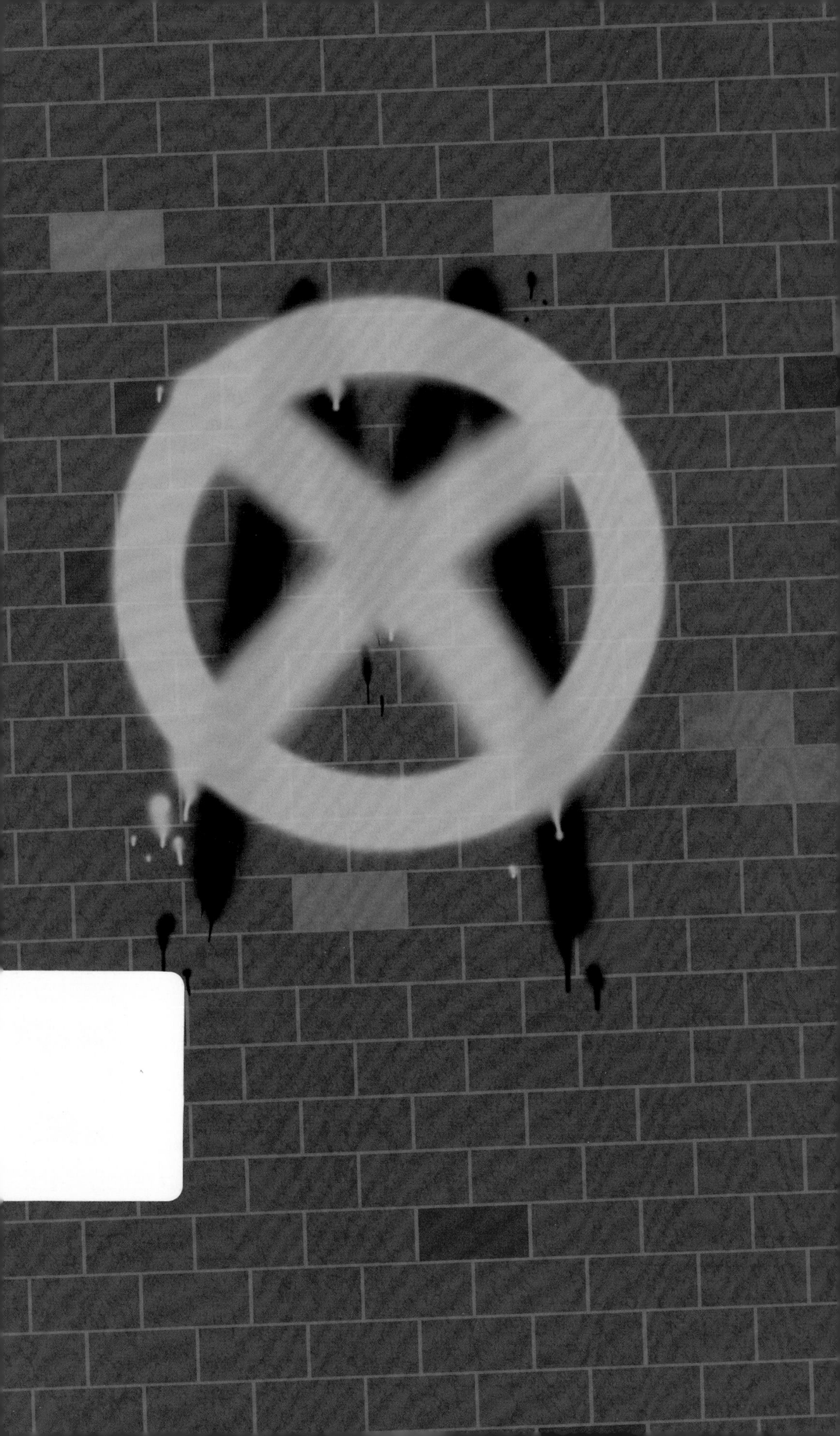

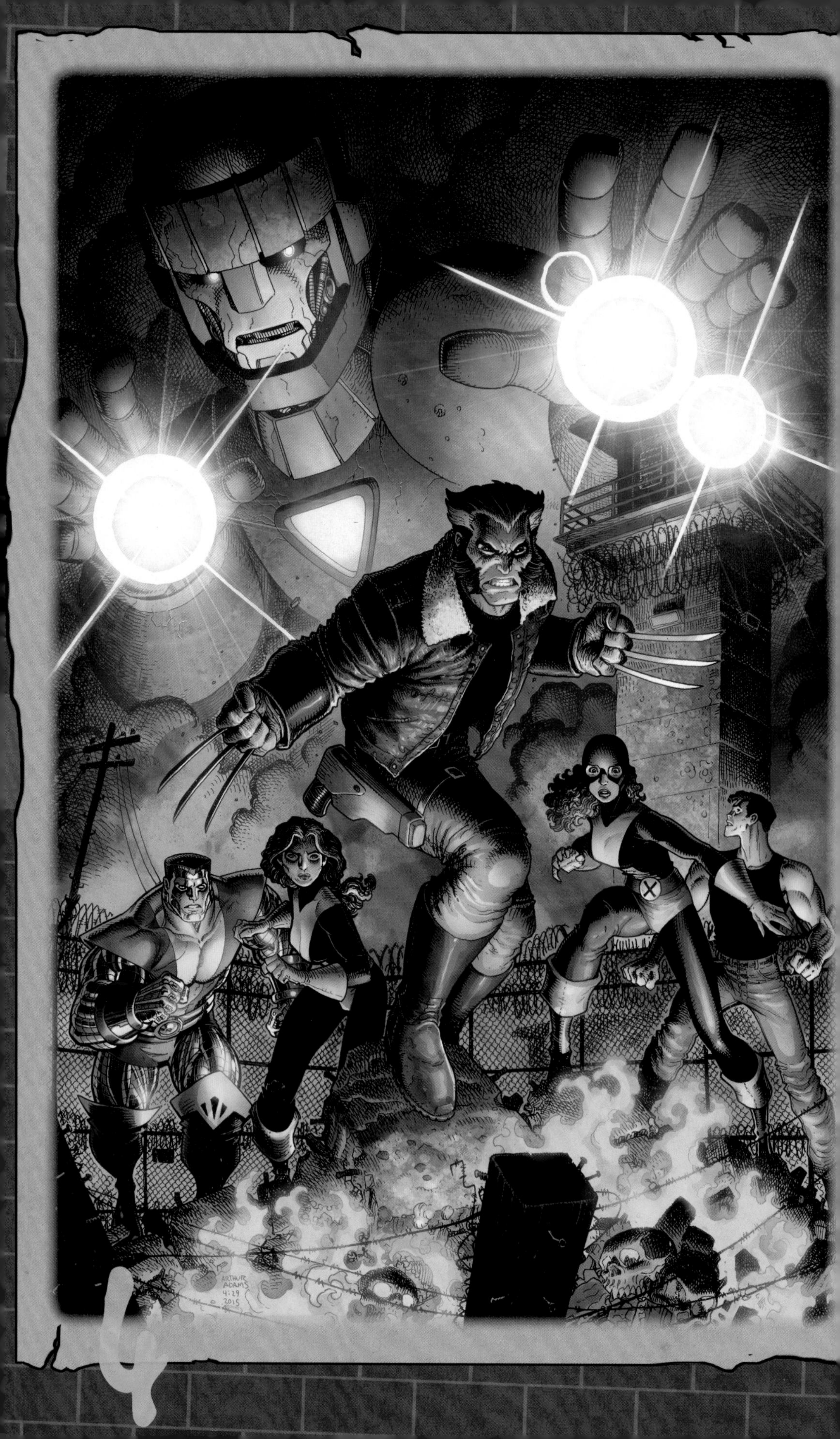
ARTHUR ADAMS 4-29 2015

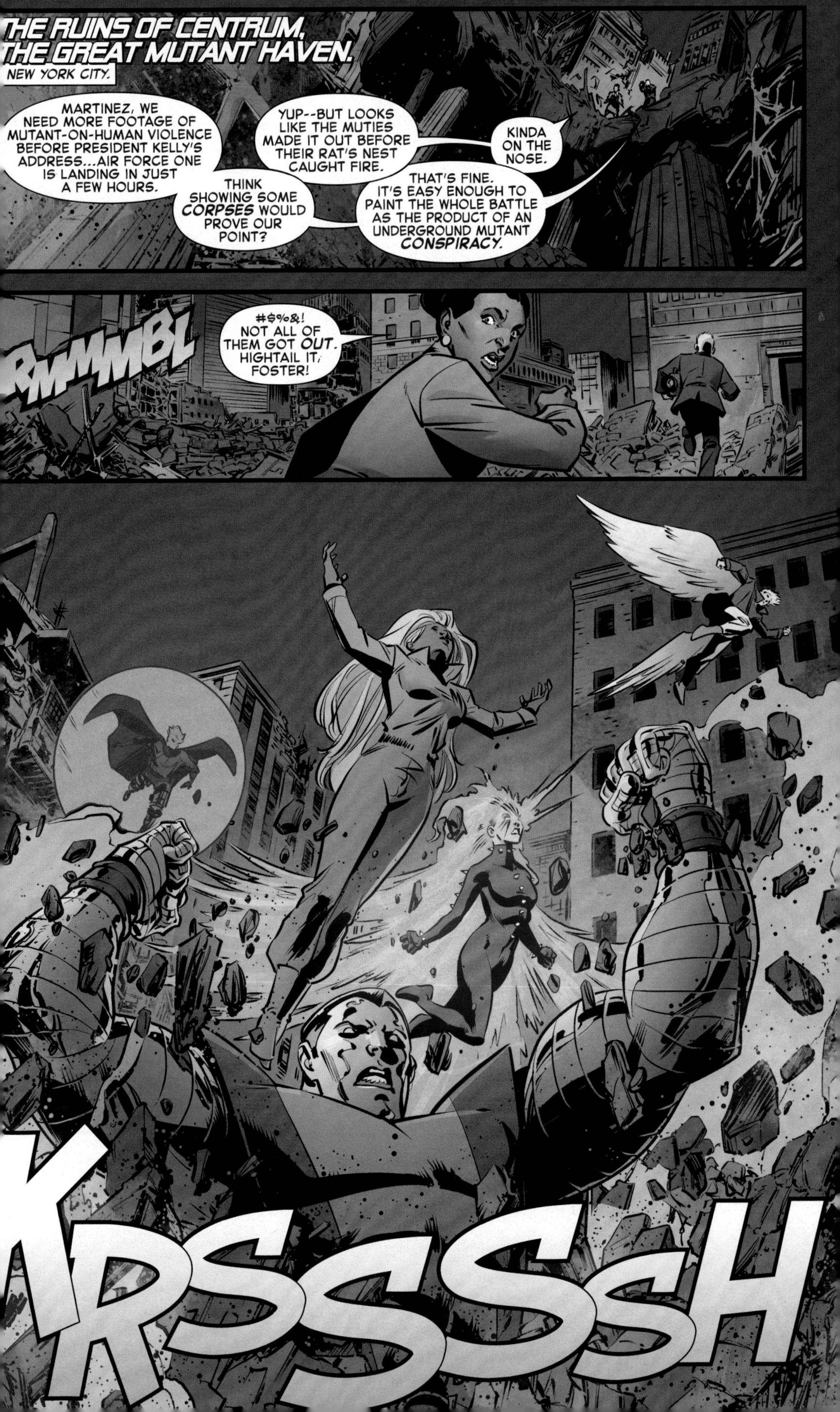
THE RUINS OF CENTRUM, THE GREAT MUTANT HAVEN.
NEW YORK CITY.
MARTINEZ, WE NEED MORE FOOTAGE OF MUTANT-ON-HUMAN VIOLENCE BEFORE PRESIDENT KELLY'S ADDRESS...AIR FORCE ONE IS LANDING IN JUST A FEW HOURS.
YUP--BUT LOOKS LIKE THE MUTIES MADE IT OUT BEFORE THEIR RAT'S NEST CAUGHT FIRE.
KINDA ON THE NOSE.
THINK SHOWING SOME CORPSES WOULD PROVE OUR POINT?
THAT'S FINE. IT'S EASY ENOUGH TO PAINT THE WHOLE BATTLE AS THE PRODUCT OF AN UNDERGROUND MUTANT CONSPIRACY.
RMMMBL
#$%&! NOT ALL OF THEM GOT OUT. HIGHTAIL IT, FOSTER!
KRSSSH

FIFTEEN YEARS THEY KEPT ME IN A LAB, LOGAN, AND *THIS* IS WHAT YOU LET THE FUTURE COME TO?

WASN'T MY JOB TO PAY THE MAID, MYSTIQUE.

STORM! CAN IT BE--?

AS WE ALL LIVE AND BREATHE.

'RORO!

OH, MY OLD MAN, DO NOT CRY! I INTEND TO DO A GREAT DEAL MORE LIVING AND BREATHING. SO PERHAPS HUG ME MORE GENTLY?

BETTER.

THE REFUGEES ARE SECURE...HIDING IN A RESERVOIR SAFE HOUSE, ANOTHER GROUP IN A WAREHOUSE BASEMENT...

KATE HAS TAKEN CAMERON AND CHRISSIE TO SEE NIGHTCRAWLER.

WHAT?! DID YOU ARRANGE THIS WITHOUT INFORMING THE REST OF US, COLOSSUS?

YES, AND THANK DOOM ON HIS THRONE, HE DID. THEY ARE TOO PRECIOUS TO RISK IN SUCH A WAY.

THEY HAVE MUCH WORK TO DO. IF WE WERE TO LOSE EVEN *ONE* OF THEM--

WE RAISED THAT GIRL FROM AN INFANT, RACHEL. TAUGHT HER NIETZSCHE WITH HER ALPHABET AND SUN TZU WITH STUFFED ANIMALS. WE MUST *PROTECT* HER.

AHH...OF COURSE, MAGNETO. I MISSPOKE.

THEN TIME FOR OUR *ENDGAME*, ERIK?

SO TO SPEAK, WARREN. OUR LAST GIFT FOR CHRISSIE...

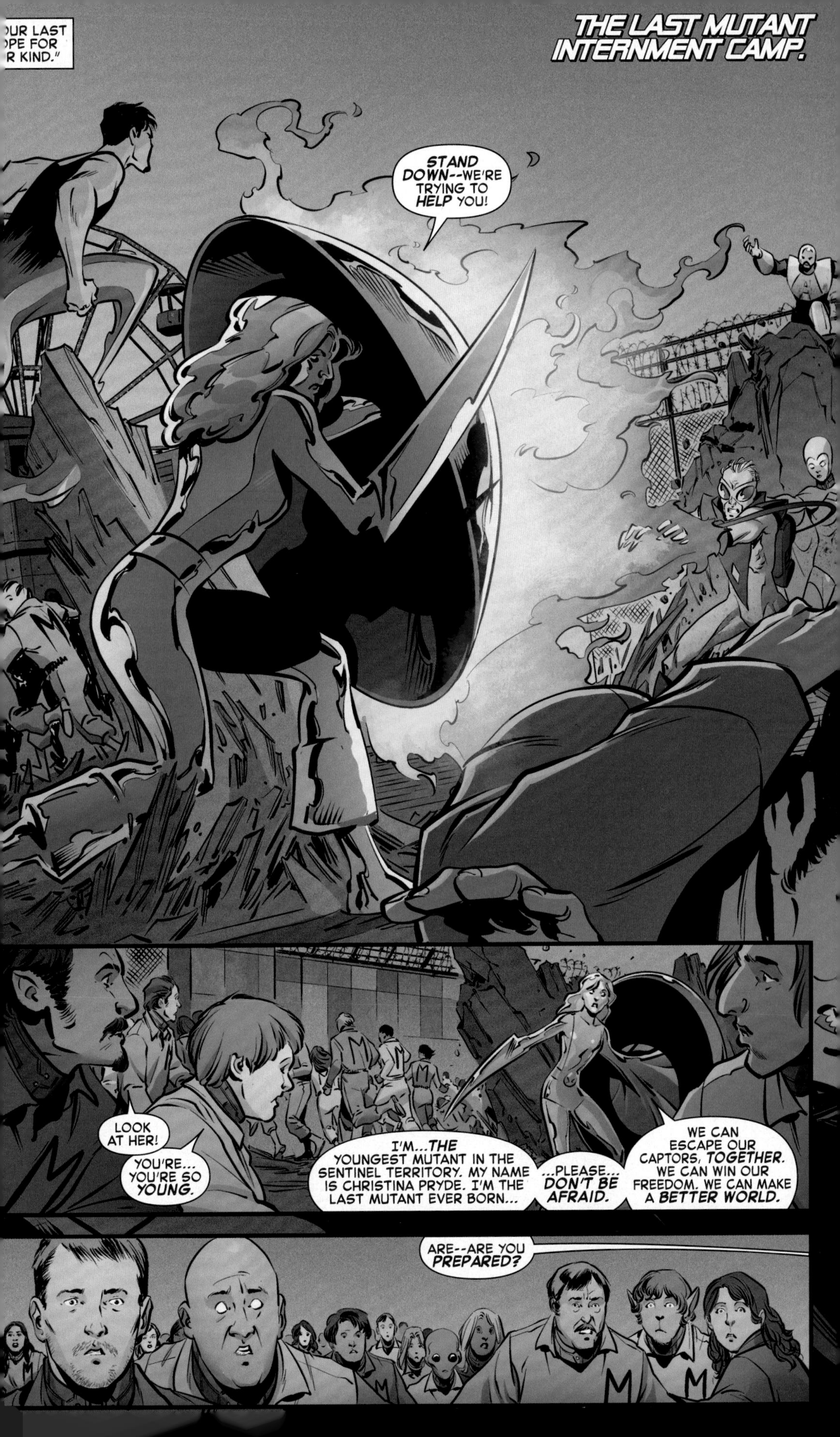

OUR LAST
OPE FOR
R KIND."
THE LAST MUTANT INTERNMENT CAMP.
STAND DOWN--WE'RE TRYING TO HELP YOU!
LOOK AT HER!
YOU'RE... YOU'RE SO YOUNG.
I'M...THE YOUNGEST MUTANT IN THE SENTINEL TERRITORY. MY NAME IS CHRISTINA PRYDE. I'M THE LAST MUTANT EVER BORN...
...PLEASE... DON'T BE AFRAID.
WE CAN ESCAPE OUR CAPTORS, TOGETHER. WE CAN WIN OUR FREEDOM. WE CAN MAKE A BETTER WORLD.
ARE--ARE YOU PREPARED?

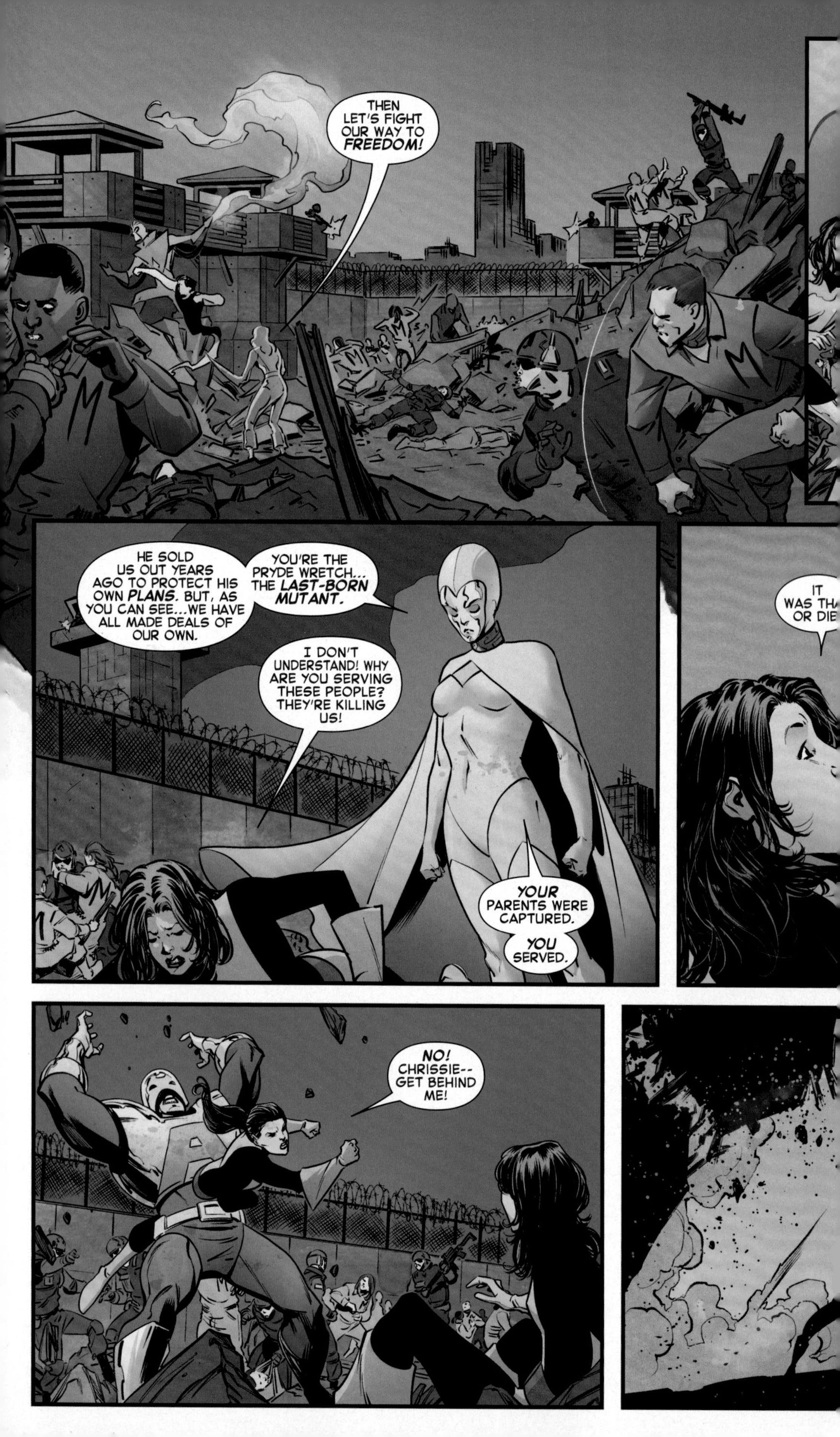
THEN LET'S FIGHT OUR WAY TO FREEDOM!
YOU'RE THE PRYDE WRETCH... THE LAST-BORN MUTANT.
HE SOLD US OUT YEARS AGO TO PROTECT HIS OWN PLANS. BUT, AS YOU CAN SEE...WE HAVE ALL MADE DEALS OF OUR OWN.
I DON'T UNDERSTAND! WHY ARE YOU SERVING THESE PEOPLE? THEY'RE KILLING US!
YOUR PARENTS WERE CAPTURED.
YOU SERVED.
NO! CHRISSIE-- GET BEHIND ME!

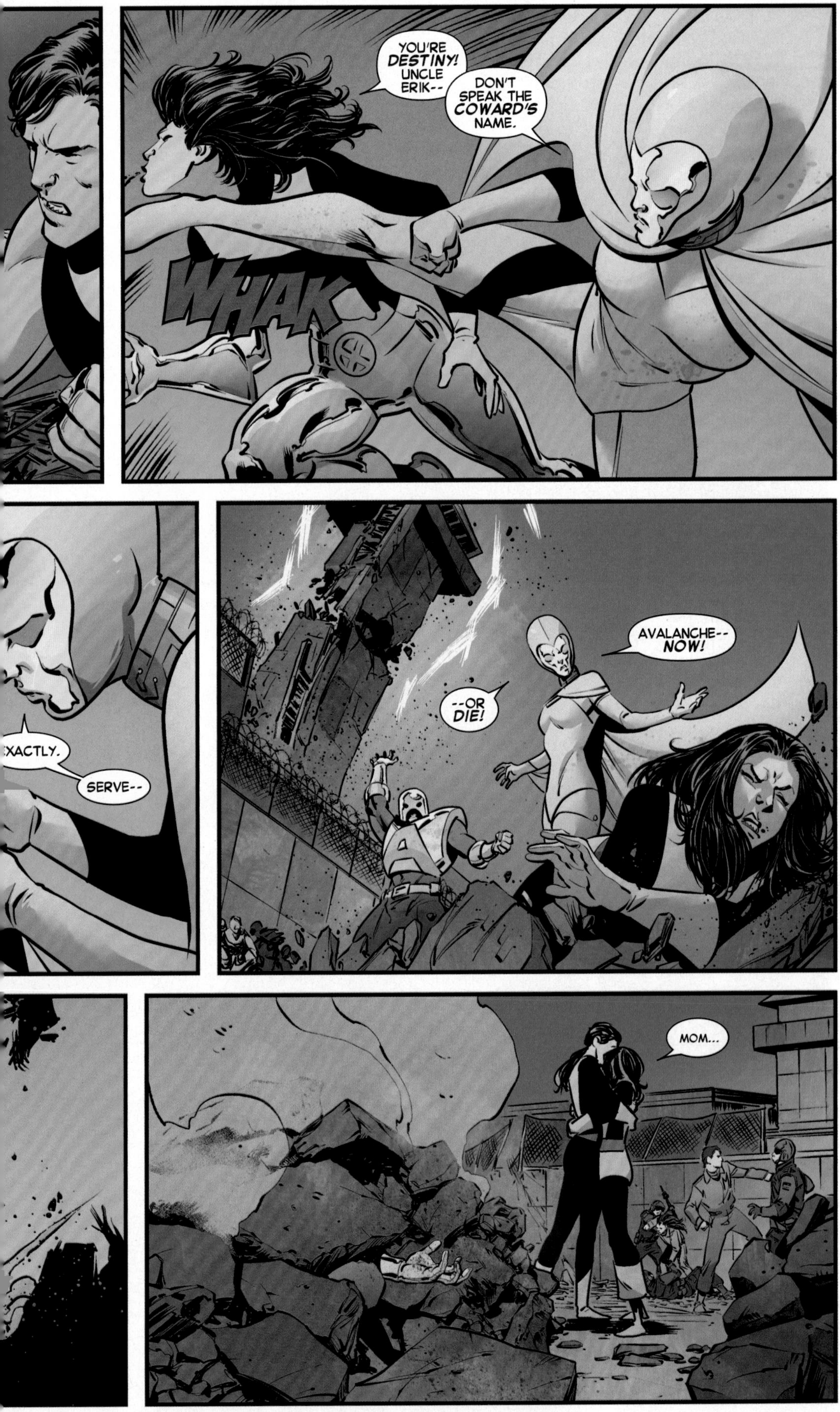
YOU'RE DESTINY! UNCLE ERIK--
DON'T SPEAK THE COWARD'S NAME.
WHAK
EXACTLY.
SERVE--
AVALANCHE-- NOW!
--OR DIE!
MOM...

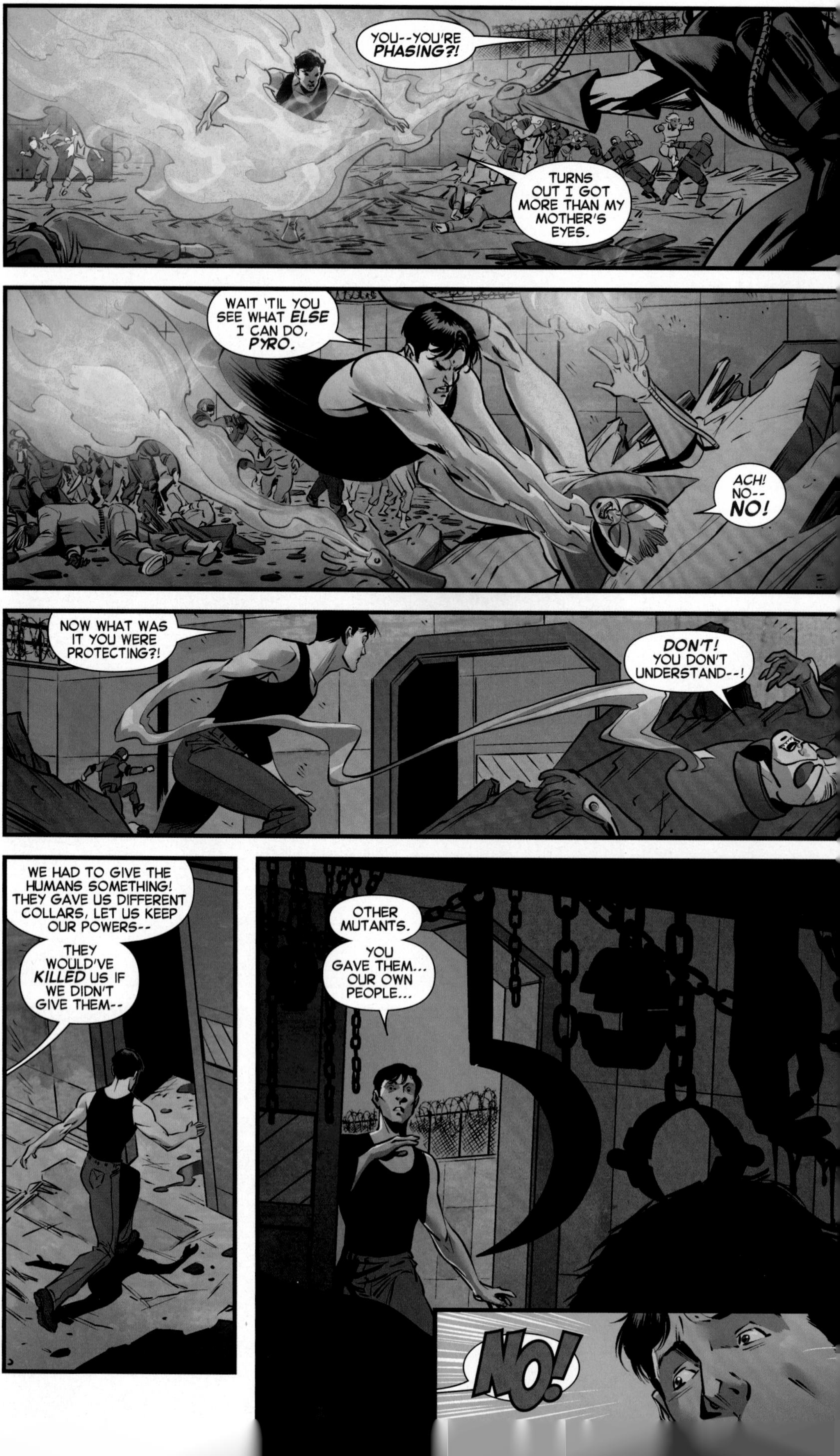
YOU--YOU'RE PHASING?!
TURNS OUT I GOT MORE THAN MY MOTHER'S EYES.
WAIT 'TIL YOU SEE WHAT ELSE I CAN DO, PYRO.
ACH! NO-- NO!
NOW WHAT WAS IT YOU WERE PROTECTING?!
DON'T! YOU DON'T UNDERSTAND--!
WE HAD TO GIVE THE HUMANS SOMETHING! THEY GAVE US DIFFERENT COLLARS, LET US KEEP OUR POWERS--
THEY WOULD'VE KILLED US IF WE DIDN'T GIVE THEM--
OTHER MUTANTS.
YOU GAVE THEM... OUR OWN PEOPLE...
NO!

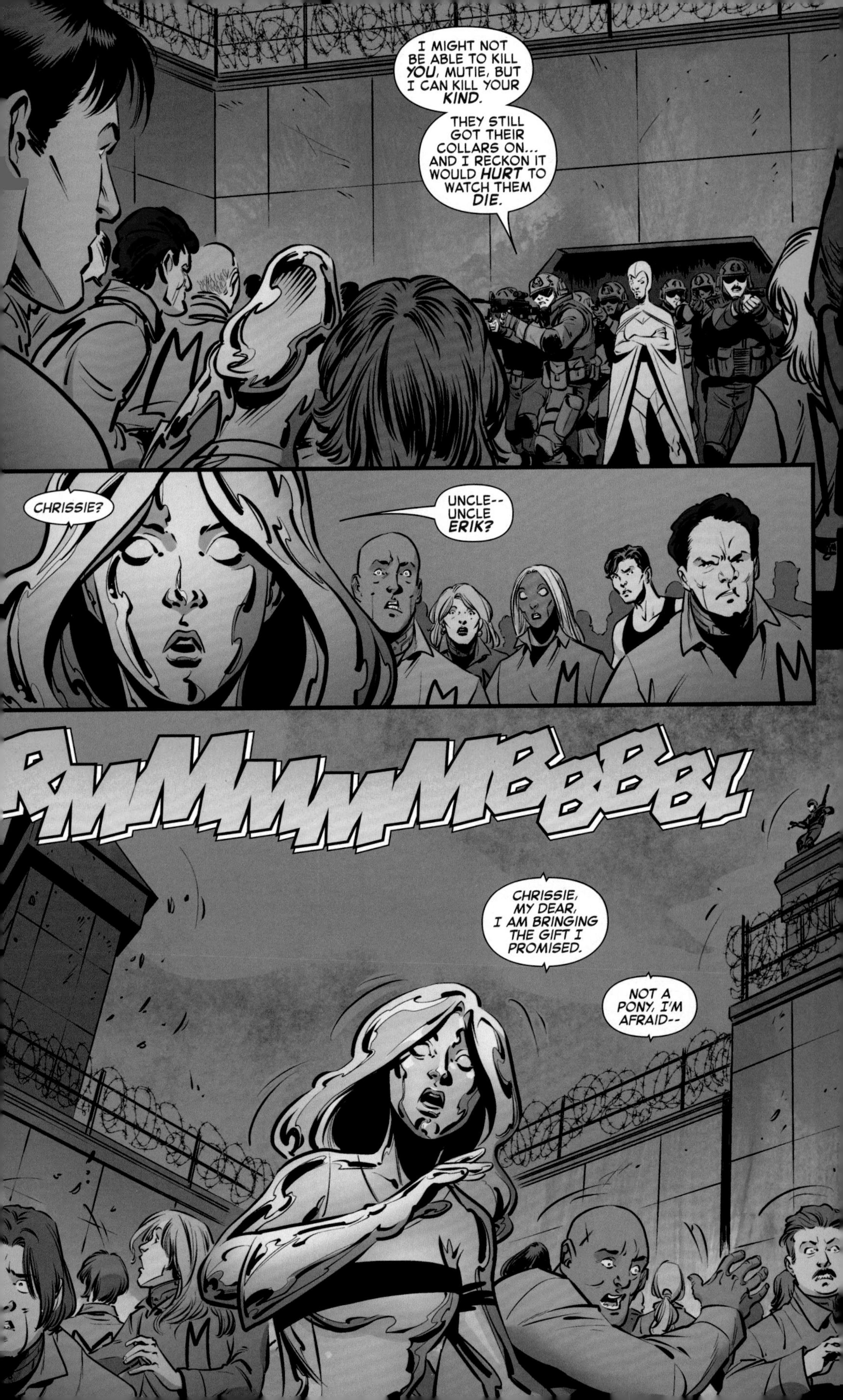
I MIGHT NOT BE ABLE TO KILL YOU, MUTIE, BUT I CAN KILL YOUR KIND.
THEY STILL GOT THEIR COLLARS ON... AND I RECKON IT WOULD HURT TO WATCH THEM DIE.
CHRISSIE?
UNCLE-- UNCLE ERIK?
RMMMMMBBBBL
CHRISSIE, MY DEAR, I AM BRINGING THE GIFT I PROMISED.
NOT A PONY, I'M AFRAID--

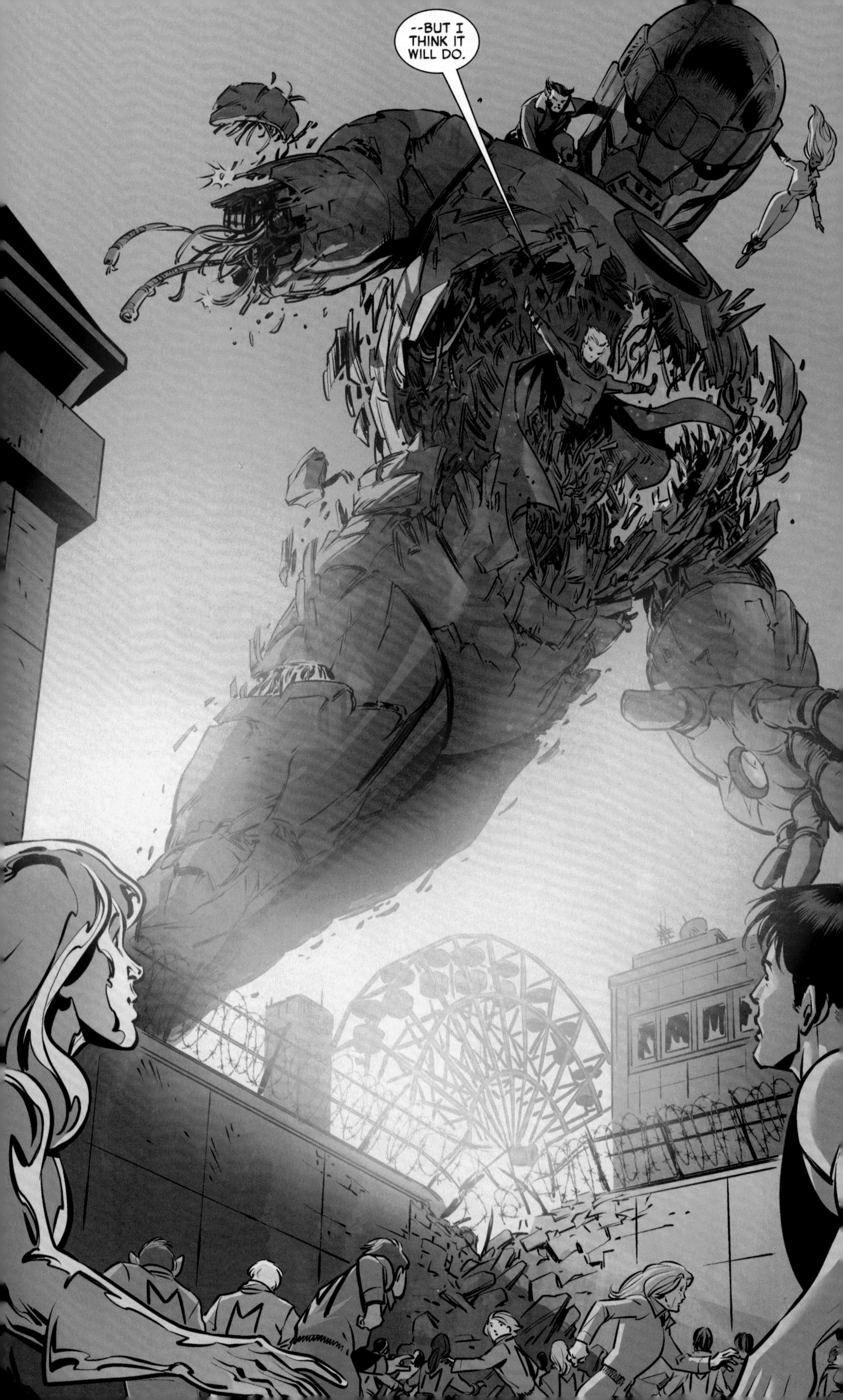
--BUT I THINK IT WILL DO.

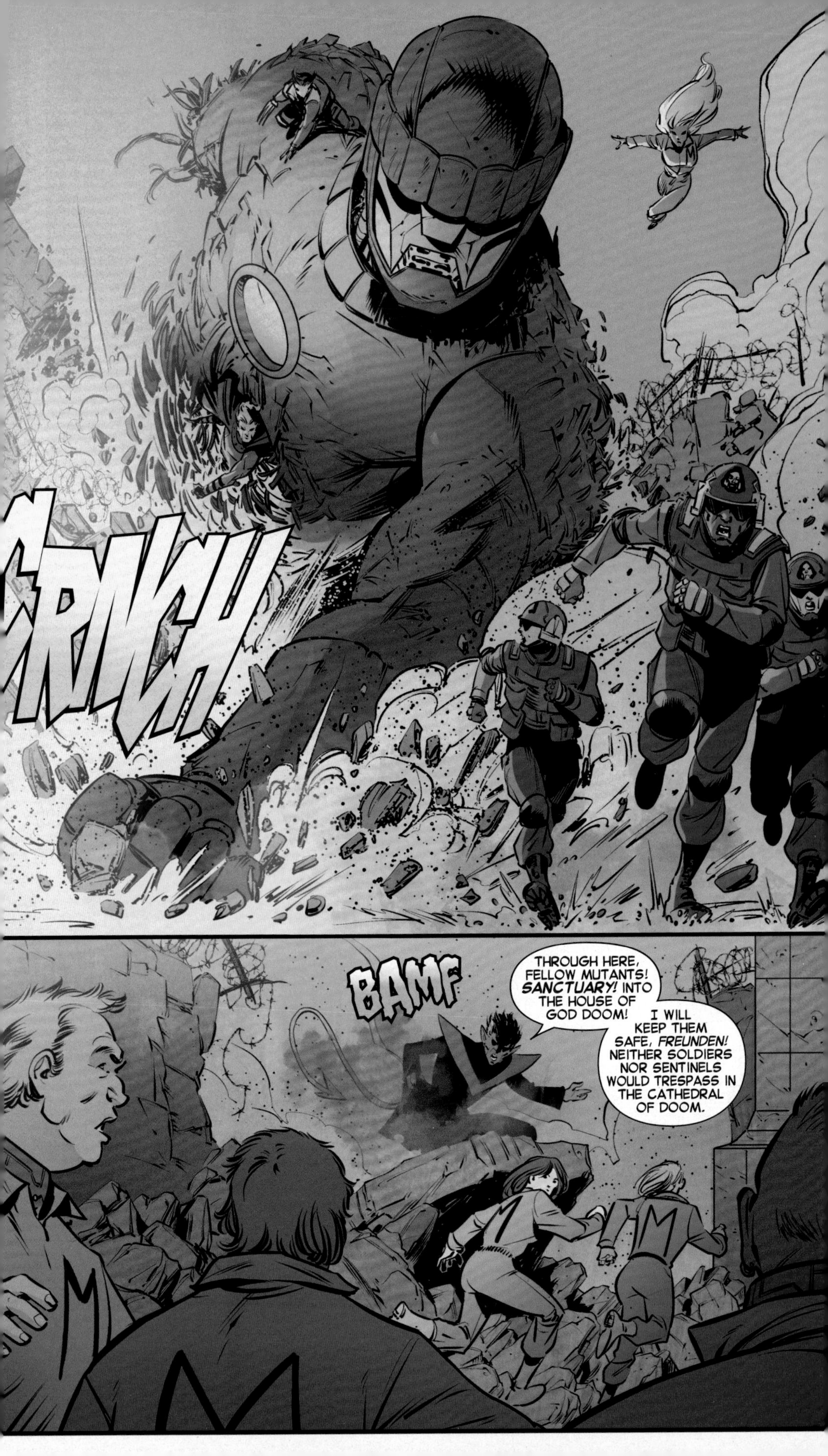
CRNCH
BAMF
THROUGH HERE, FELLOW MUTANTS! SANCTUARY! INTO THE HOUSE OF GOD DOOM!
I WILL KEEP THEM SAFE, FREUNDEN! NEITHER SOLDIERS NOR SENTINELS WOULD TRESPASS IN THE CATHEDRAL OF DOOM.

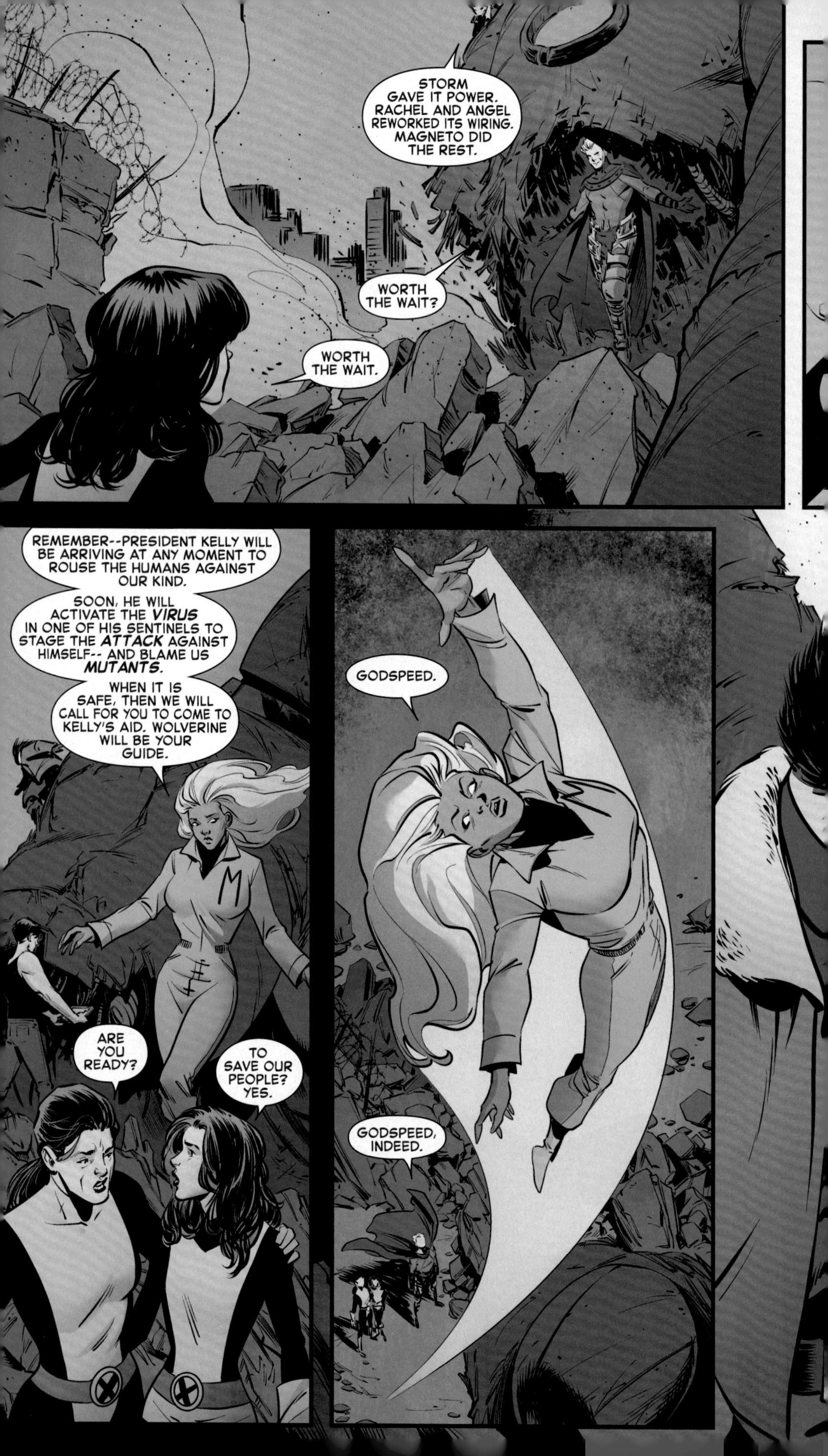
STORM GAVE IT POWER. RACHEL AND ANGEL REWORKED ITS WIRING. MAGNETO DID THE REST.
WORTH THE WAIT?
WORTH THE WAIT.
REMEMBER--PRESIDENT KELLY WILL BE ARRIVING AT ANY MOMENT TO ROUSE THE HUMANS AGAINST OUR KIND.
SOON, HE WILL ACTIVATE THE VIRUS IN ONE OF HIS SENTINELS TO STAGE THE ATTACK AGAINST HIMSELF-- AND BLAME US MUTANTS.
WHEN IT IS SAFE, THEN WE WILL CALL FOR YOU TO COME TO KELLY'S AID. WOLVERINE WILL BE YOUR GUIDE.
ARE YOU READY?
TO SAVE OUR PEOPLE? YES.
GODSPEED.
GODSPEED, INDEED.

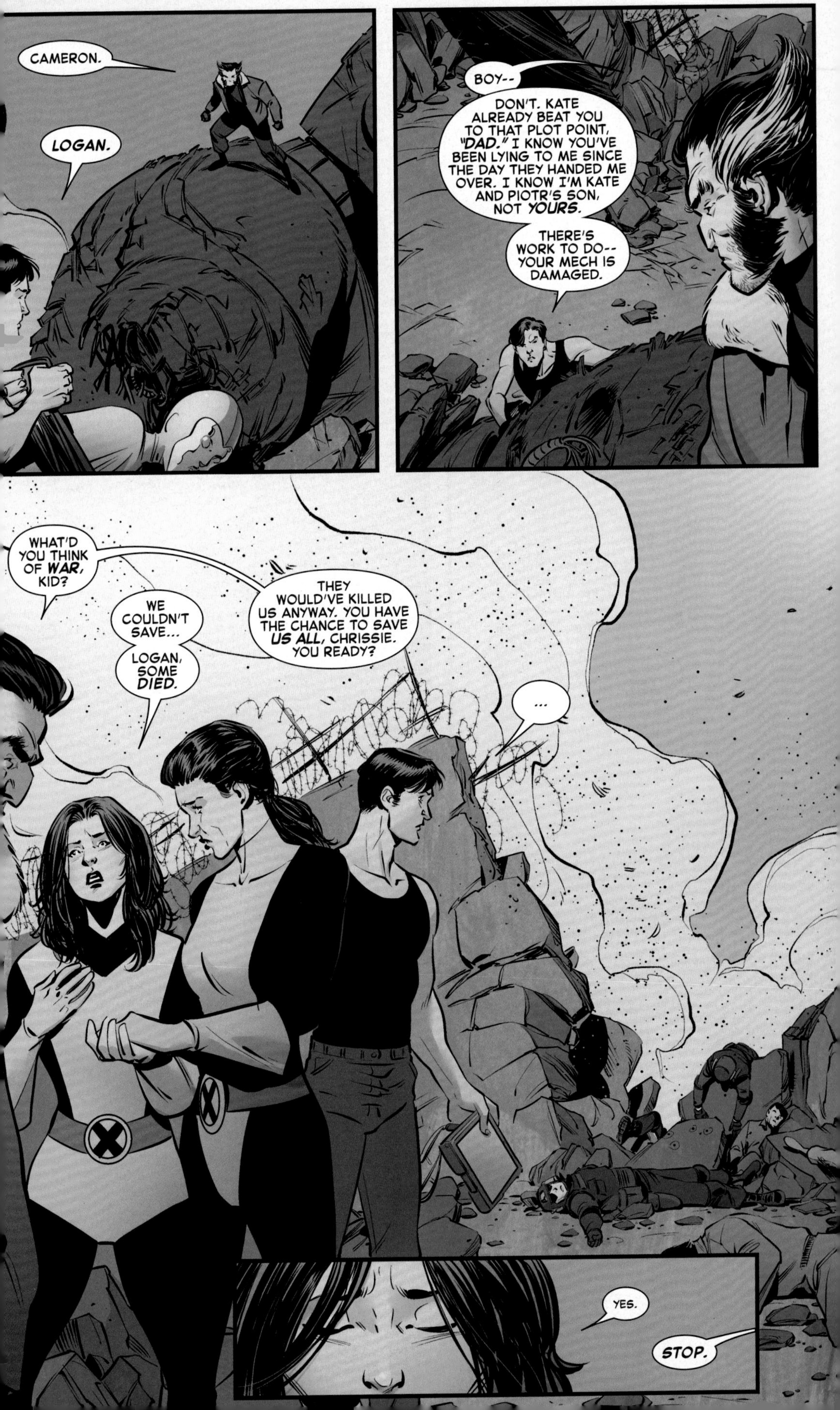
CAMERON.
LOGAN.
BOY--
DON'T. KATE ALREADY BEAT YOU TO THAT PLOT POINT, "DAD." I KNOW YOU'VE BEEN LYING TO ME SINCE THE DAY THEY HANDED ME OVER. I KNOW I'M KATE AND PIOTR'S SON, NOT YOURS.
THERE'S WORK TO DO-- YOUR MECH IS DAMAGED.
WHAT'D YOU THINK OF WAR, KID?
WE COULDN'T SAVE...
LOGAN, SOME DIED.
THEY WOULD'VE KILLED US ANYWAY. YOU HAVE THE CHANCE TO SAVE US ALL, CHRISSIE. YOU READY?
...
YES.
STOP.

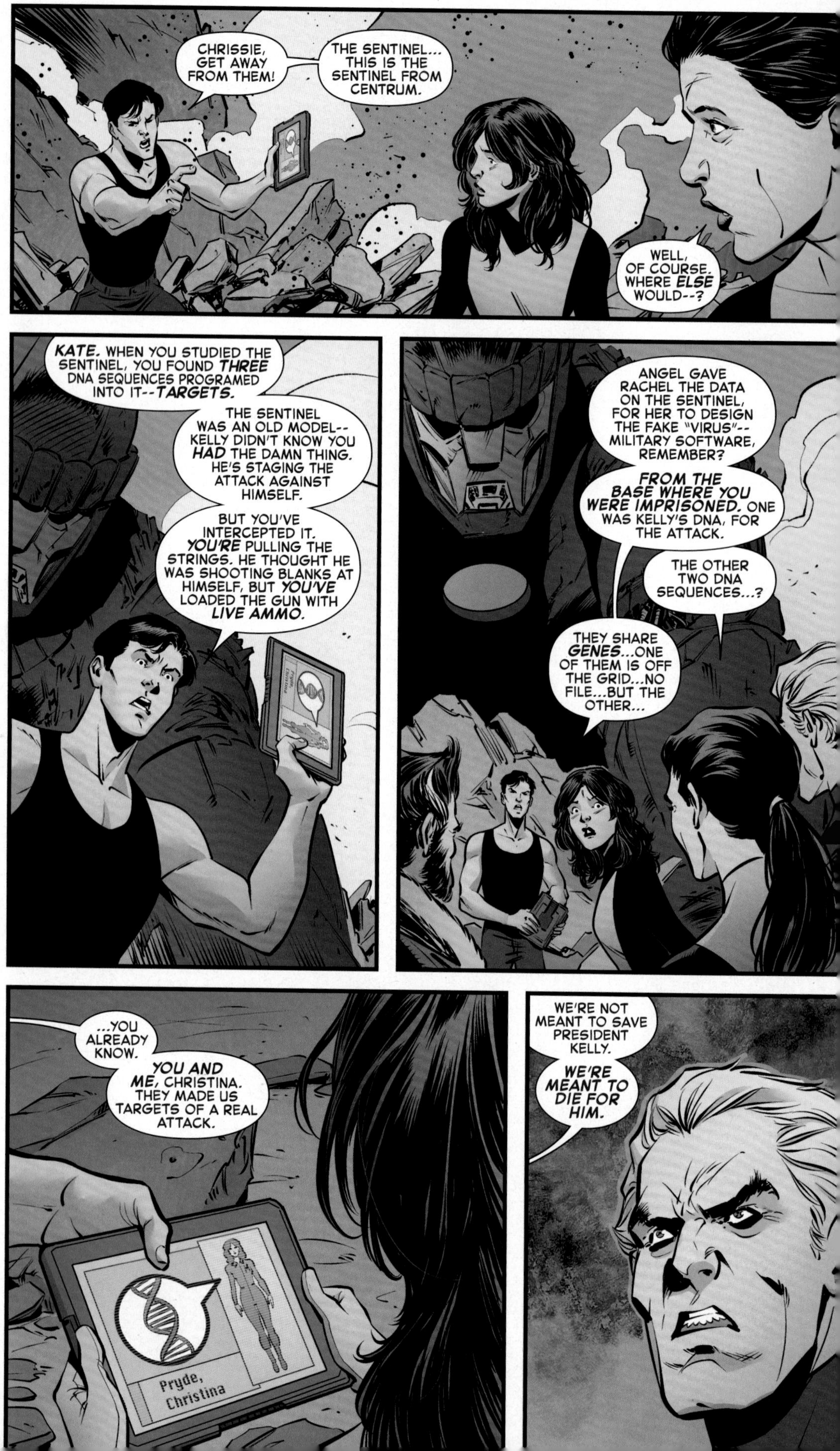
CHRISSIE, GET AWAY FROM THEM!
THE SENTINEL... THIS IS THE SENTINEL FROM CENTRUM.
WELL, OF COURSE. WHERE *ELSE* WOULD--?
KATE. WHEN YOU STUDIED THE SENTINEL, YOU FOUND *THREE* DNA SEQUENCES PROGRAMED INTO IT--*TARGETS.*
THE SENTINEL WAS AN OLD MODEL-- KELLY DIDN'T KNOW YOU *HAD* THE DAMN THING. HE'S STAGING THE ATTACK AGAINST HIMSELF.
BUT YOU'VE INTERCEPTED IT. *YOU'RE* PULLING THE STRINGS. HE THOUGHT HE WAS SHOOTING BLANKS AT HIMSELF, BUT *YOU'VE* LOADED THE GUN WITH *LIVE AMMO.*
ANGEL GAVE RACHEL THE DATA ON THE SENTINEL, FOR HER TO DESIGN THE FAKE "VIRUS"-- MILITARY SOFTWARE, REMEMBER?
FROM THE BASE WHERE YOU WERE IMPRISONED. ONE WAS KELLY'S DNA, FOR THE ATTACK.
THE OTHER TWO DNA SEQUENCES...?
THEY SHARE *GENES*...ONE OF THEM IS OFF THE GRID...NO FILE...BUT THE OTHER...
...YOU ALREADY KNOW.
YOU AND ME, CHRISTINA. THEY MADE US TARGETS OF A REAL ATTACK.
Pryde, Christina
WE'RE NOT MEANT TO SAVE PRESIDENT KELLY.
WE'RE MEANT TO DIE FOR HIM.

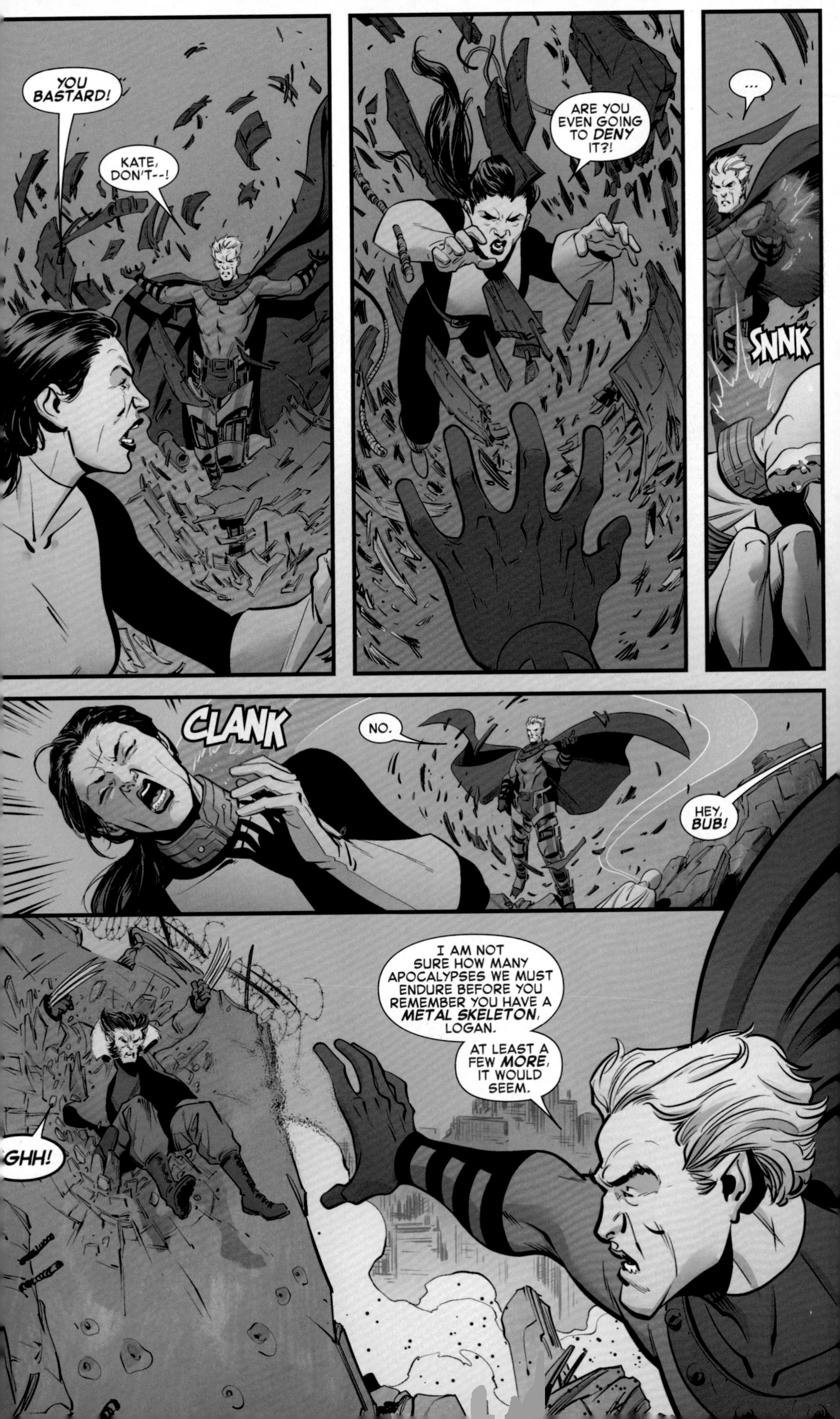
YOU BASTARD!
KATE, DON'T--!
ARE YOU EVEN GOING TO *DENY* IT?!
...
SNNK
CLANK
NO.
HEY, *BUB!*
I AM NOT SURE HOW MANY APOCALYPSES WE MUST ENDURE BEFORE YOU REMEMBER YOU HAVE A *METAL SKELETON*, LOGAN.
AT LEAST A FEW *MORE*, IT WOULD SEEM.
GHH!

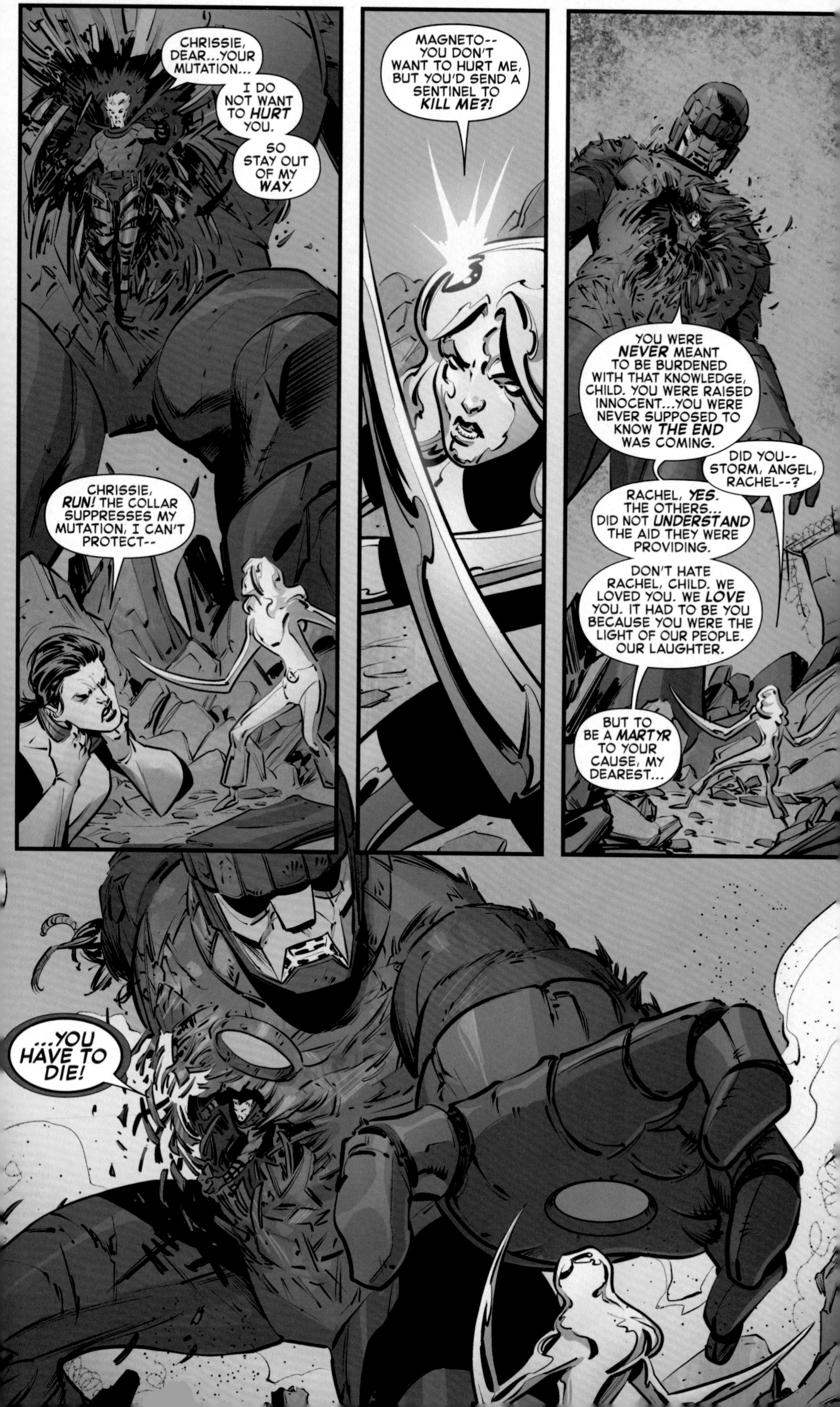

CHRISSIE, DEAR...YOUR MUTATION...
I DO NOT WANT TO HURT YOU.
SO STAY OUT OF MY WAY.
CHRISSIE, RUN! THE COLLAR SUPPRESSES MY MUTATION, I CAN'T PROTECT--
MAGNETO--YOU DON'T WANT TO HURT ME, BUT YOU'D SEND A SENTINEL TO KILL ME?!
YOU WERE NEVER MEANT TO BE BURDENED WITH THAT KNOWLEDGE, CHILD. YOU WERE RAISED INNOCENT...YOU WERE NEVER SUPPOSED TO KNOW THE END WAS COMING.
DID YOU--STORM, ANGEL, RACHEL--?
RACHEL, YES. THE OTHERS... DID NOT UNDERSTAND THE AID THEY WERE PROVIDING.
DON'T HATE RACHEL, CHILD. WE LOVED YOU. WE LOVE YOU. IT HAD TO BE YOU BECAUSE YOU WERE THE LIGHT OF OUR PEOPLE. OUR LAUGHTER.
BUT TO BE A MARTYR TO YOUR CAUSE, MY DEAREST...
...YOU HAVE TO DIE!

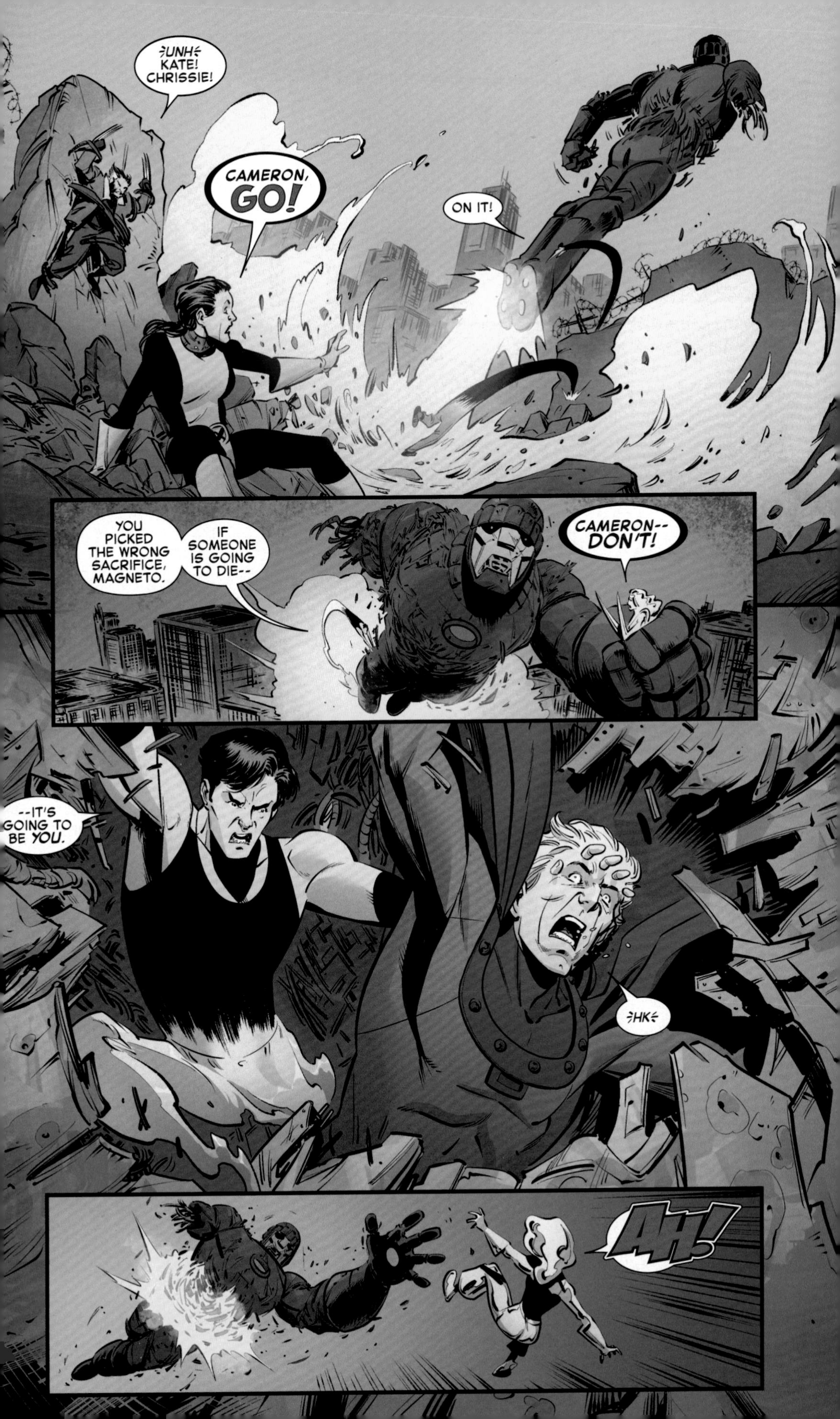

UNH KATE! CHRISSIE!
CAMERON, GO!
ON IT!
YOU PICKED THE WRONG SACRIFICE, MAGNETO.
IF SOMEONE IS GOING TO DIE--
CAMERON-- DON'T!
--IT'S GOING TO BE YOU.
HK
AH!

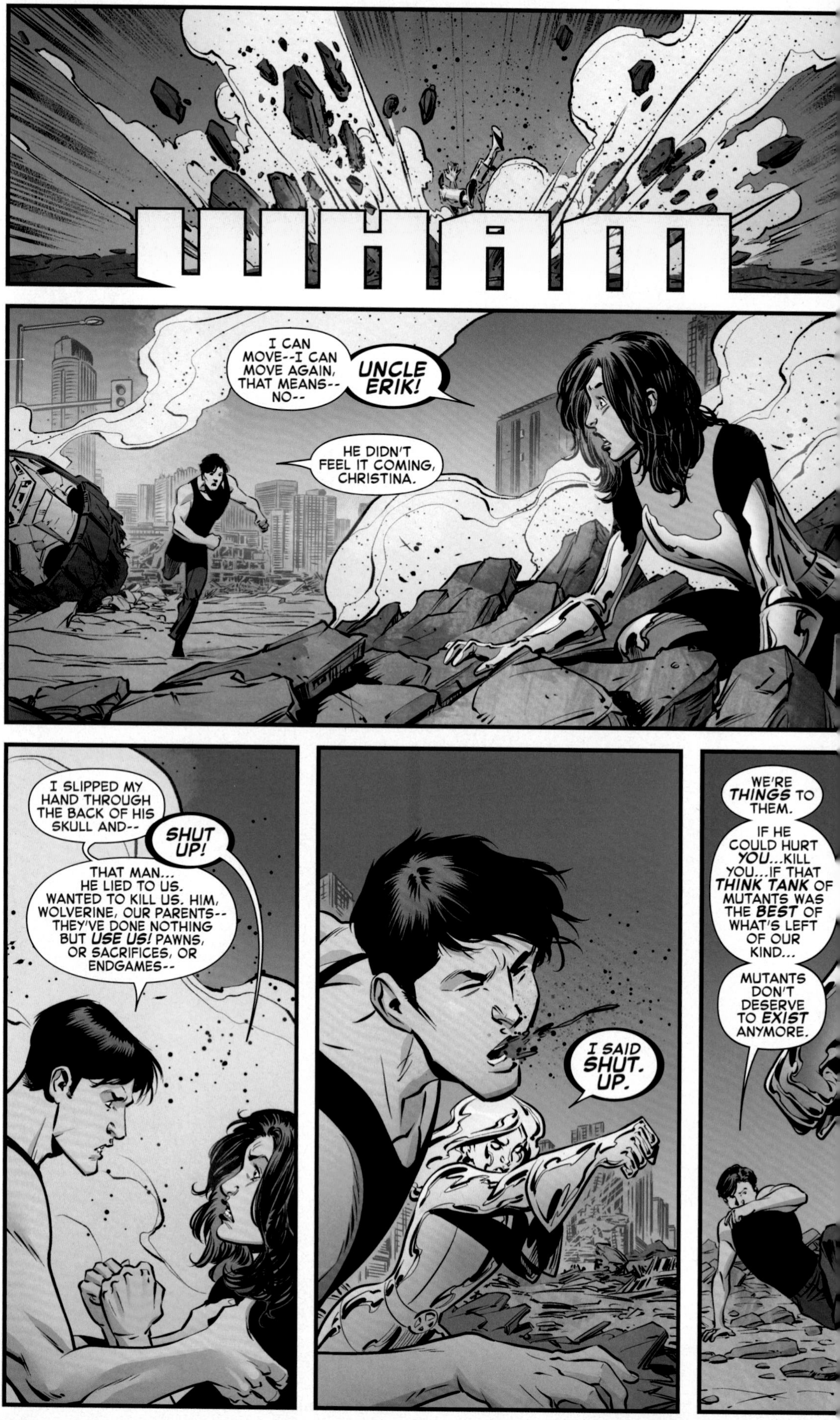
WHAM
I CAN MOVE--I CAN MOVE AGAIN, THAT MEANS-- NO--
UNCLE ERIK!
HE DIDN'T FEEL IT COMING, CHRISTINA.
I SLIPPED MY HAND THROUGH THE BACK OF HIS SKULL AND--
SHUT UP!
THAT MAN... HE LIED TO US. WANTED TO KILL US. HIM, WOLVERINE, OUR PARENTS-- THEY'VE DONE NOTHING BUT USE US! PAWNS, OR SACRIFICES, OR ENDGAMES--
I SAID SHUT. UP.
WE'RE THINGS TO THEM.
IF HE COULD HURT YOU...KILL YOU...IF THAT THINK TANK OF MUTANTS WAS THE BEST OF WHAT'S LEFT OF OUR KIND...
MUTANTS DON'T DESERVE TO EXIST ANYMORE.

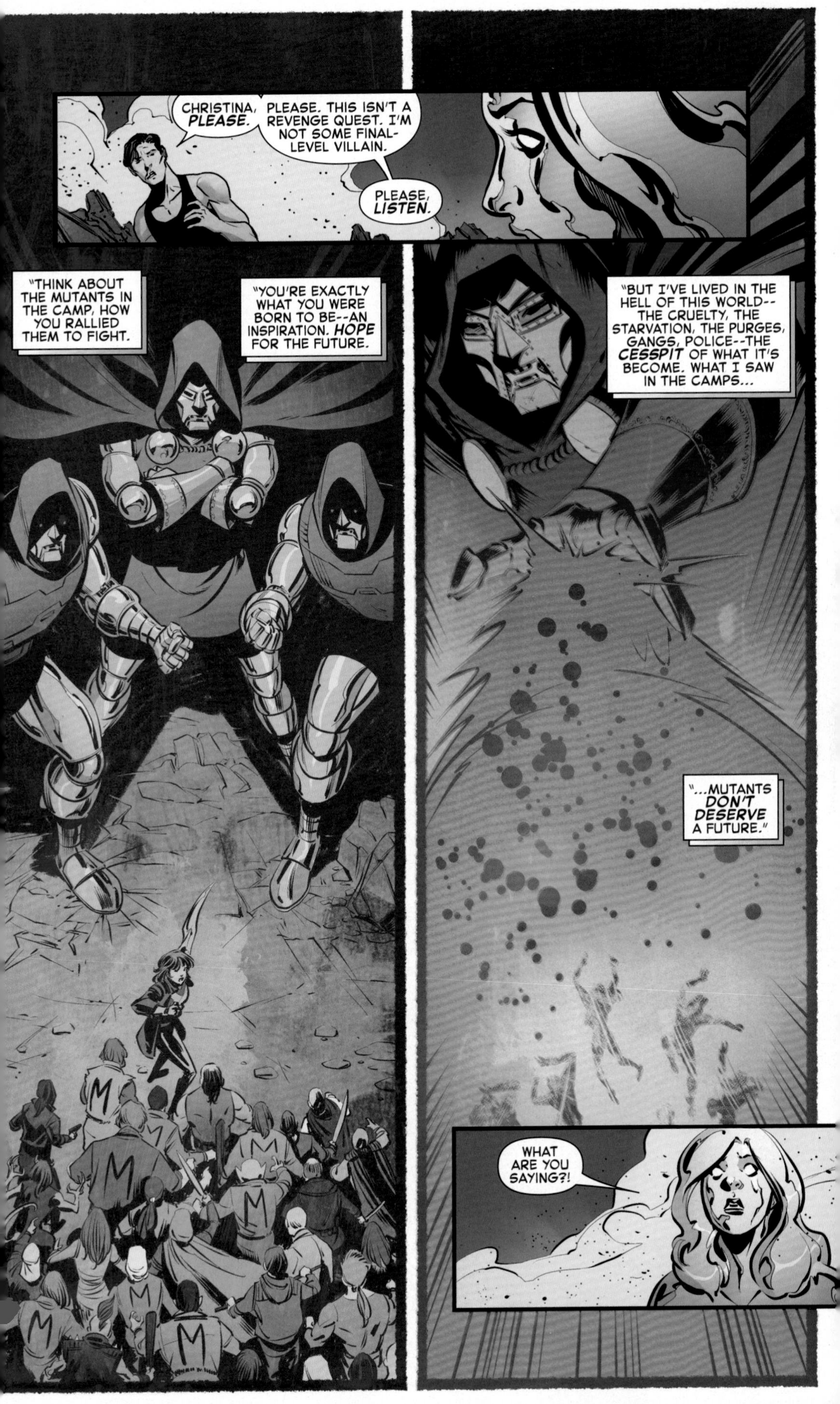
CHRISTINA, PLEASE.
PLEASE. THIS ISN'T A REVENGE QUEST. I'M NOT SOME FINAL-LEVEL VILLAIN.
PLEASE, LISTEN.
"THINK ABOUT THE MUTANTS IN THE CAMP, HOW YOU RALLIED THEM TO FIGHT.
"YOU'RE EXACTLY WHAT YOU WERE BORN TO BE--AN INSPIRATION. HOPE FOR THE FUTURE.
"BUT I'VE LIVED IN THE HELL OF THIS WORLD-- THE CRUELTY, THE STARVATION, THE PURGES, GANGS, POLICE--THE CESSPIT OF WHAT IT'S BECOME. WHAT I SAW IN THE CAMPS...
"...MUTANTS DON'T DESERVE A FUTURE."
WHAT ARE YOU SAYING?!

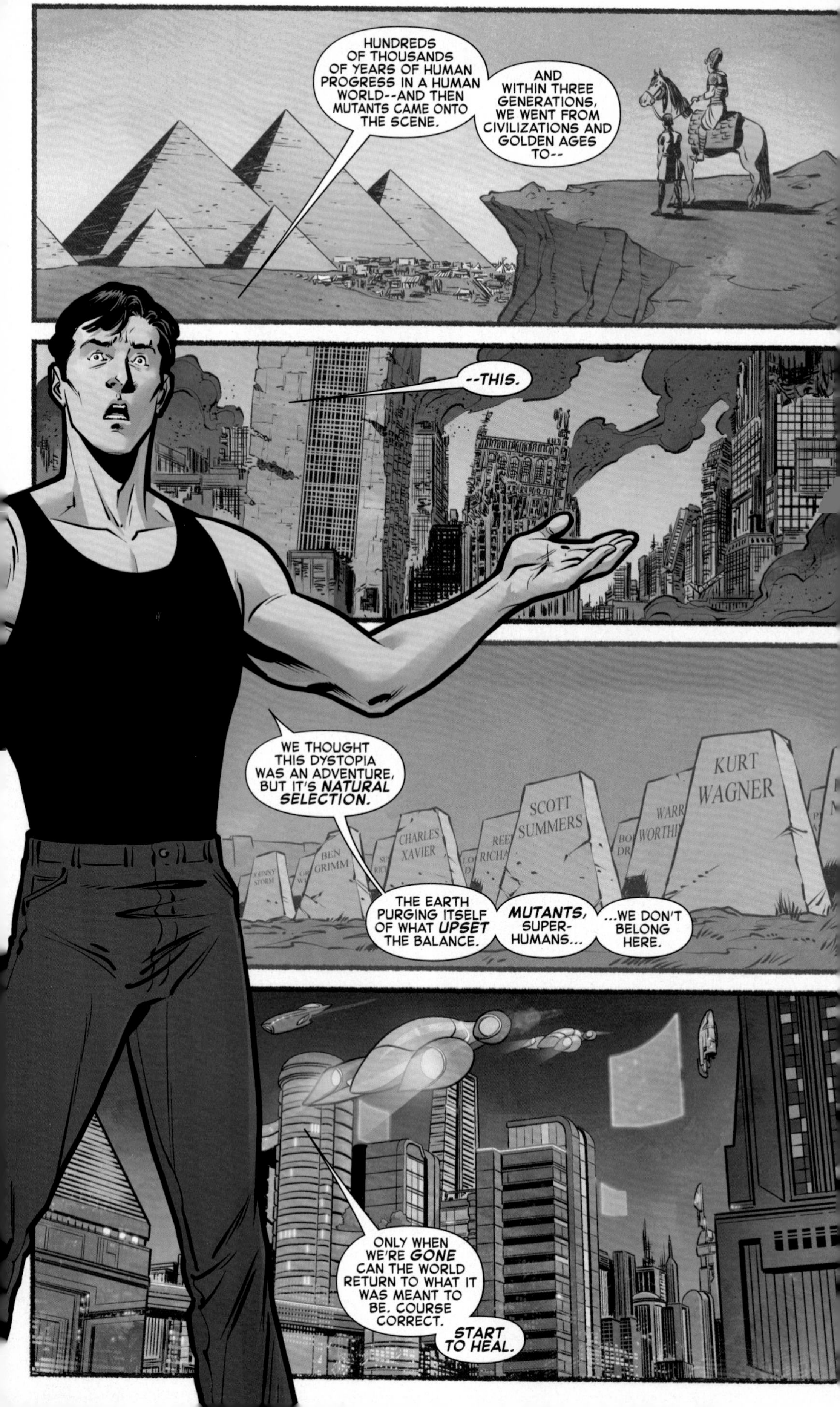
HUNDREDS OF THOUSANDS OF YEARS OF HUMAN PROGRESS IN A HUMAN WORLD--AND THEN MUTANTS CAME ONTO THE SCENE.
AND WITHIN THREE GENERATIONS, WE WENT FROM CIVILIZATIONS AND GOLDEN AGES TO--
--THIS.
WE THOUGHT THIS DYSTOPIA WAS AN ADVENTURE, BUT IT'S NATURAL SELECTION.
KURT WAGNER
SCOTT SUMMERS
CHARLES XAVIER
BEN GRIMM
JOHNNY STORM
THE EARTH PURGING ITSELF OF WHAT UPSET THE BALANCE.
MUTANTS, SUPER-HUMANS...
...WE DON'T BELONG HERE.
ONLY WHEN WE'RE GONE CAN THE WORLD RETURN TO WHAT IT WAS MEANT TO BE. COURSE CORRECT.
START TO HEAL.

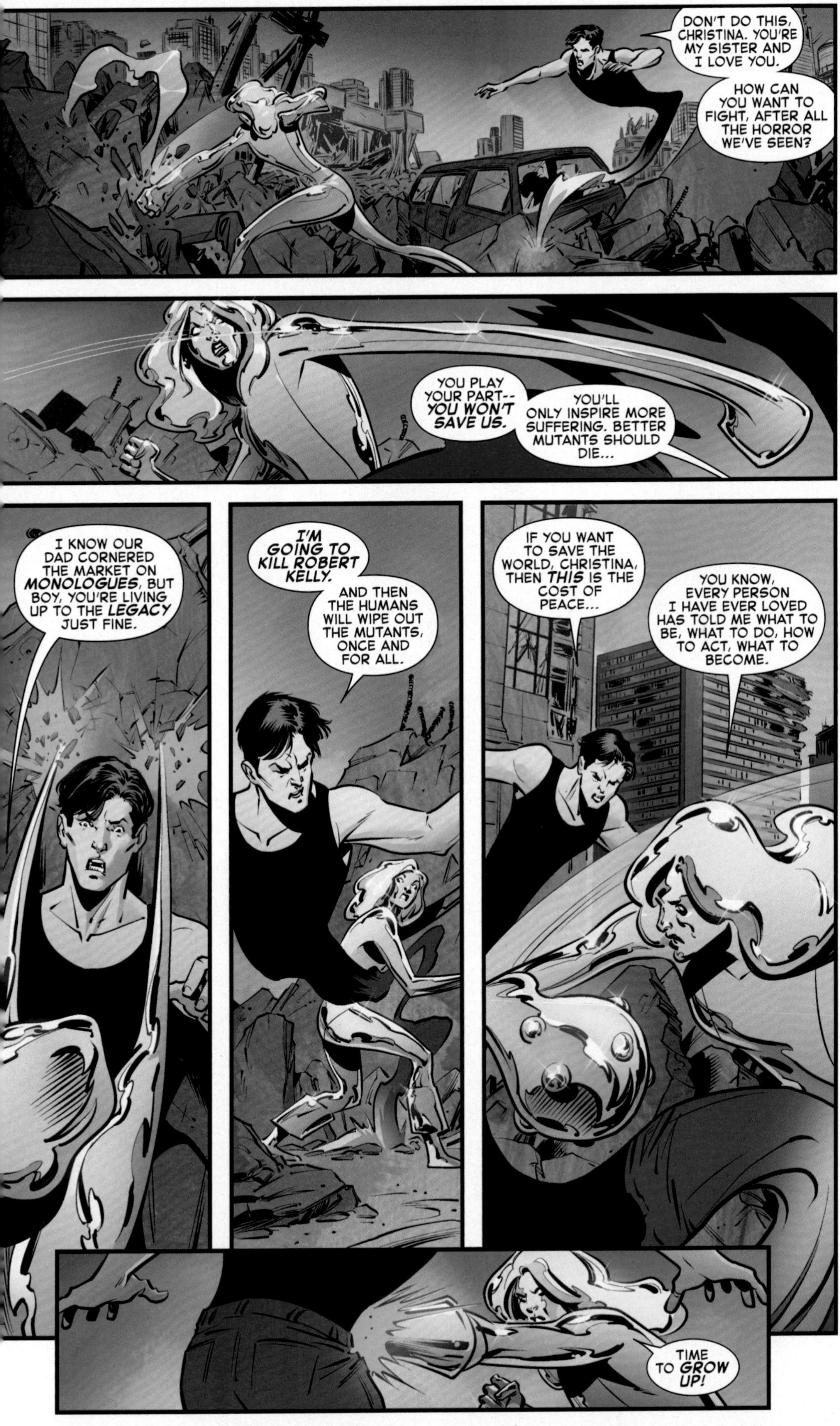

DON'T DO THIS, CHRISTINA. YOU'RE MY SISTER AND I LOVE YOU.
HOW CAN YOU WANT TO FIGHT, AFTER ALL THE HORROR WE'VE SEEN?
YOU PLAY YOUR PART-- *YOU WON'T SAVE US.*
YOU'LL ONLY INSPIRE MORE SUFFERING. BETTER MUTANTS SHOULD DIE...
I KNOW OUR DAD CORNERED THE MARKET ON *MONOLOGUES*, BUT BOY, YOU'RE LIVING UP TO THE *LEGACY* JUST FINE.
I'M GOING TO KILL ROBERT KELLY.
AND THEN THE HUMANS WILL WIPE OUT THE MUTANTS, ONCE AND FOR ALL.
IF YOU WANT TO SAVE THE WORLD, CHRISTINA, THEN *THIS* IS THE COST OF PEACE...
YOU KNOW, EVERY PERSON I HAVE EVER LOVED HAS TOLD ME WHAT TO BE, WHAT TO DO, HOW TO ACT, WHAT TO BECOME.
TIME TO *GROW UP!*

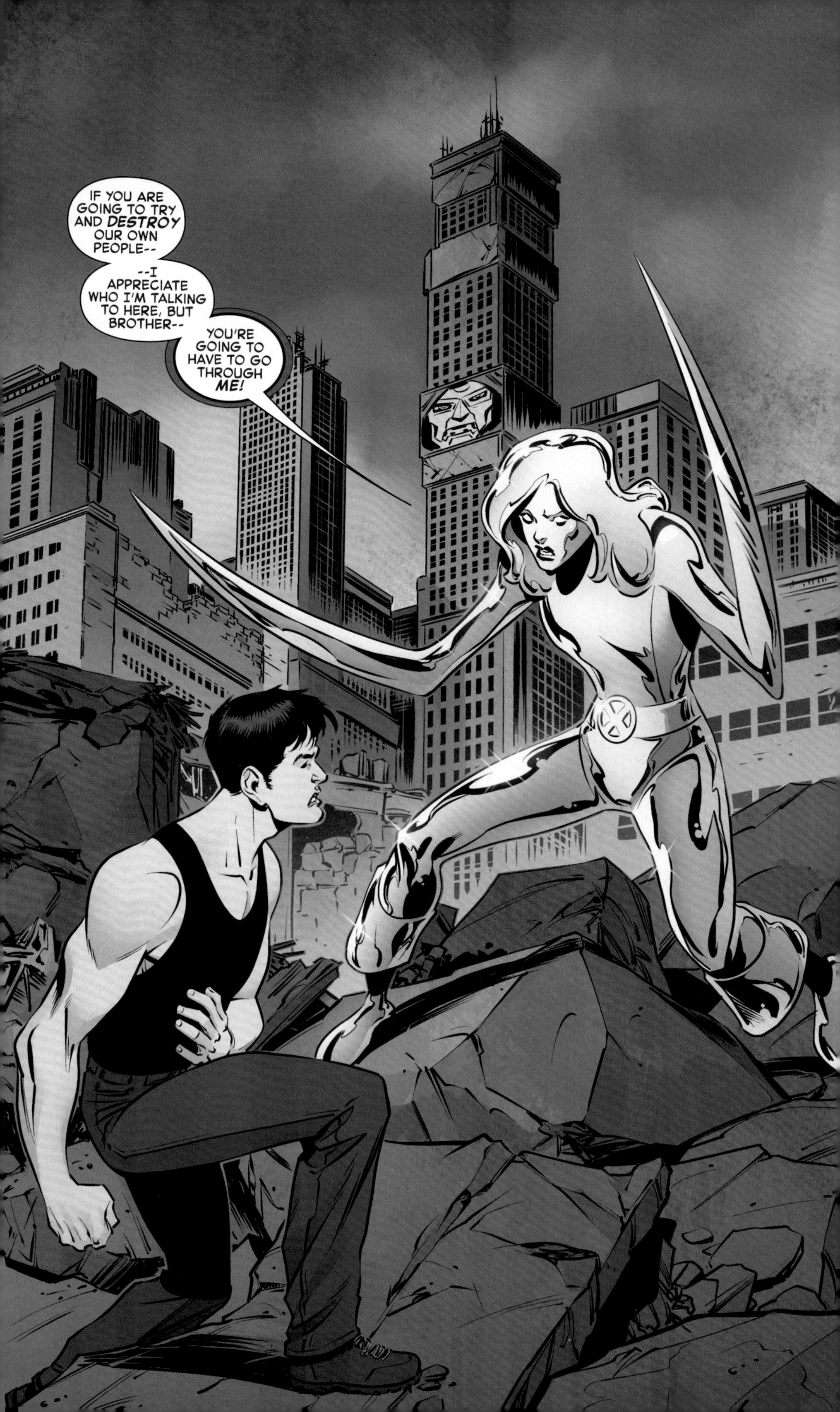
IF YOU ARE GOING TO TRY AND DESTROY OUR OWN PEOPLE--
--I APPRECIATE WHO I'M TALKING TO HERE, BUT BROTHER--
YOU'RE GOING TO HAVE TO GO THROUGH ME!

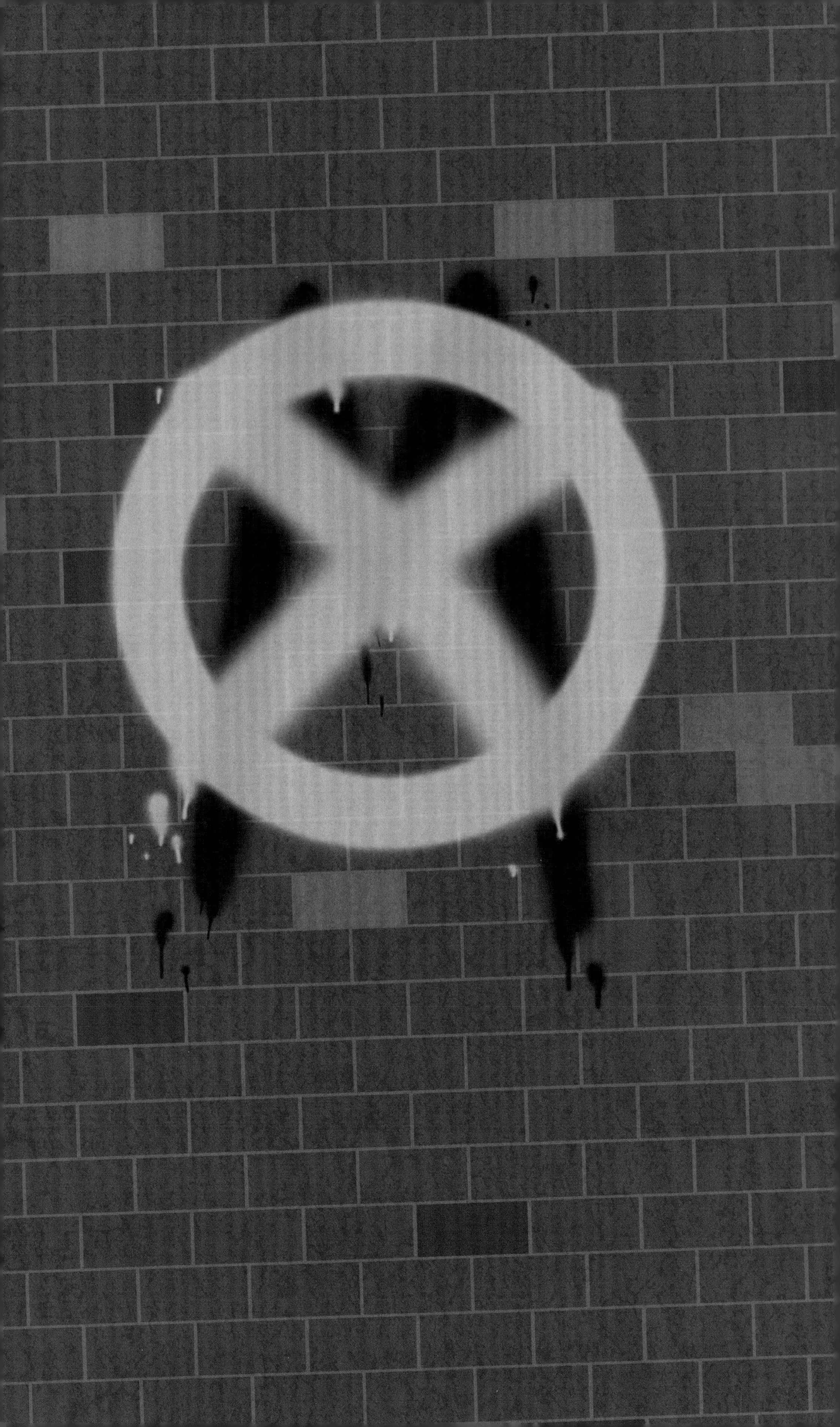

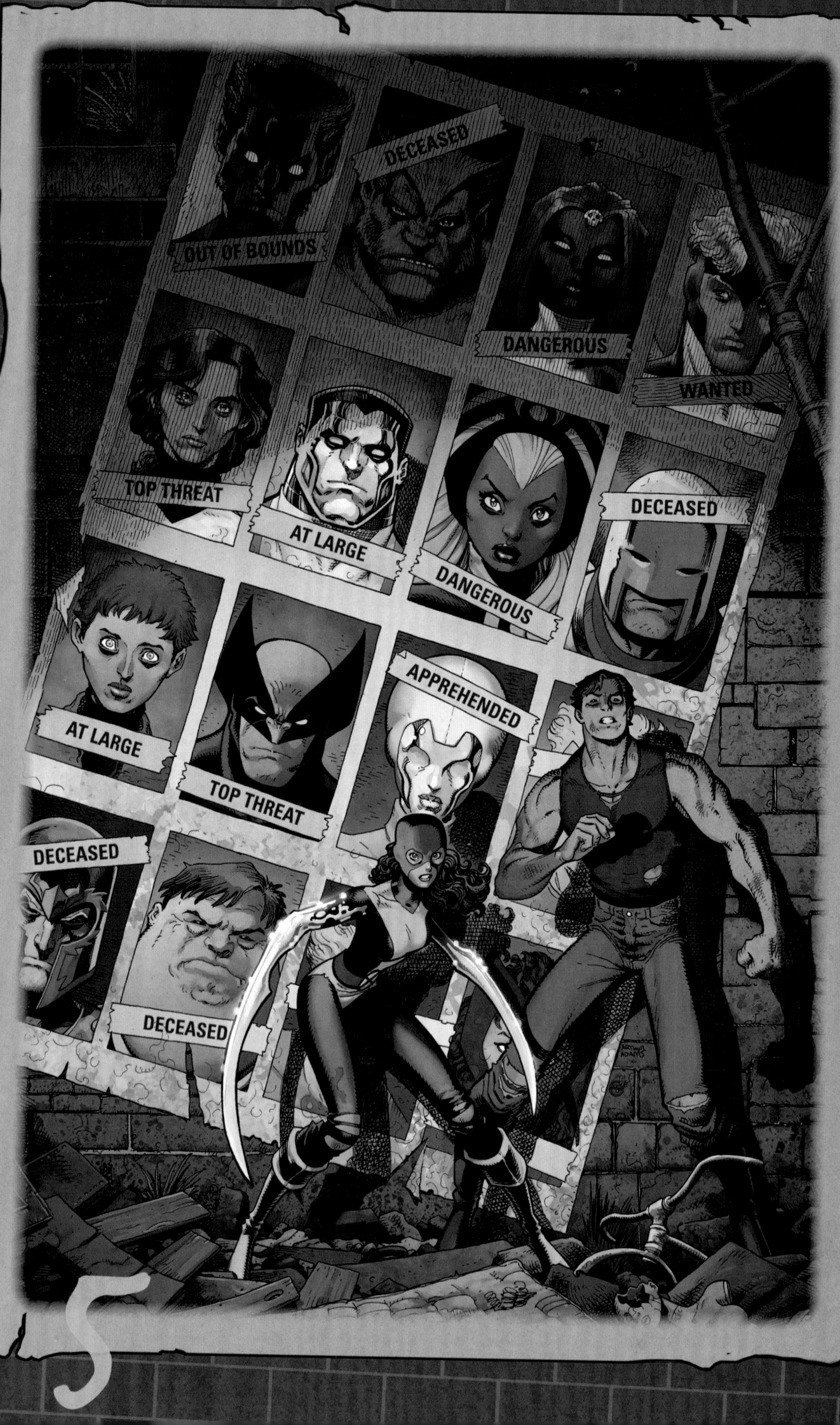
OUT OF BOUNDS
DECEASED
DANGEROUS
WANTED
TOP THREAT
AT LARGE
DANGEROUS
DECEASED
AT LARGE
TOP THREAT
APPREHENDED
DECEASED
DECEASED
5

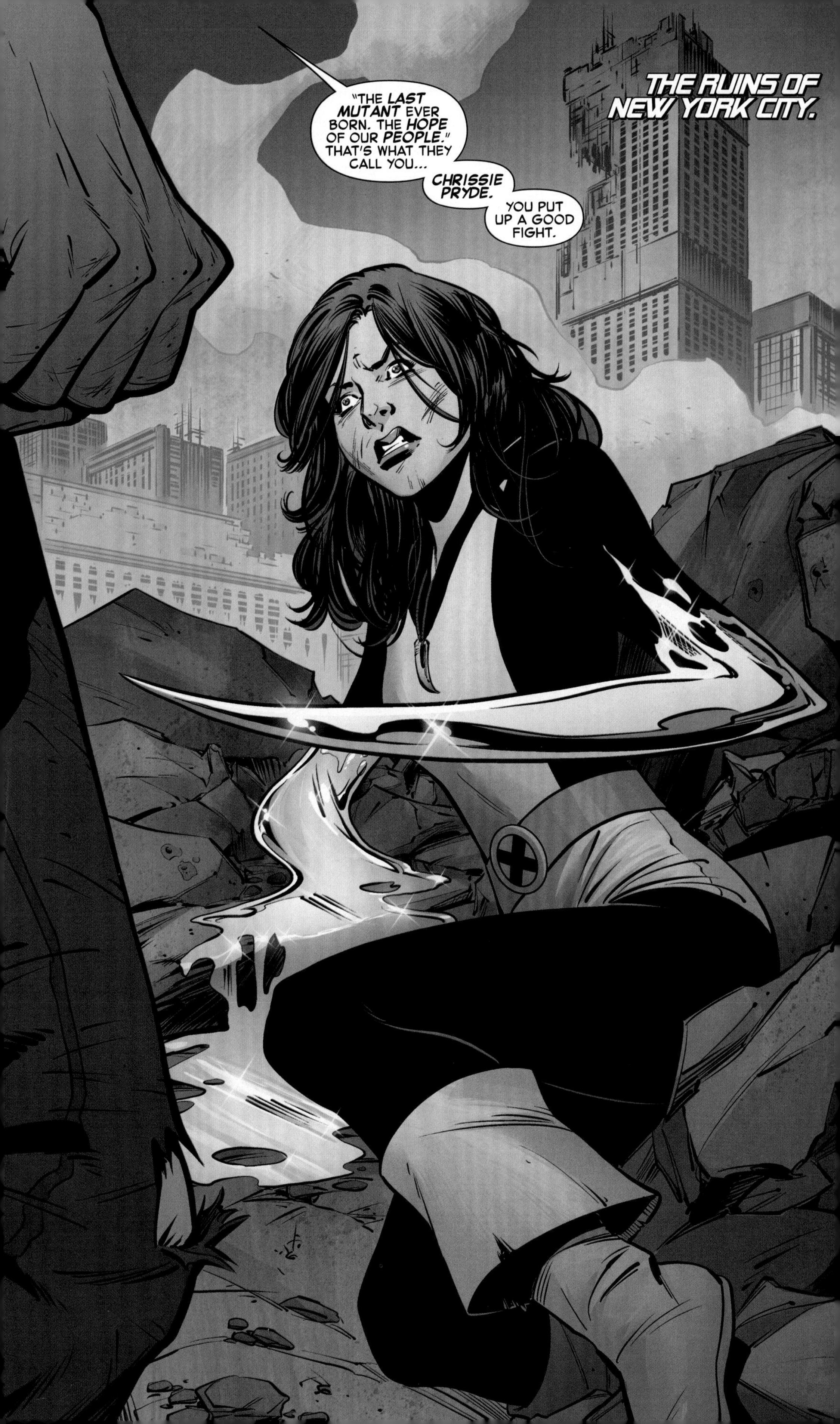
THE RUINS OF NEW YORK CITY.
"THE LAST MUTANT EVER BORN. THE HOPE OF OUR PEOPLE." THAT'S WHAT THEY CALL YOU...
CHRISSIE PRYDE.
YOU PUT UP A GOOD FIGHT.

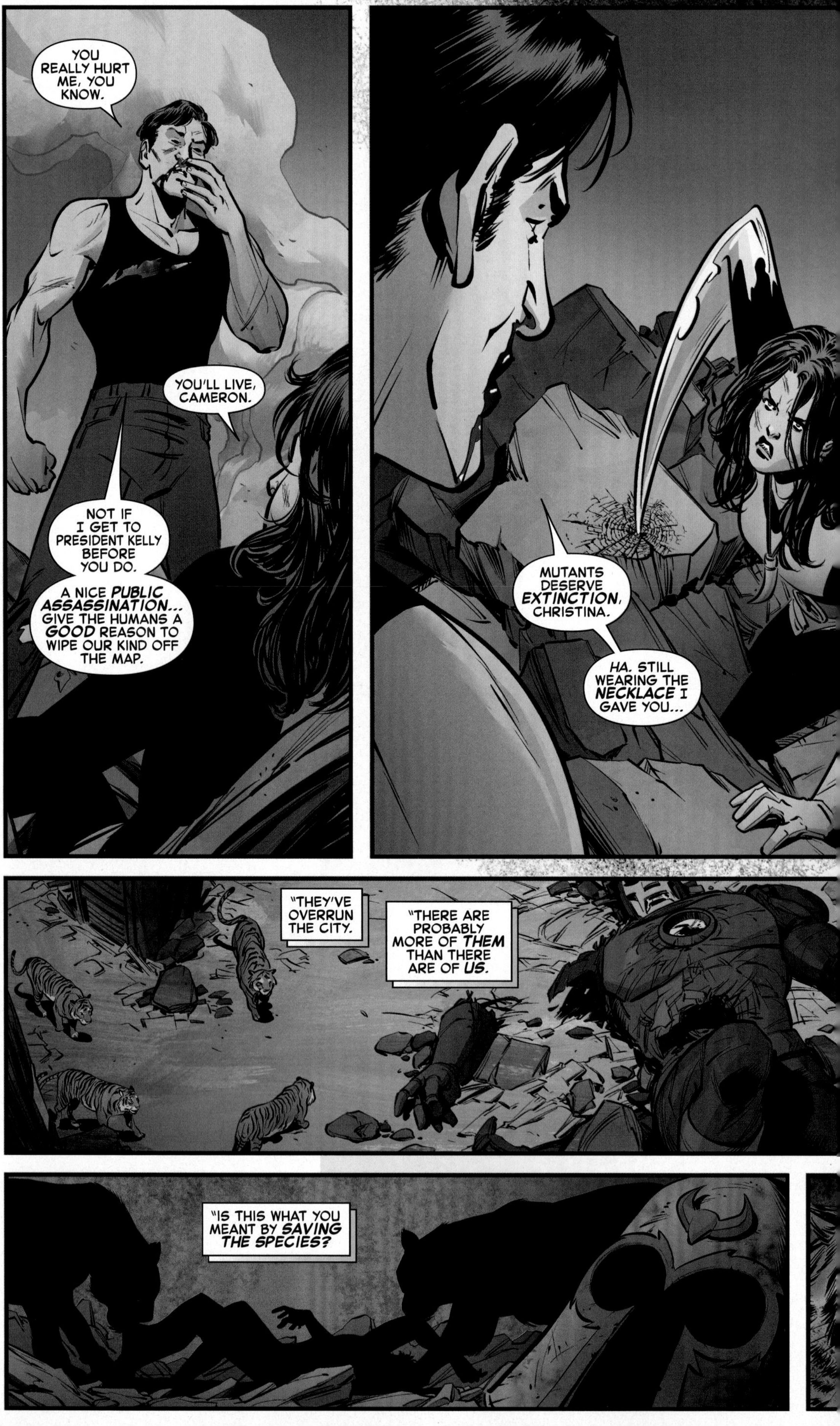
YOU REALLY HURT ME, YOU KNOW.
YOU'LL LIVE, CAMERON.
NOT IF I GET TO PRESIDENT KELLY BEFORE YOU DO.
A NICE *PUBLIC ASSASSINATION...* GIVE THE HUMANS A *GOOD* REASON TO WIPE OUR KIND OFF THE MAP.
MUTANTS DESERVE *EXTINCTION*, CHRISTINA.
HA. STILL WEARING THE *NECKLACE* I GAVE YOU...
"THEY'VE OVERRUN THE CITY.
"THERE ARE PROBABLY MORE OF *THEM* THAN THERE ARE OF *US*.
"IS THIS WHAT YOU MEANT BY *SAVING THE SPECIES?*

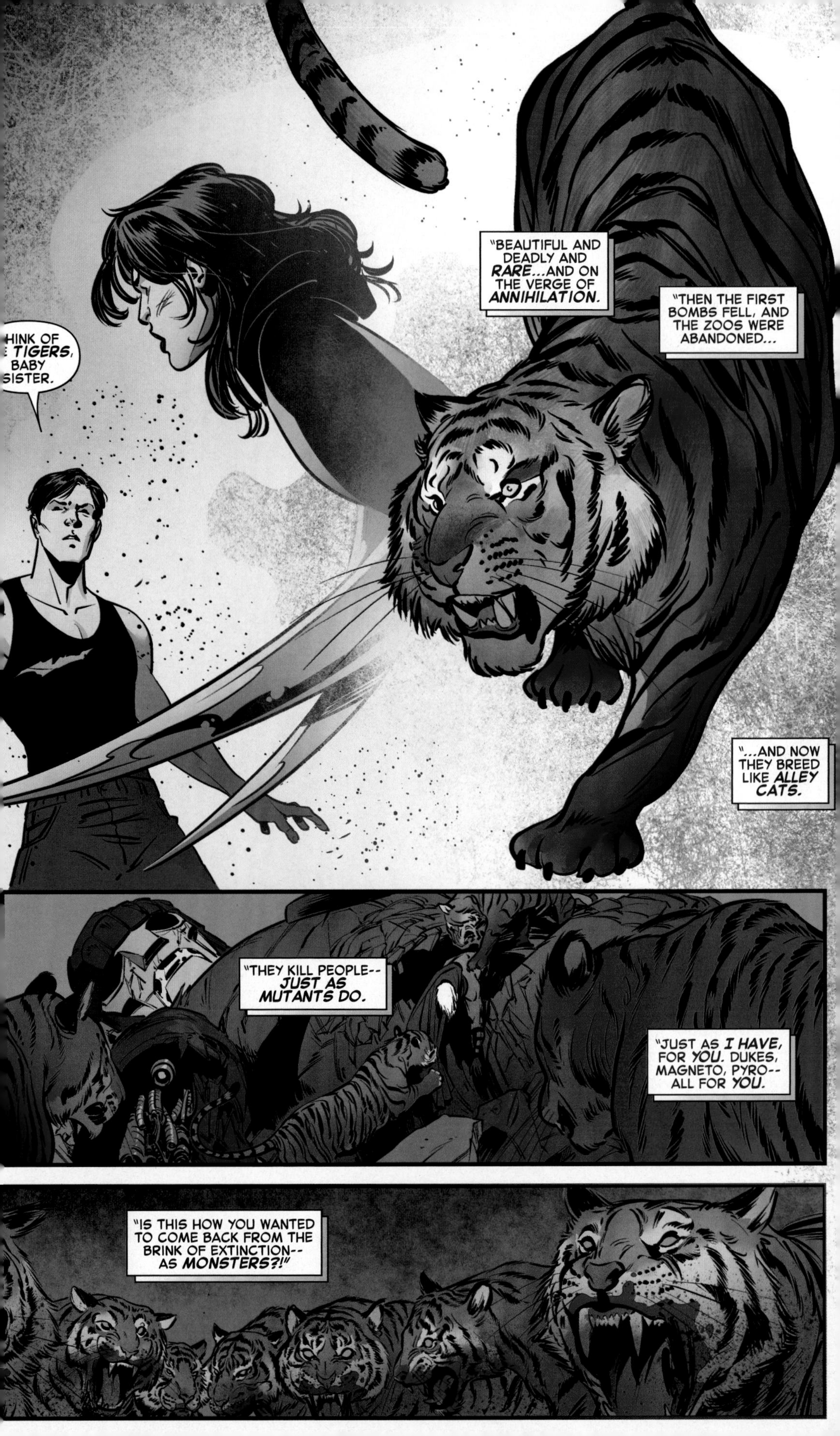

HINK OF
E TIGERS,
BABY
SISTER.
"BEAUTIFUL AND DEADLY AND RARE...AND ON THE VERGE OF ANNIHILATION.
"THEN THE FIRST BOMBS FELL, AND THE ZOOS WERE ABANDONED...
"...AND NOW THEY BREED LIKE ALLEY CATS.
"THEY KILL PEOPLE-- JUST AS MUTANTS DO.
"JUST AS I HAVE, FOR YOU. DUKES, MAGNETO, PYRO-- ALL FOR YOU.
"IS THIS HOW YOU WANTED TO COME BACK FROM THE BRINK OF EXTINCTION-- AS MONSTERS?!"

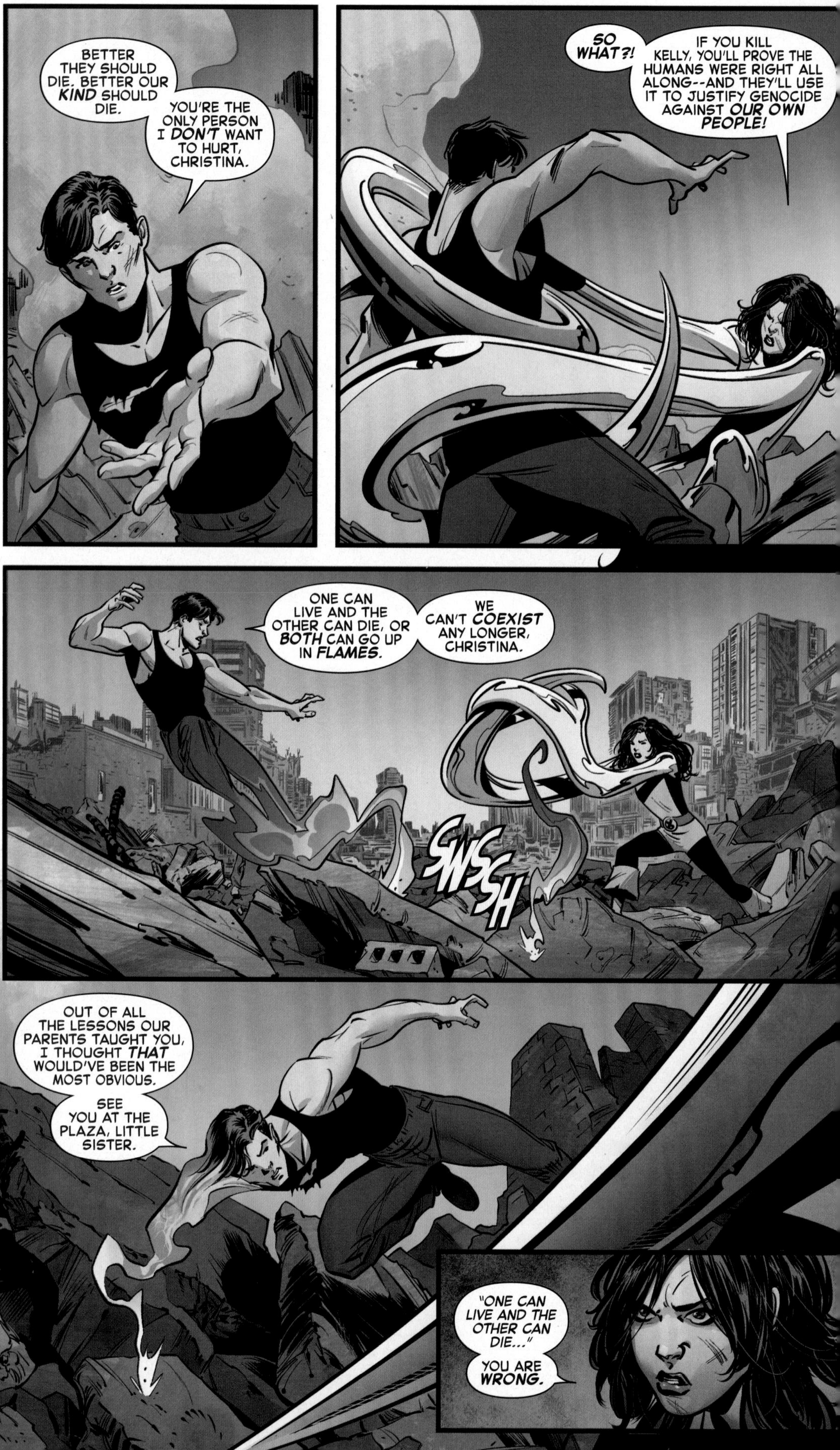
BETTER THEY SHOULD DIE. BETTER OUR KIND SHOULD DIE.
YOU'RE THE ONLY PERSON I DON'T WANT TO HURT, CHRISTINA.
SO WHAT?!
IF YOU KILL KELLY, YOU'LL PROVE THE HUMANS WERE RIGHT ALL ALONG--AND THEY'LL USE IT TO JUSTIFY GENOCIDE AGAINST OUR OWN PEOPLE!
ONE CAN LIVE AND THE OTHER CAN DIE, OR BOTH CAN GO UP IN FLAMES.
WE CAN'T COEXIST ANY LONGER, CHRISTINA.
SWSSH
OUT OF ALL THE LESSONS OUR PARENTS TAUGHT YOU, I THOUGHT THAT WOULD'VE BEEN THE MOST OBVIOUS.
SEE YOU AT THE PLAZA, LITTLE SISTER.
"ONE CAN LIVE AND THE OTHER CAN DIE..."
YOU ARE WRONG.

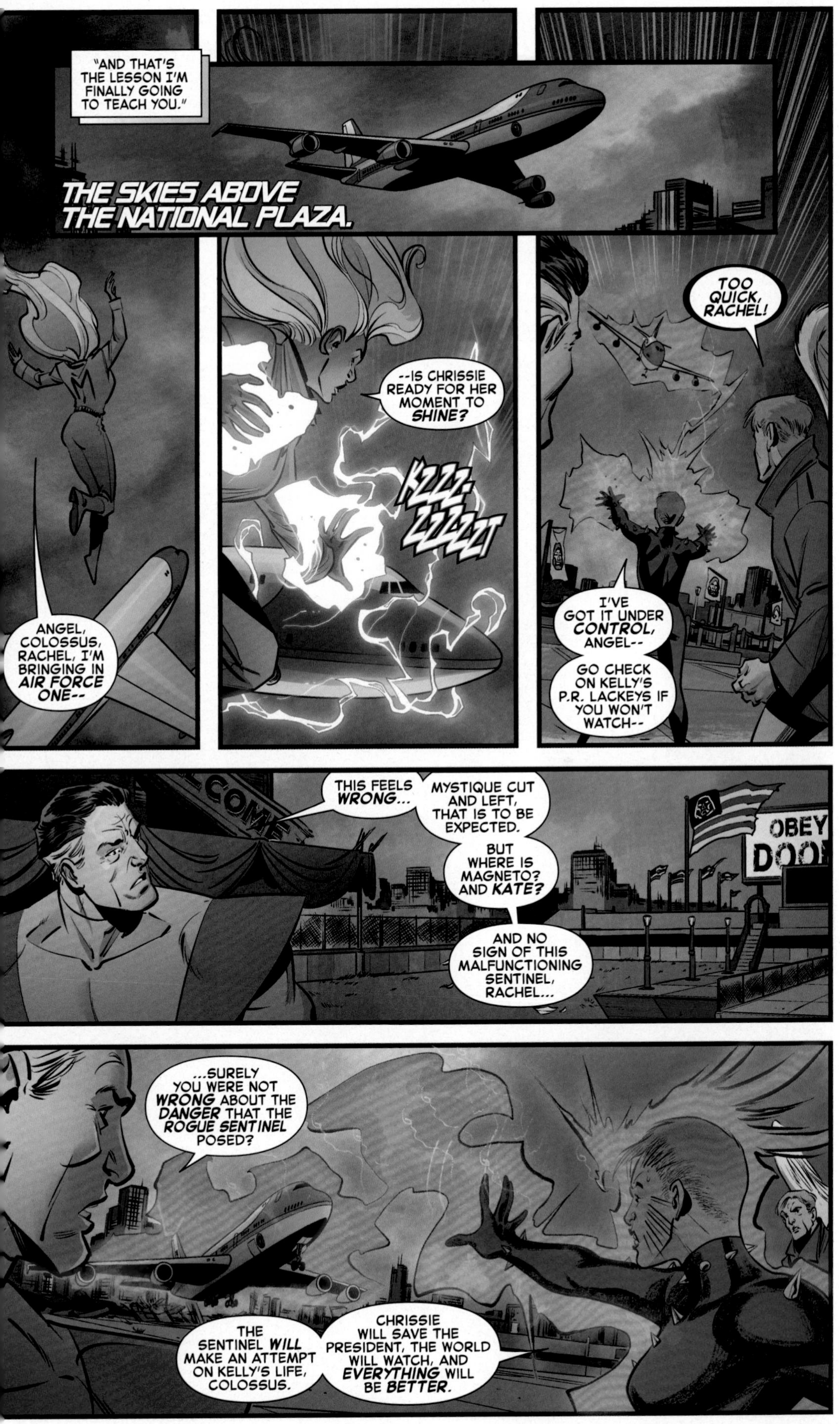
"AND THAT'S THE LESSON I'M FINALLY GOING TO TEACH YOU."
THE SKIES ABOVE THE NATIONAL PLAZA.
ANGEL, COLOSSUS, RACHEL, I'M BRINGING IN AIR FORCE ONE--
--IS CHRISSIE READY FOR HER MOMENT TO SHINE?
KZZZ-ZZZZZT
TOO QUICK, RACHEL!
I'VE GOT IT UNDER CONTROL, ANGEL--
GO CHECK ON KELLY'S P.R. LACKEYS IF YOU WON'T WATCH--
THIS FEELS WRONG...
MYSTIQUE CUT AND LEFT, THAT IS TO BE EXPECTED.
BUT WHERE IS MAGNETO? AND KATE?
AND NO SIGN OF THIS MALFUNCTIONING SENTINEL, RACHEL...
OBEY DOO
...SURELY YOU WERE NOT WRONG ABOUT THE DANGER THAT THE ROGUE SENTINEL POSED?
THE SENTINEL WILL MAKE AN ATTEMPT ON KELLY'S LIFE, COLOSSUS.
CHRISSIE WILL SAVE THE PRESIDENT, THE WORLD WILL WATCH, AND EVERYTHING WILL BE BETTER.

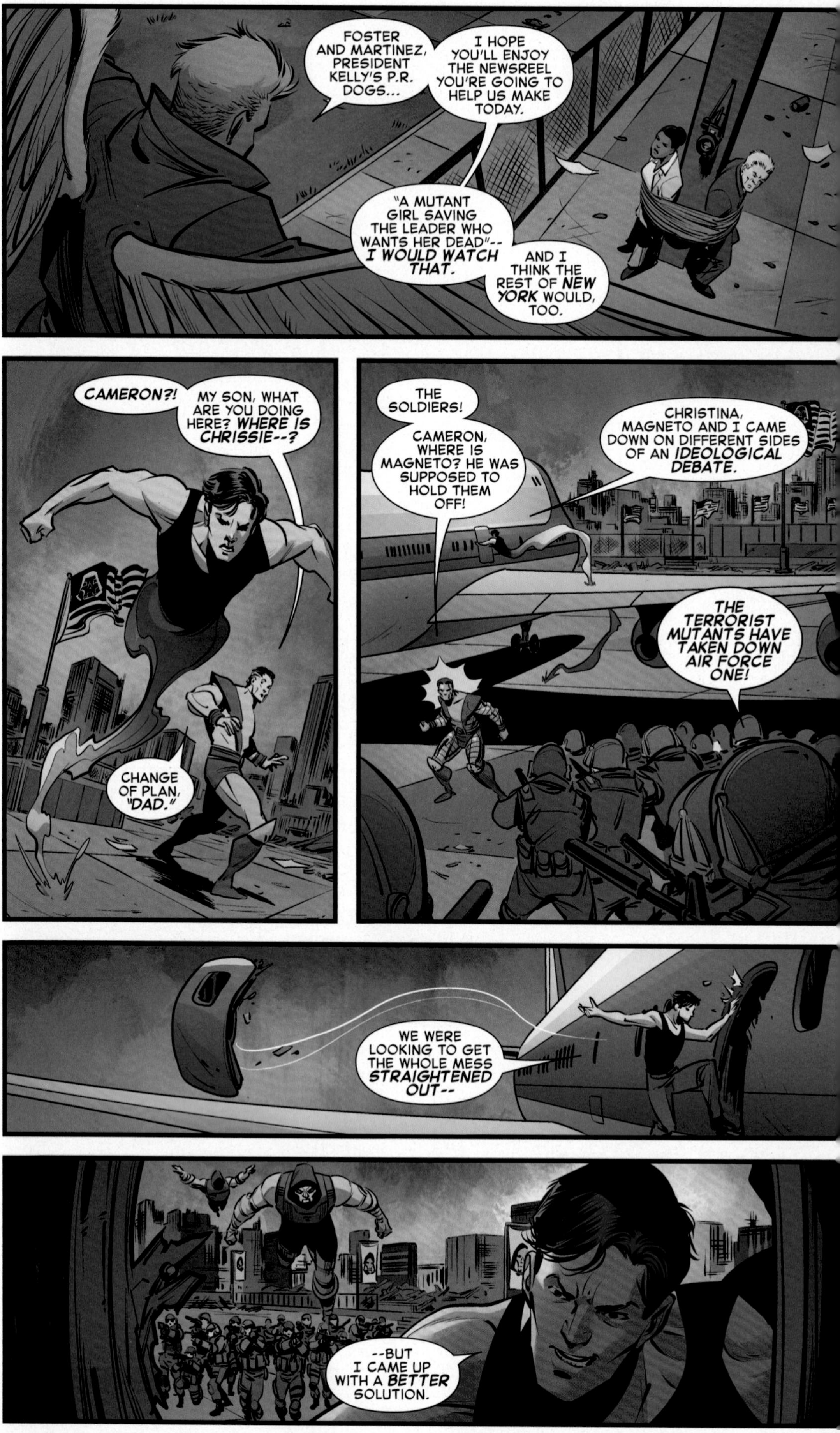
FOSTER AND MARTINEZ, PRESIDENT KELLY'S P.R. DOGS...
I HOPE YOU'LL ENJOY THE NEWSREEL YOU'RE GOING TO HELP US MAKE TODAY.
"A MUTANT GIRL SAVING THE LEADER WHO WANTS HER DEAD"-- I WOULD WATCH THAT.
AND I THINK THE REST OF NEW YORK WOULD, TOO.
CAMERON?!
MY SON, WHAT ARE YOU DOING HERE? WHERE IS CHRISSIE--?
CHANGE OF PLAN, "DAD."
THE SOLDIERS!
CAMERON, WHERE IS MAGNETO? HE WAS SUPPOSED TO HOLD THEM OFF!
CHRISTINA, MAGNETO AND I CAME DOWN ON DIFFERENT SIDES OF AN IDEOLOGICAL DEBATE.
THE TERRORIST MUTANTS HAVE TAKEN DOWN AIR FORCE ONE!
WE WERE LOOKING TO GET THE WHOLE MESS STRAIGHTENED OUT--
--BUT I CAME UP WITH A BETTER SOLUTION.

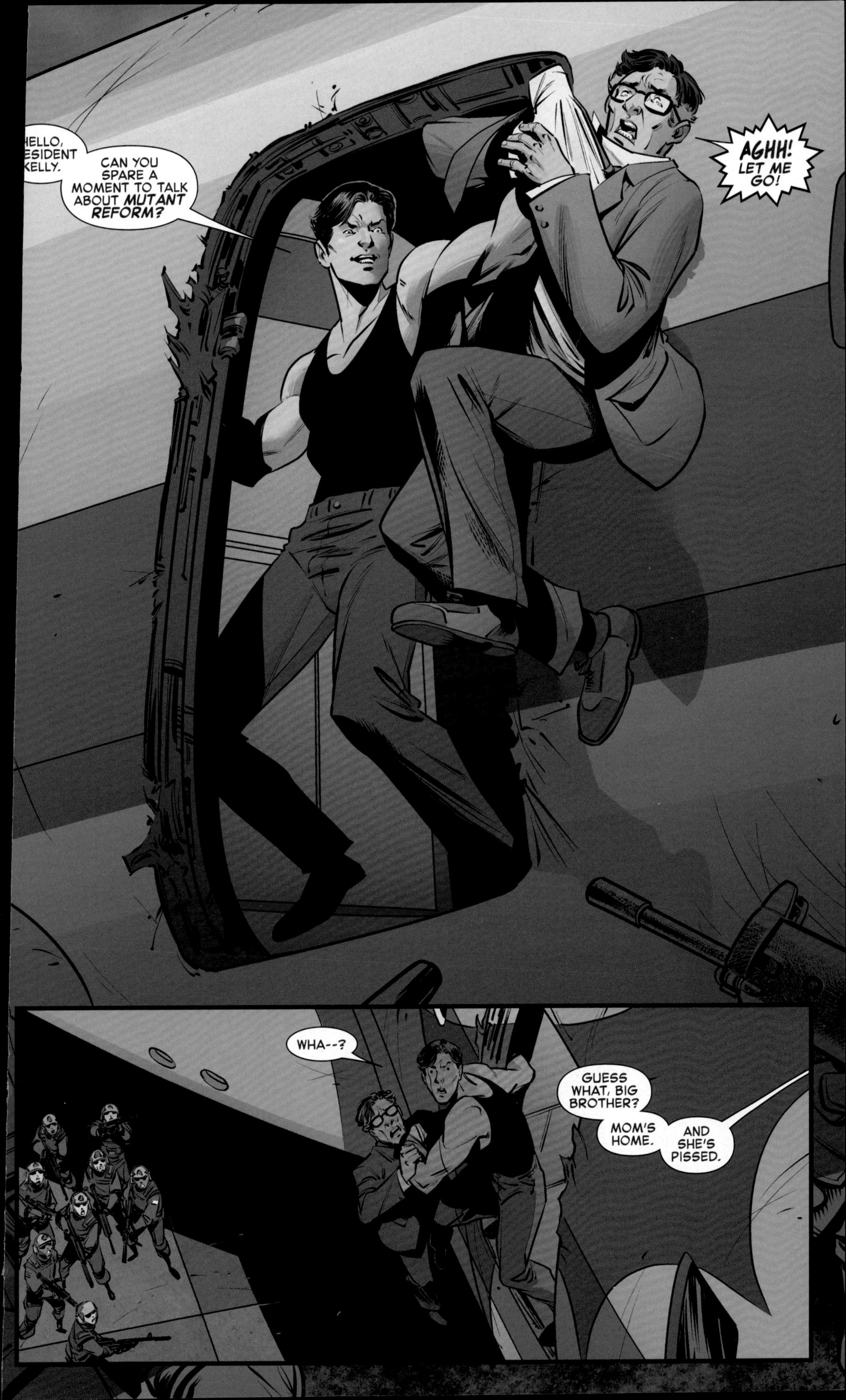
HELLO, ESIDENT KELLY.
CAN YOU SPARE A MOMENT TO TALK ABOUT MUTANT REFORM?
AGHH! LET ME GO!
WHA--?
GUESS WHAT, BIG BROTHER?
MOM'S HOME.
AND SHE'S PISSED.

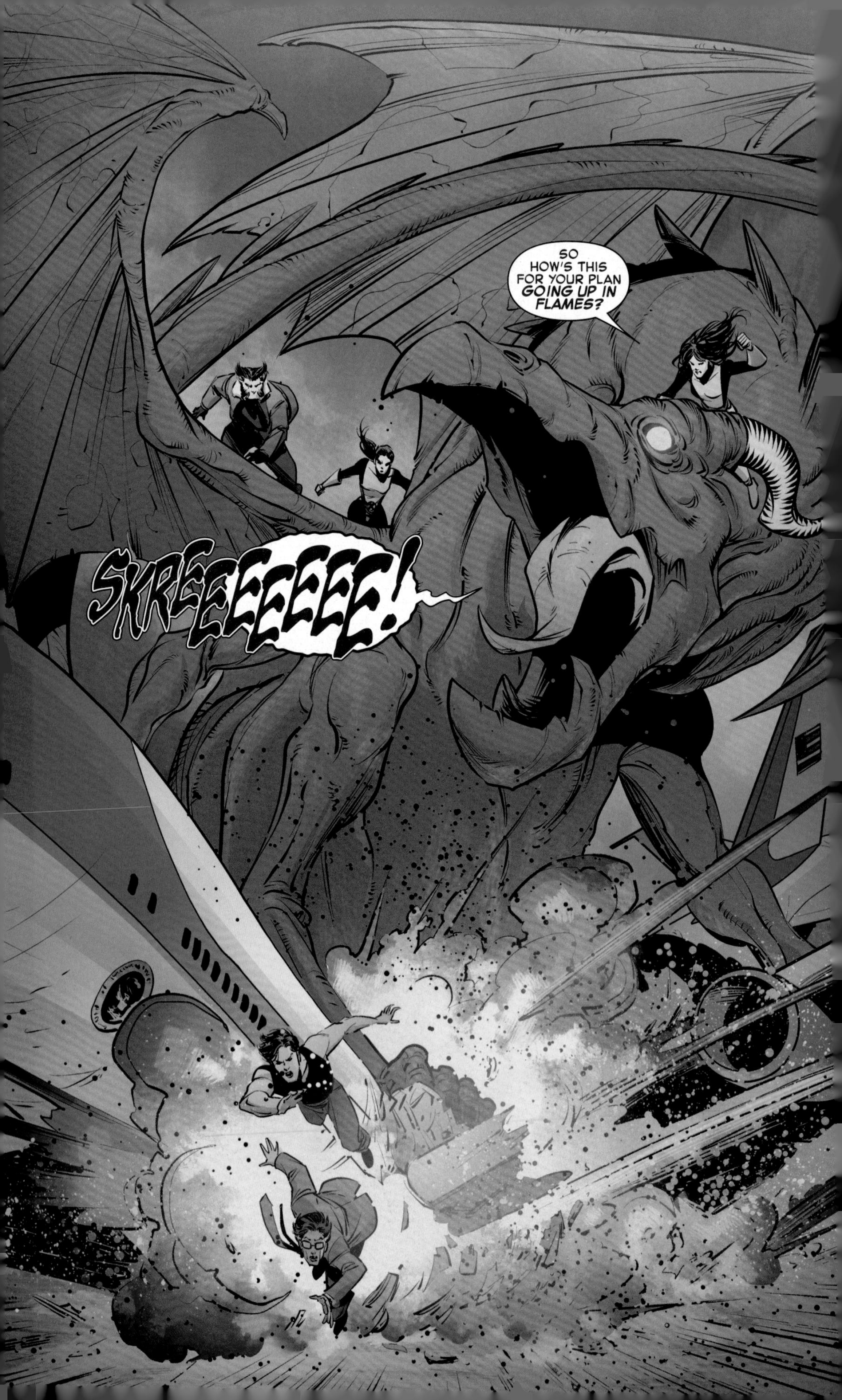
SO HOW'S THIS FOR YOUR PLAN GOING UP IN FLAMES?
SKREEEEEEEEE!

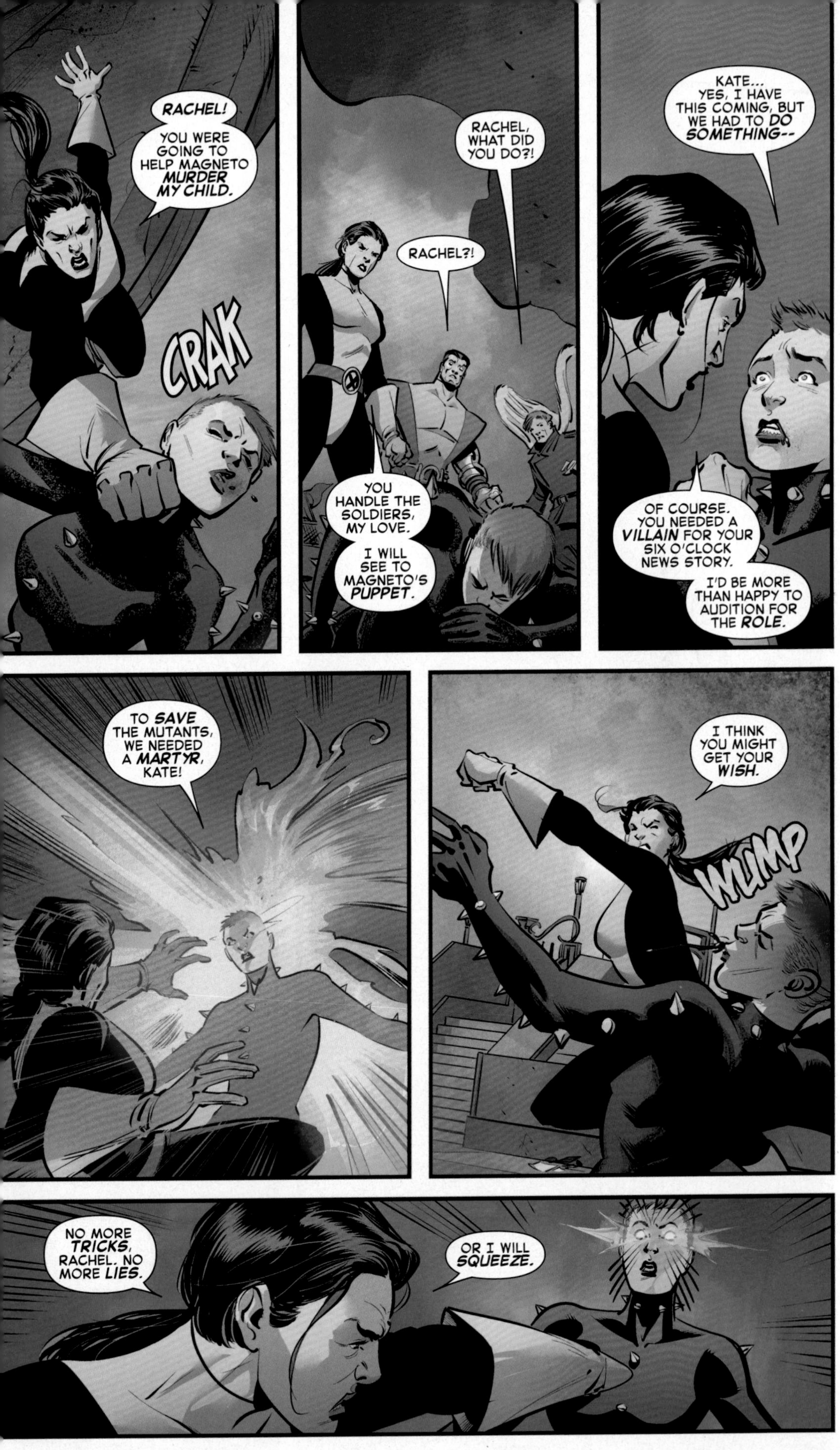
RACHEL!
YOU WERE GOING TO HELP MAGNETO MURDER MY CHILD.
CRAK
RACHEL, WHAT DID YOU DO?!
RACHEL?!
YOU HANDLE THE SOLDIERS, MY LOVE.
I WILL SEE TO MAGNETO'S PUPPET.
KATE... YES, I HAVE THIS COMING, BUT WE HAD TO DO SOMETHING--
OF COURSE. YOU NEEDED A VILLAIN FOR YOUR SIX O'CLOCK NEWS STORY.
I'D BE MORE THAN HAPPY TO AUDITION FOR THE ROLE.
TO SAVE THE MUTANTS, WE NEEDED A MARTYR, KATE!
I THINK YOU MIGHT GET YOUR WISH.
WUMP
NO MORE TRICKS, RACHEL. NO MORE LIES.
OR I WILL SQUEEZE.

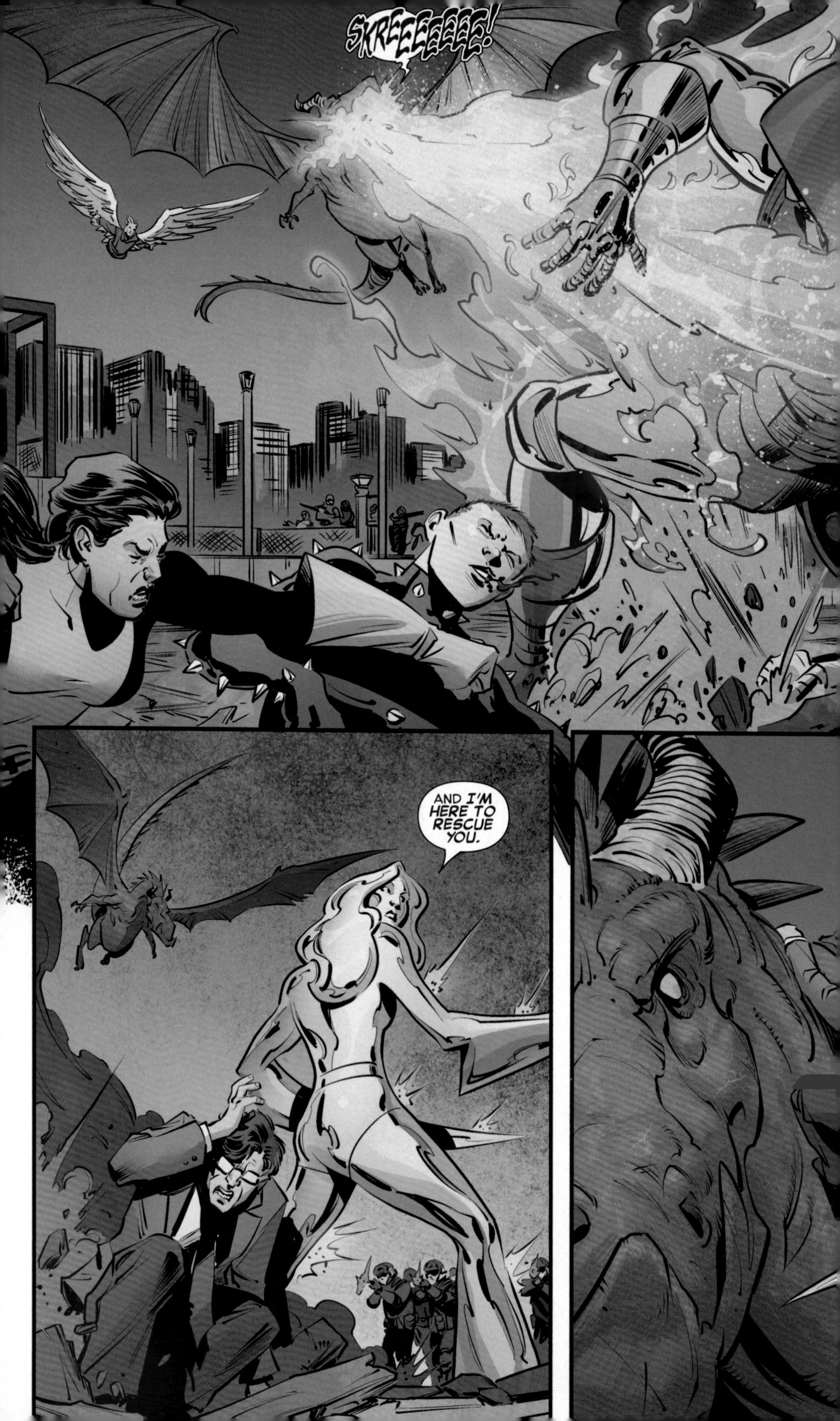
SKREEEEEEEE!
AND I'M HERE TO RESCUE YOU.

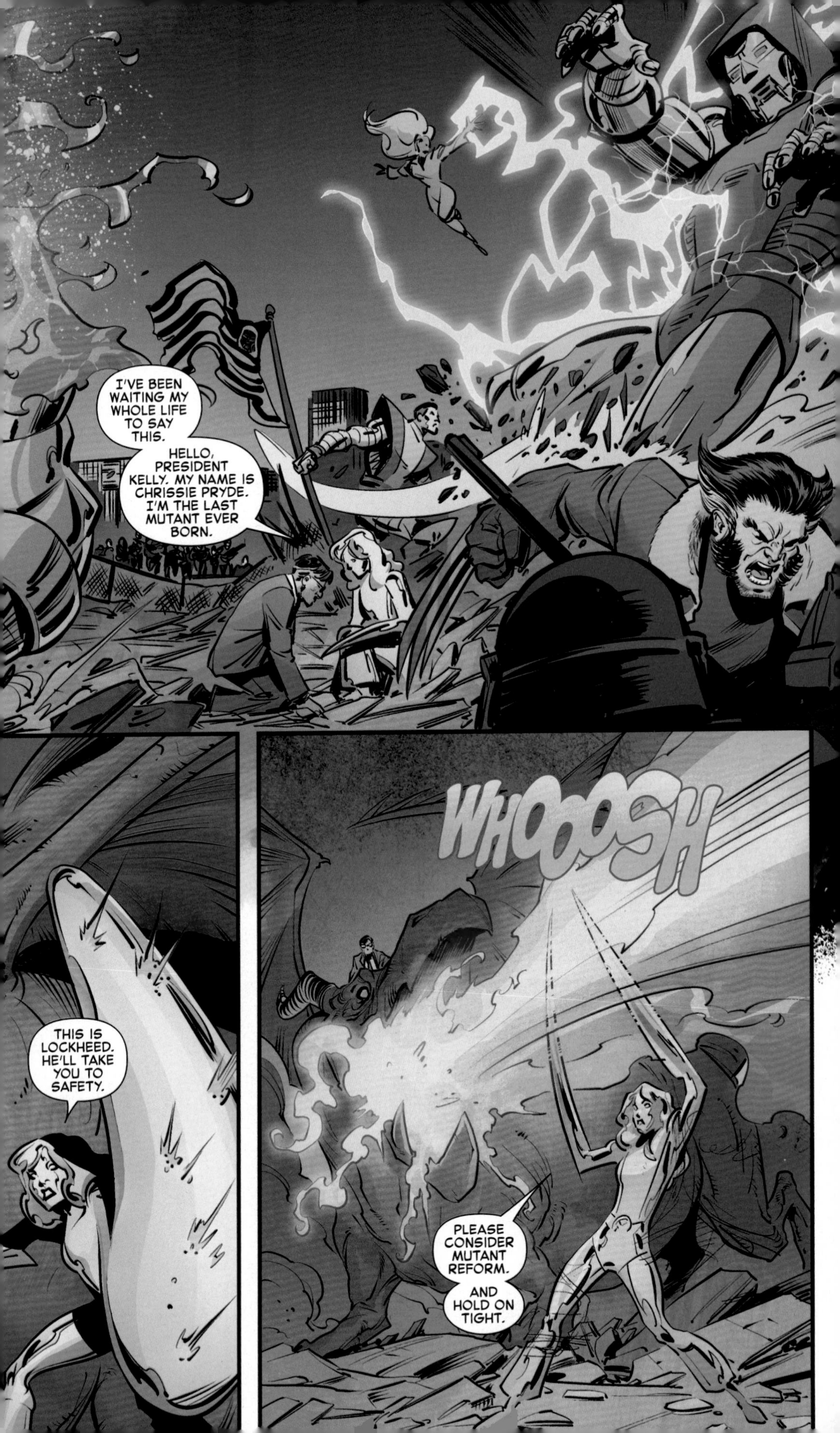
I'VE BEEN WAITING MY WHOLE LIFE TO SAY THIS.
HELLO, PRESIDENT KELLY. MY NAME IS CHRISSIE PRYDE. I'M THE LAST MUTANT EVER BORN.
THIS IS LOCKHEED. HE'LL TAKE YOU TO SAFETY.
WHOOOOSH
PLEASE CONSIDER MUTANT REFORM.
AND HOLD ON TIGHT.

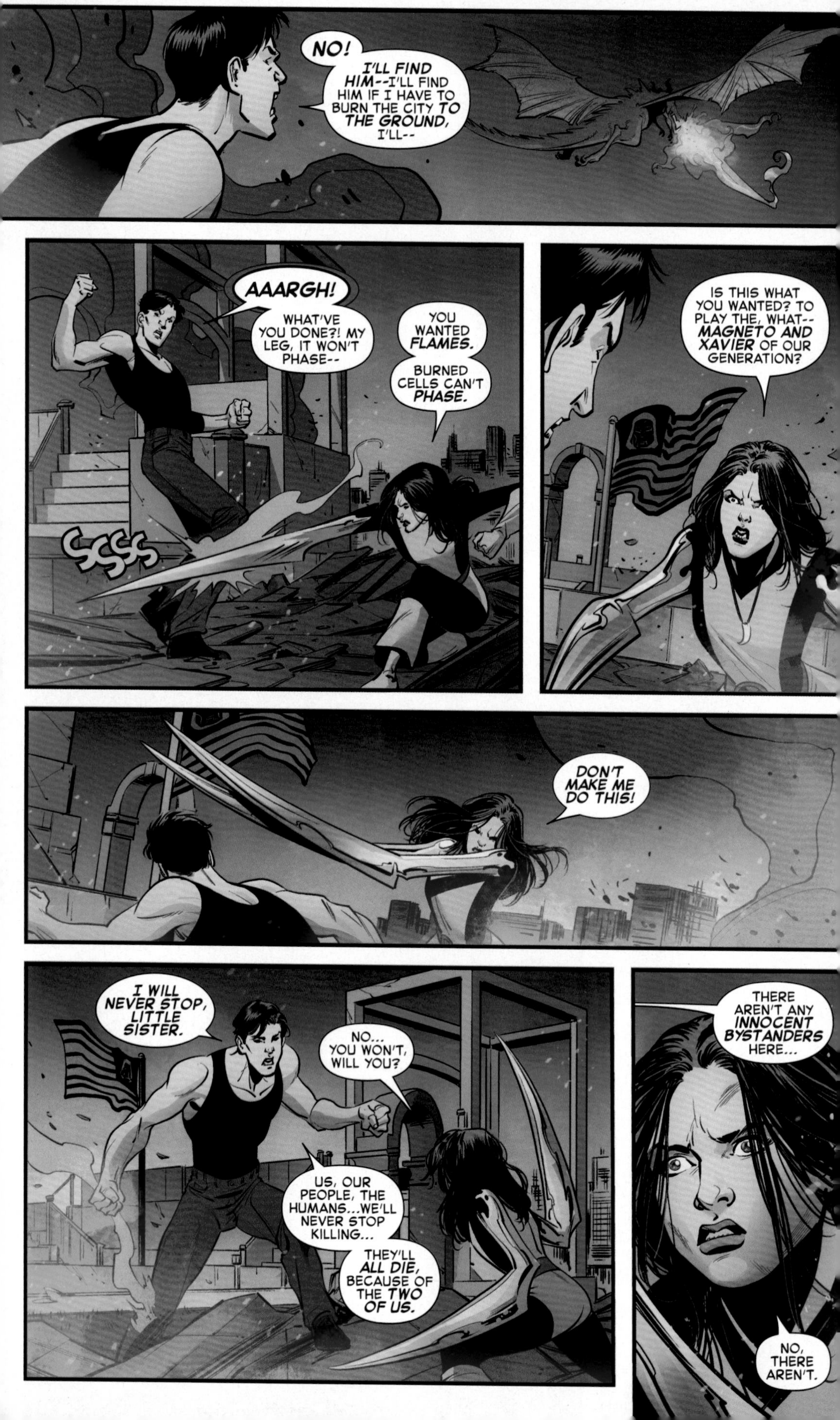
NO!
I'LL FIND HIM--I'LL FIND HIM IF I HAVE TO BURN THE CITY TO THE GROUND, I'LL--
AAARGH!
WHAT'VE YOU DONE?! MY LEG, IT WON'T PHASE--
YOU WANTED FLAMES.
BURNED CELLS CAN'T PHASE.
SSSS
IS THIS WHAT YOU WANTED? TO PLAY THE, WHAT--MAGNETO AND XAVIER OF OUR GENERATION?
DON'T MAKE ME DO THIS!
I WILL NEVER STOP, LITTLE SISTER.
NO... YOU WON'T, WILL YOU?
US, OUR PEOPLE, THE HUMANS...WE'LL NEVER STOP KILLING...
THEY'LL ALL DIE, BECAUSE OF THE TWO OF US.
THERE AREN'T ANY INNOCENT BYSTANDERS HERE...
NO, THERE AREN'T.

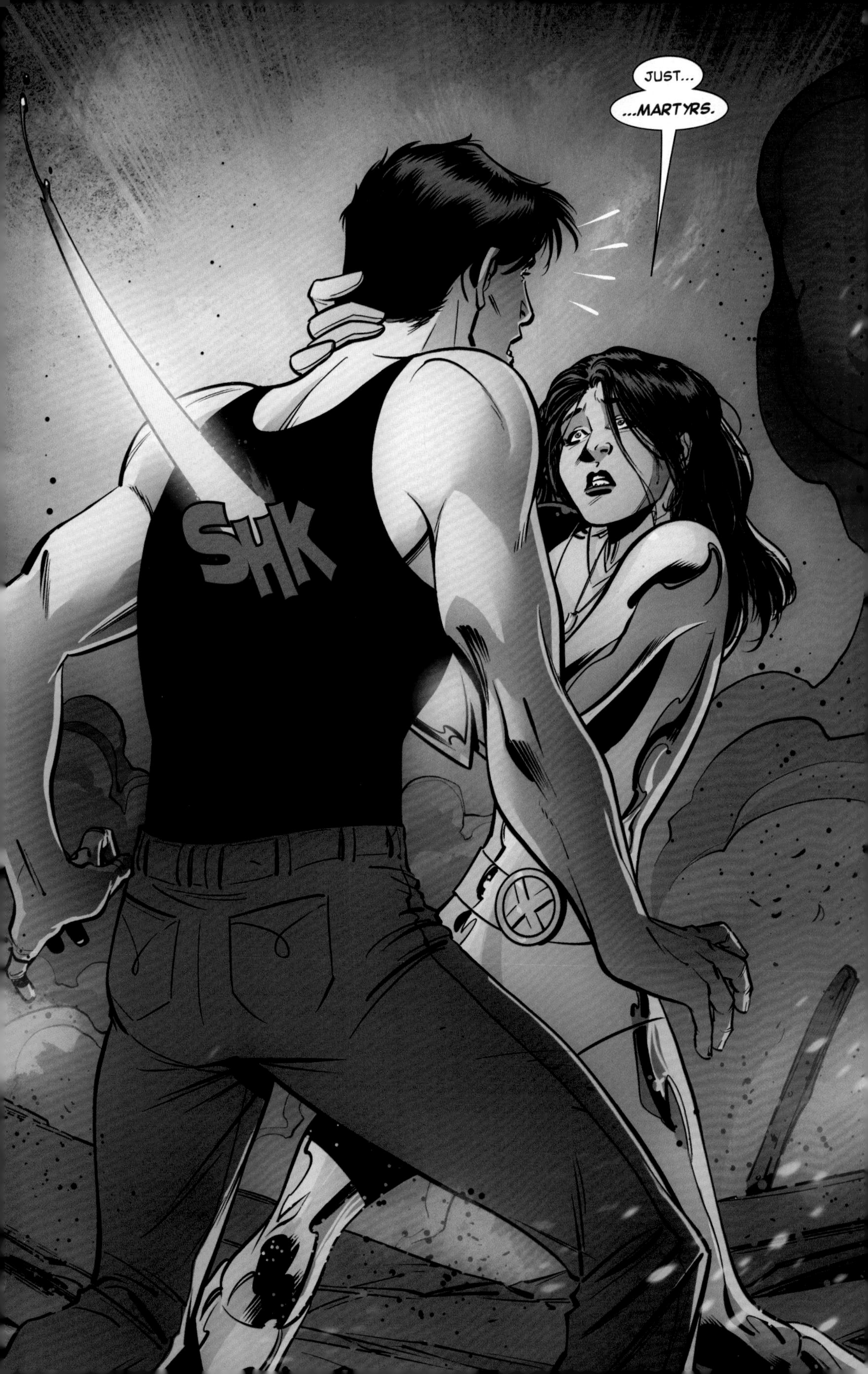
JUST...
...MARTYRS.
SHK

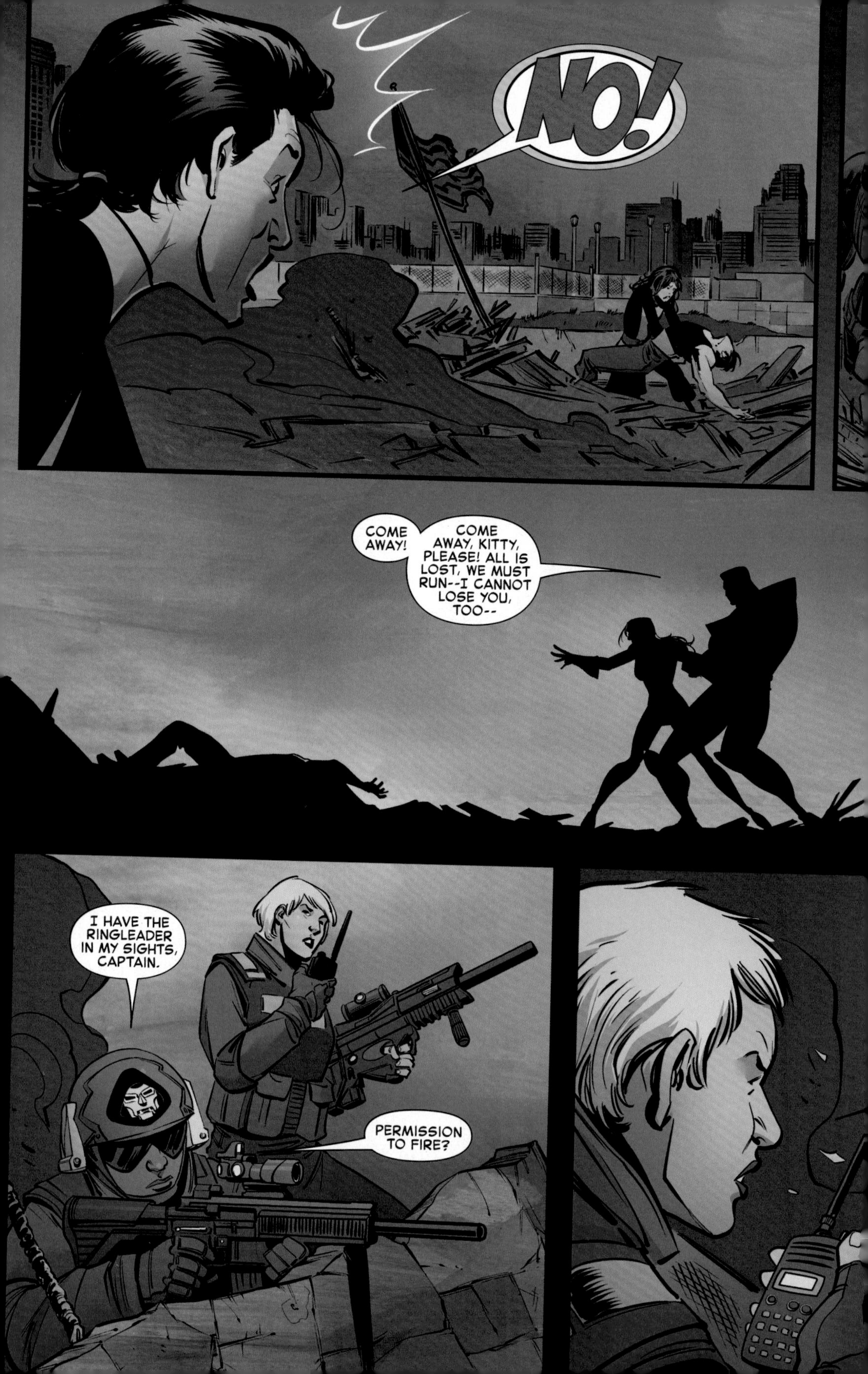
NO!
COME AWAY!
COME AWAY, KITTY, PLEASE! ALL IS LOST, WE MUST RUN--I CANNOT LOSE YOU, TOO--
I HAVE THE RINGLEADER IN MY SIGHTS, CAPTAIN.
PERMISSION TO FIRE?

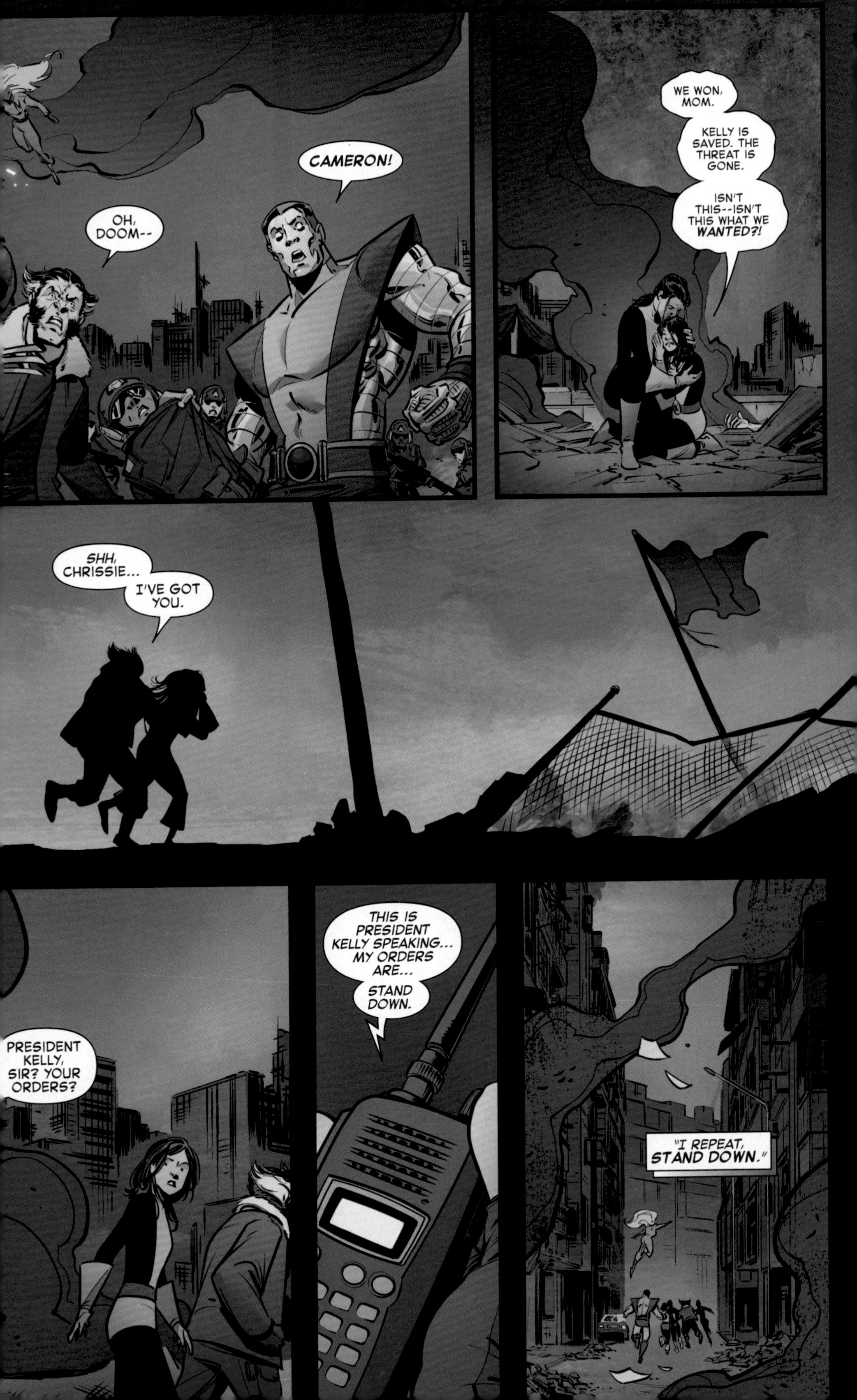

CAMERON!
OH, DOOM--
WE WON, MOM.
KELLY IS SAVED. THE THREAT IS GONE.
ISN'T THIS--ISN'T THIS WHAT WE WANTED?!
SHH, CHRISSIE...
I'VE GOT YOU.
PRESIDENT KELLY, SIR? YOUR ORDERS?
THIS IS PRESIDENT KELLY SPEAKING... MY ORDERS ARE...
STAND DOWN.
"I REPEAT, STAND DOWN."

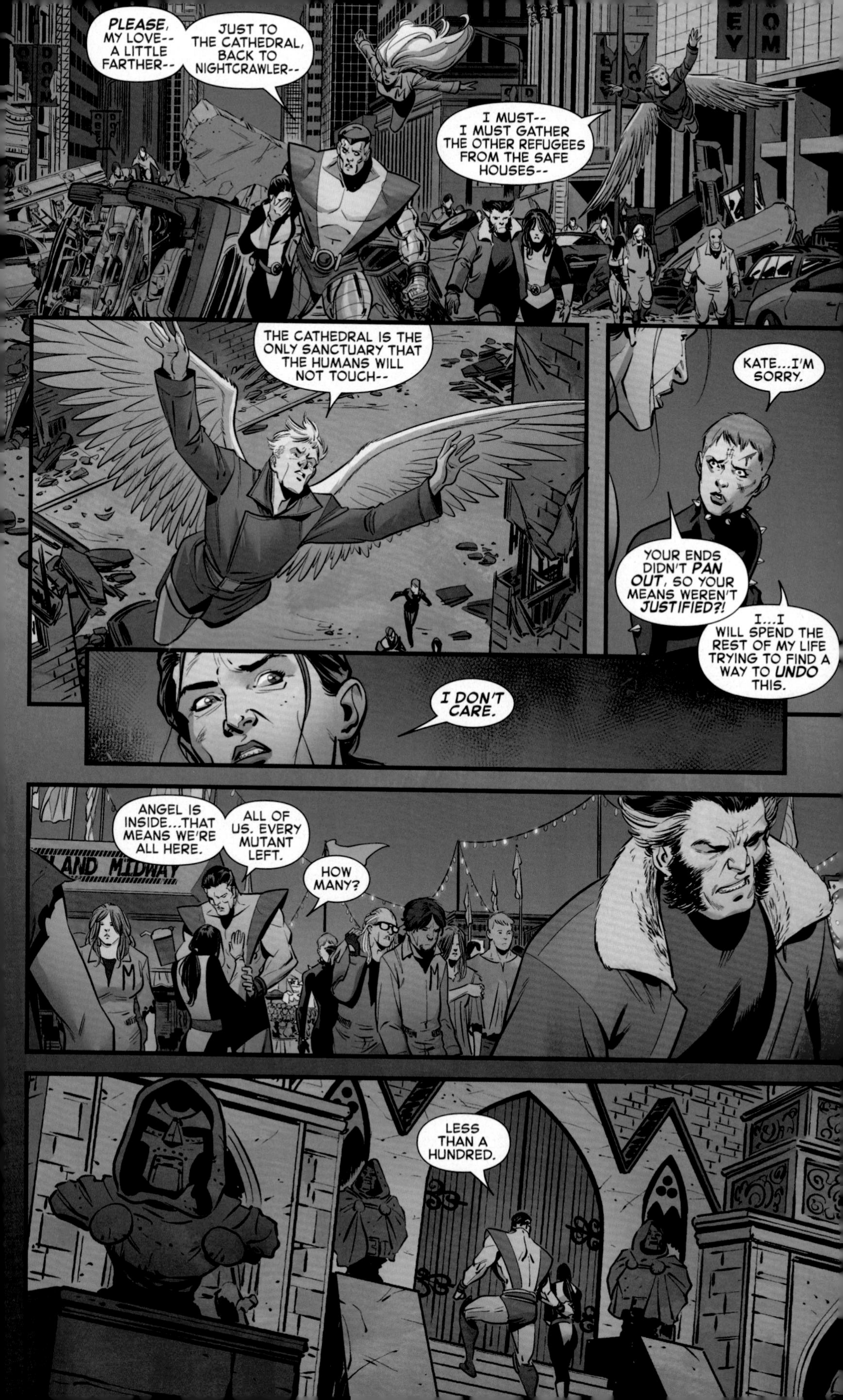
PLEASE, MY LOVE-- A LITTLE FARTHER--
JUST TO THE CATHEDRAL, BACK TO NIGHTCRAWLER--
I MUST-- I MUST GATHER THE OTHER REFUGEES FROM THE SAFE HOUSES--
THE CATHEDRAL IS THE ONLY SANCTUARY THAT THE HUMANS WILL NOT TOUCH--
KATE...I'M SORRY.
YOUR ENDS DIDN'T PAN OUT, SO YOUR MEANS WEREN'T JUSTIFIED?!
I...I WILL SPEND THE REST OF MY LIFE TRYING TO FIND A WAY TO UNDO THIS.
I DON'T CARE.
ANGEL IS INSIDE...THAT MEANS WE'RE ALL HERE.
ALL OF US. EVERY MUTANT LEFT.
HOW MANY?
LAND MIDWAY
LESS THAN A HUNDRED.

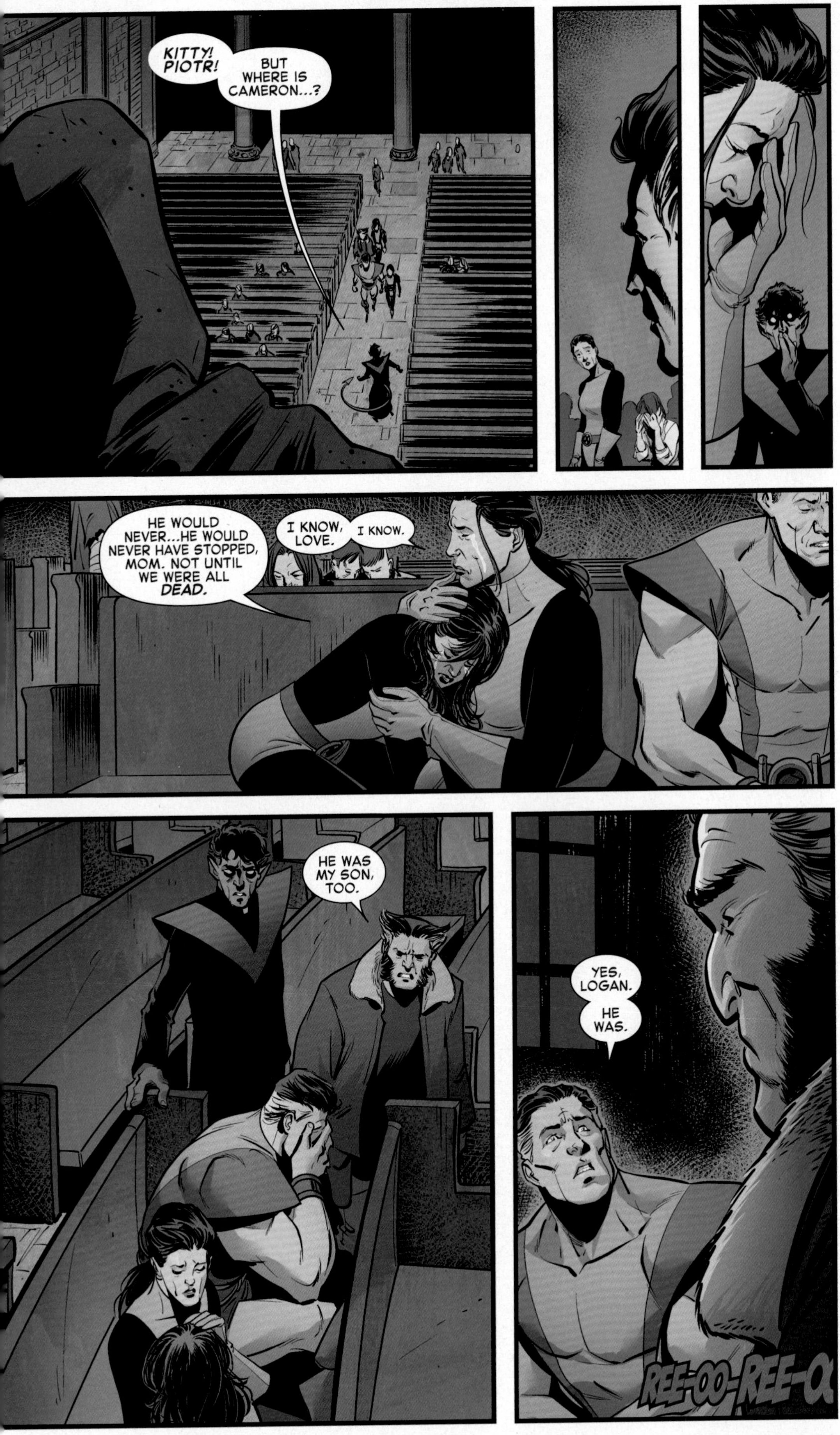
KITTY! PIOTR!
BUT WHERE IS CAMERON...?
HE WOULD NEVER...HE WOULD NEVER HAVE STOPPED, MOM. NOT UNTIL WE WERE ALL DEAD.
I KNOW, LOVE.
I KNOW.
HE WAS MY SON, TOO.
YES, LOGAN.
HE WAS.
REE-OO-REE-OO

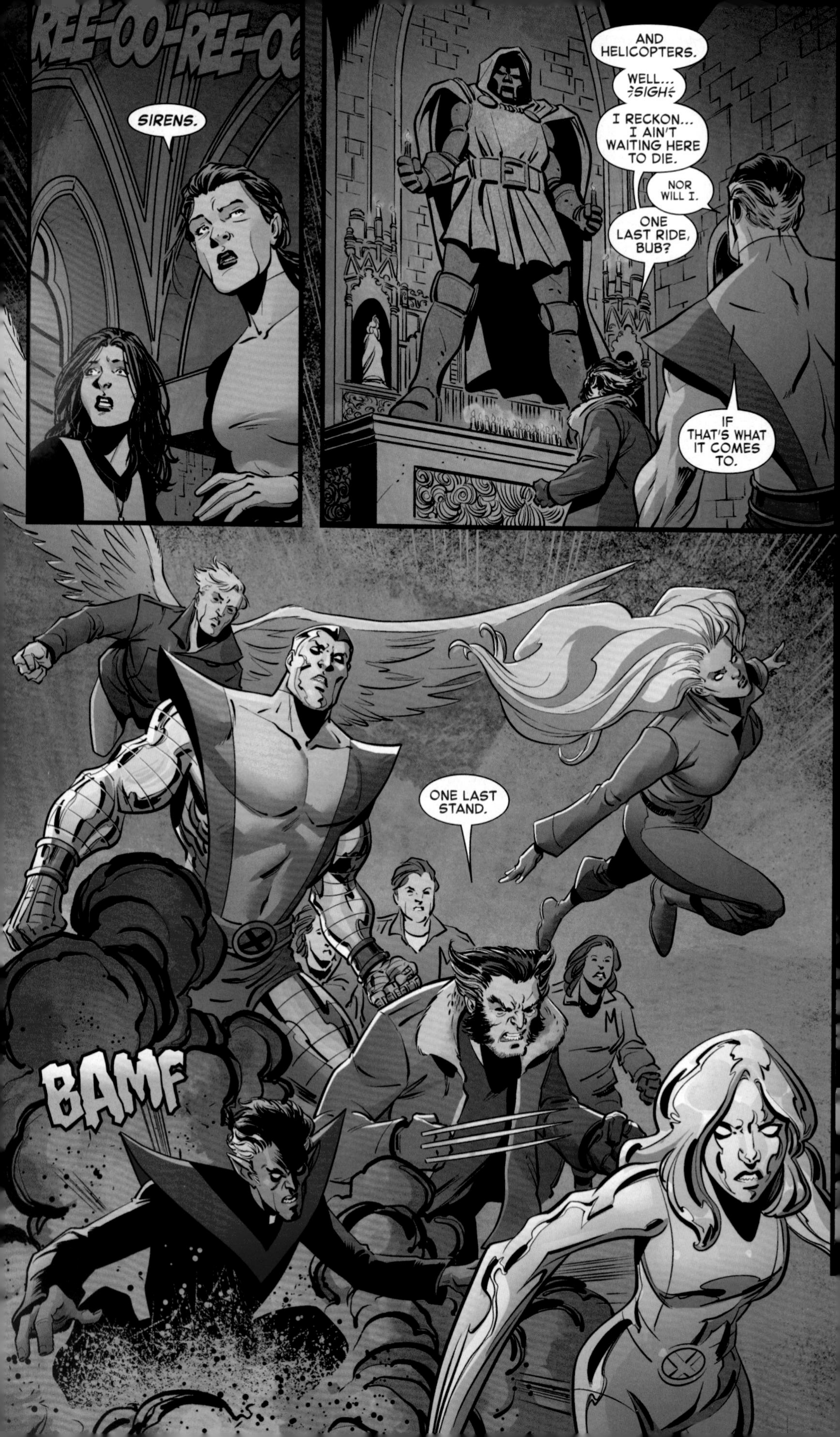
REE-OO-REE-OO
SIRENS.
AND HELICOPTERS.
WELL... SIGH
I RECKON... I AIN'T WAITING HERE TO DIE.
NOR WILL I.
ONE LAST RIDE, BUB?
IF THAT'S WHAT IT COMES TO.
ONE LAST STAND.
BAMF

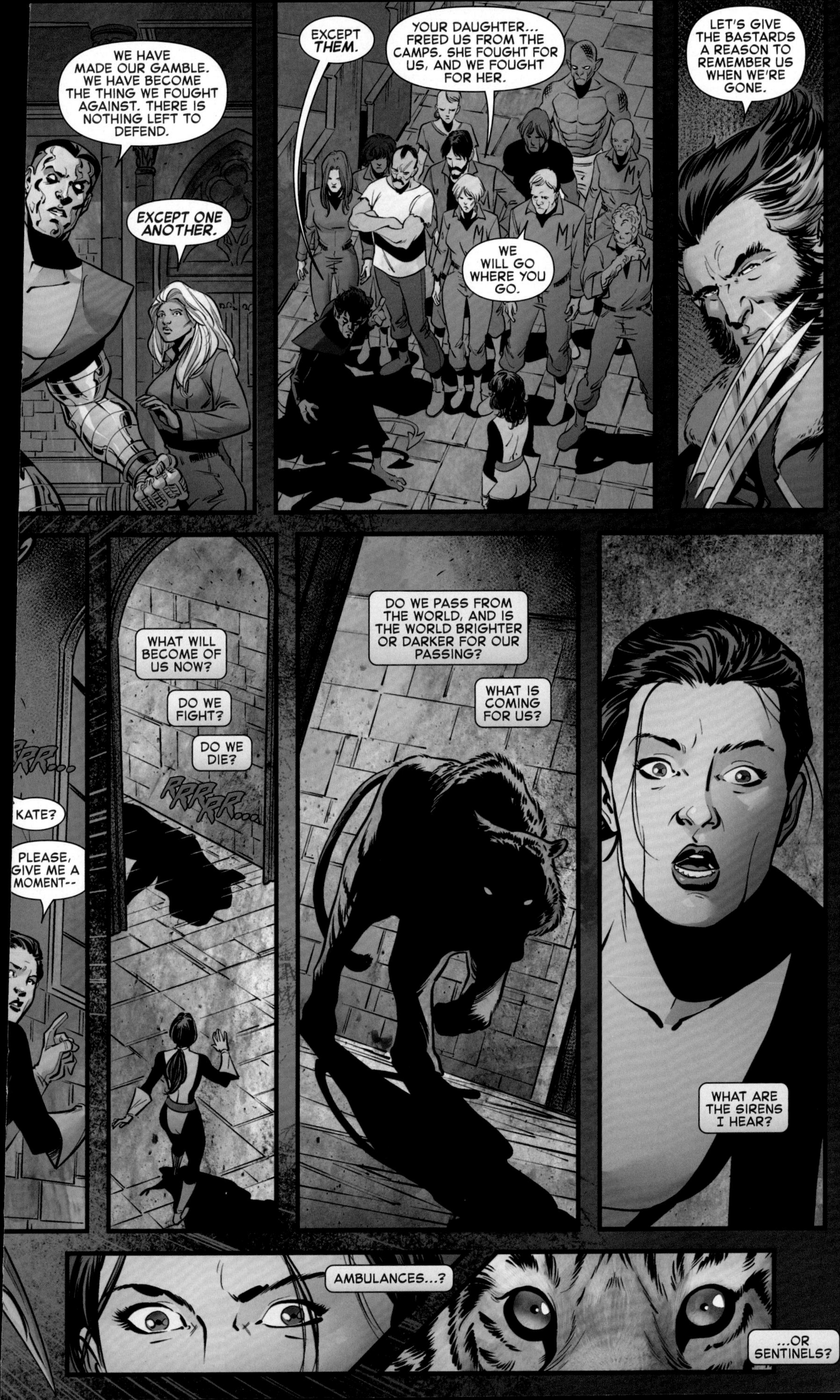
WE HAVE MADE OUR GAMBLE. WE HAVE BECOME THE THING WE FOUGHT AGAINST. THERE IS NOTHING LEFT TO DEFEND.
EXCEPT ONE ANOTHER.
EXCEPT THEM.
YOUR DAUGHTER... FREED US FROM THE CAMPS. SHE FOUGHT FOR US, AND WE FOUGHT FOR HER.
WE WILL GO WHERE YOU GO.
LET'S GIVE THE BASTARDS A REASON TO REMEMBER US WHEN WE'RE GONE.
RRR...
KATE?
PLEASE, GIVE ME A MOMENT--
WHAT WILL BECOME OF US NOW?
DO WE FIGHT?
DO WE DIE?
RRRRR...
DO WE PASS FROM THE WORLD, AND IS THE WORLD BRIGHTER OR DARKER FOR OUR PASSING?
WHAT IS COMING FOR US?
WHAT ARE THE SIRENS I HEAR?
AMBULANCES...?
...OR SENTINELS?

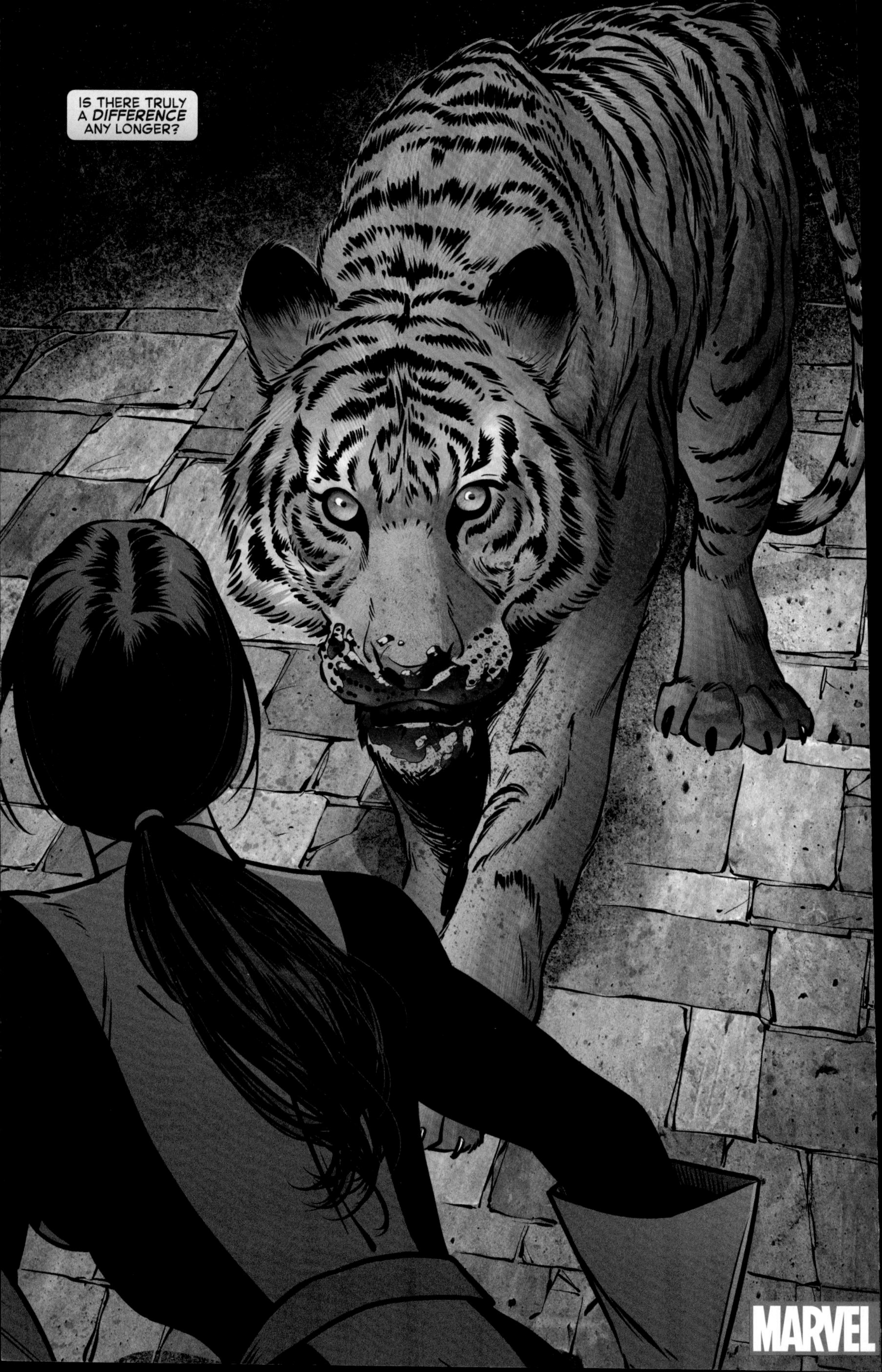
IS THERE TRULY A *DIFFERENCE* ANY LONGER?
MARVEL

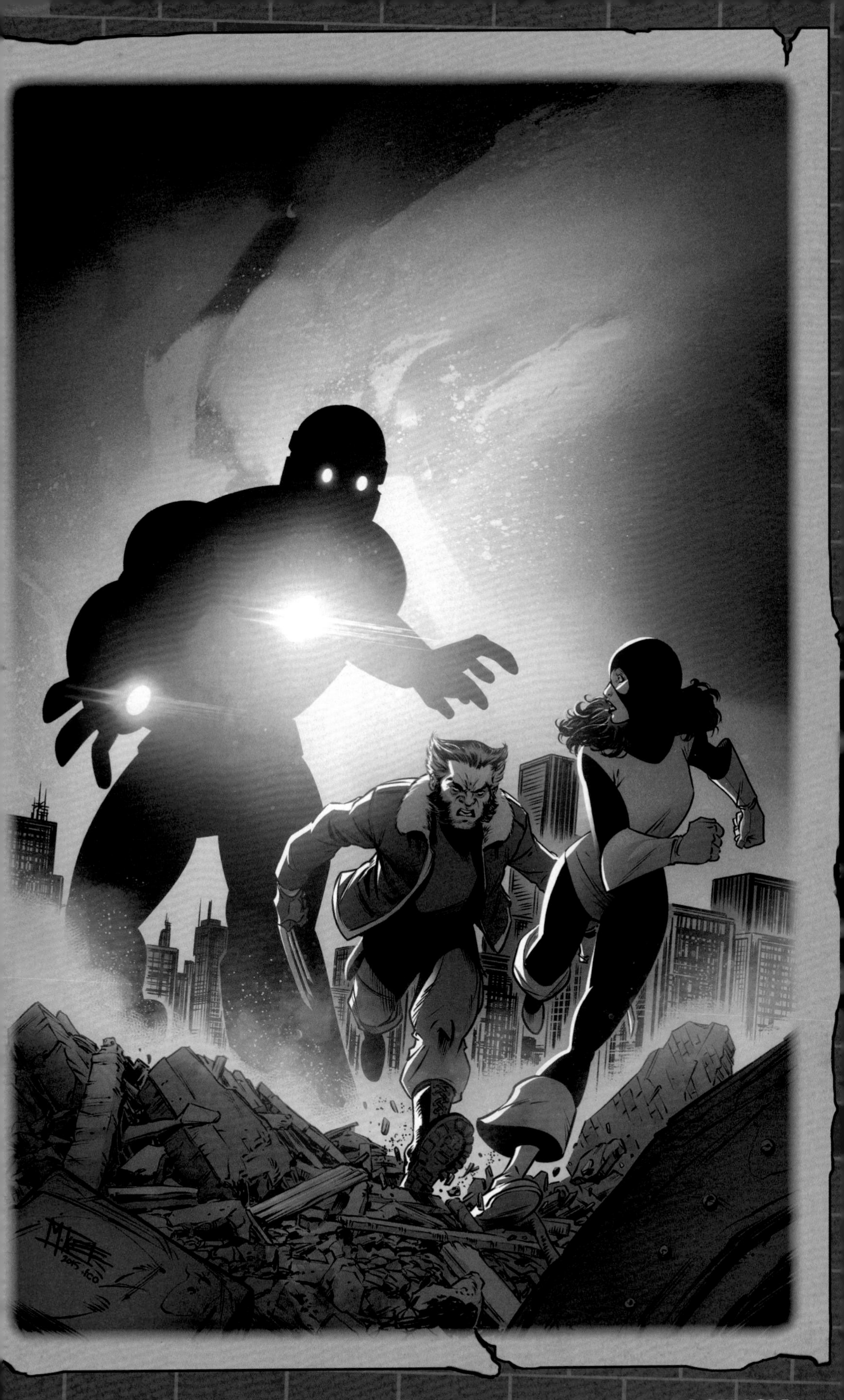
M. NORTON 2015 FCO

#1 Variant by **MIKE NORTON** & **FCO PLASCENCIA**

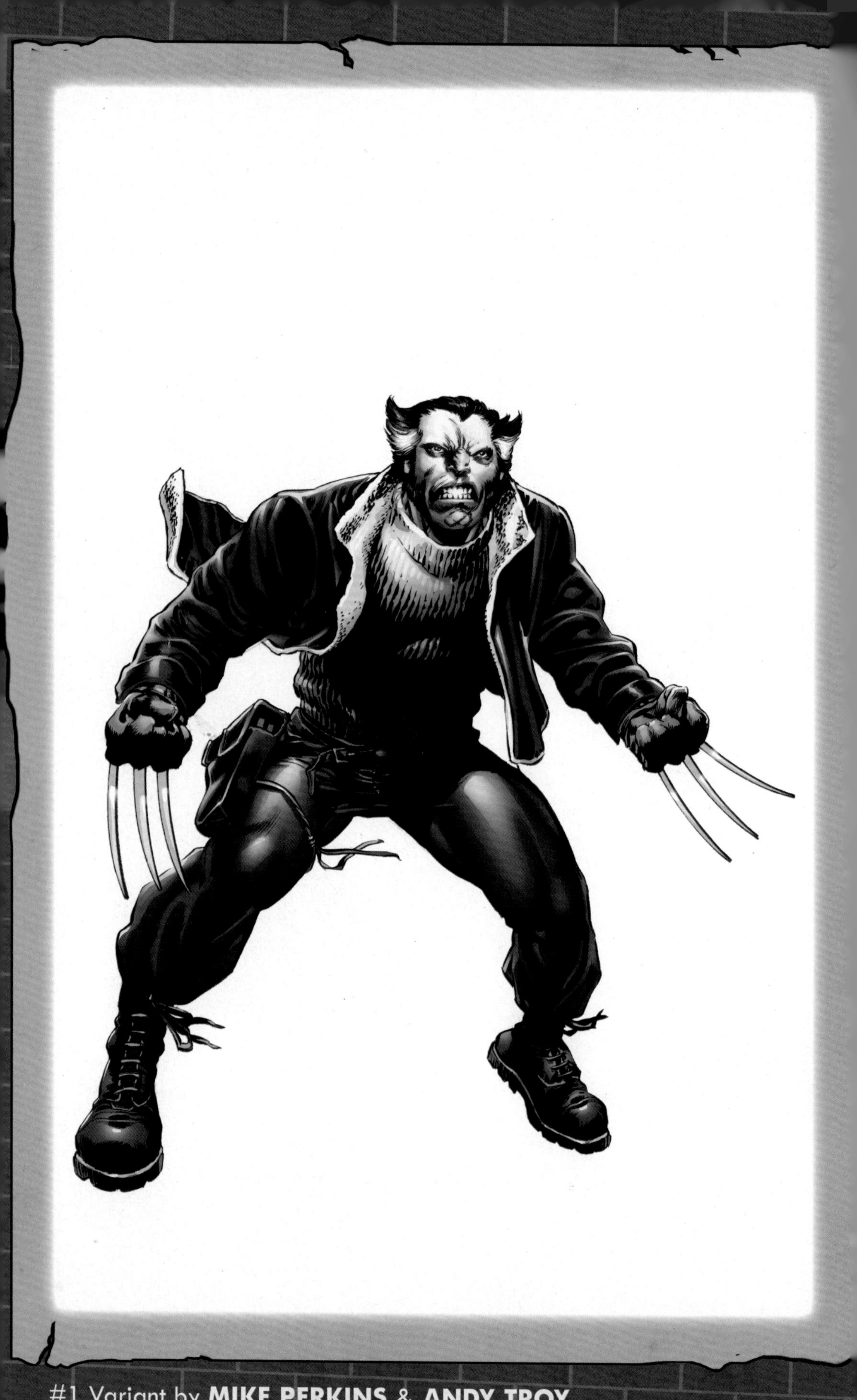

#1 Variant by **MIKE PERKINS** & **ANDY TROY**

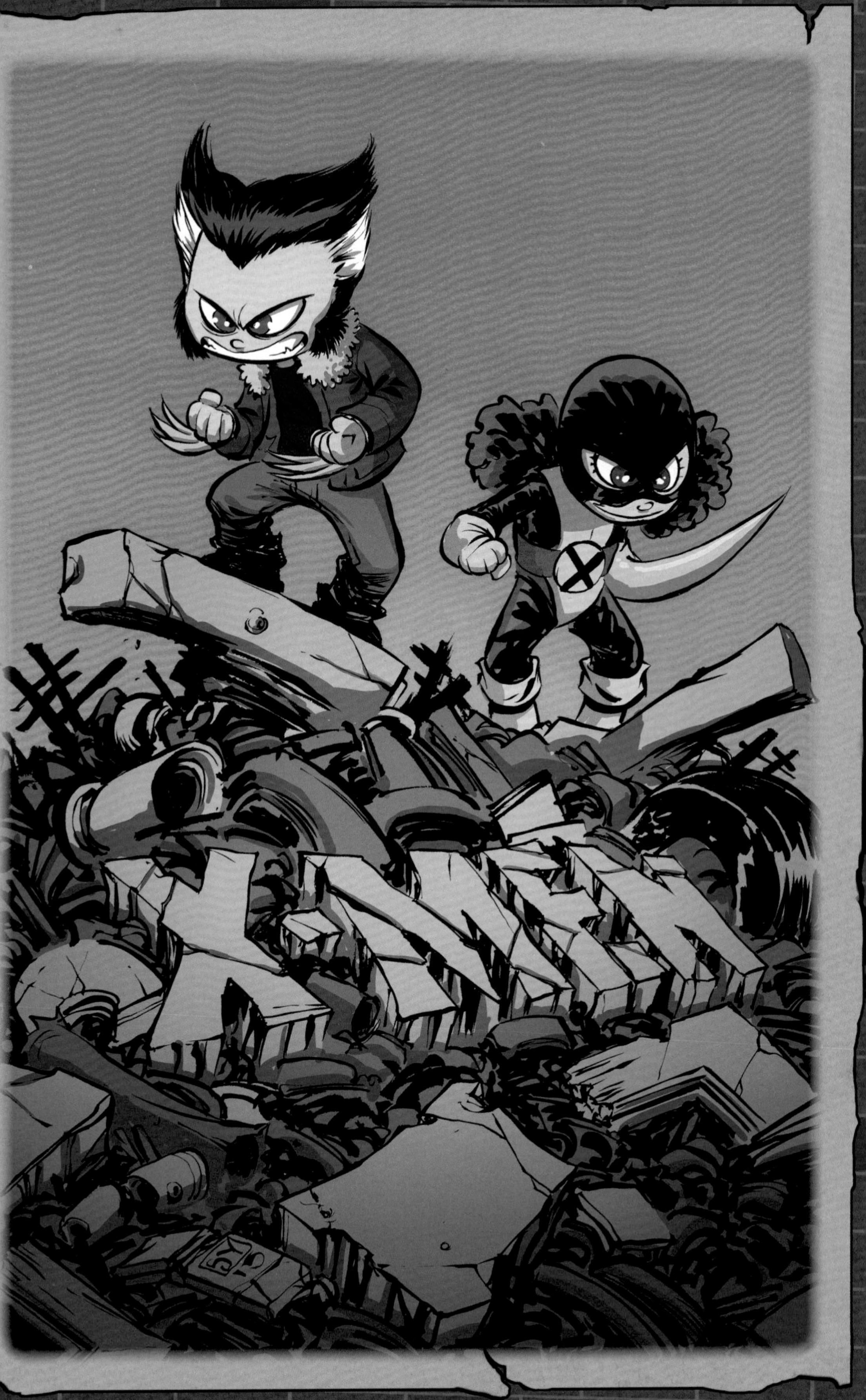

#1 Variant by **SKOTTIE YOUNG**

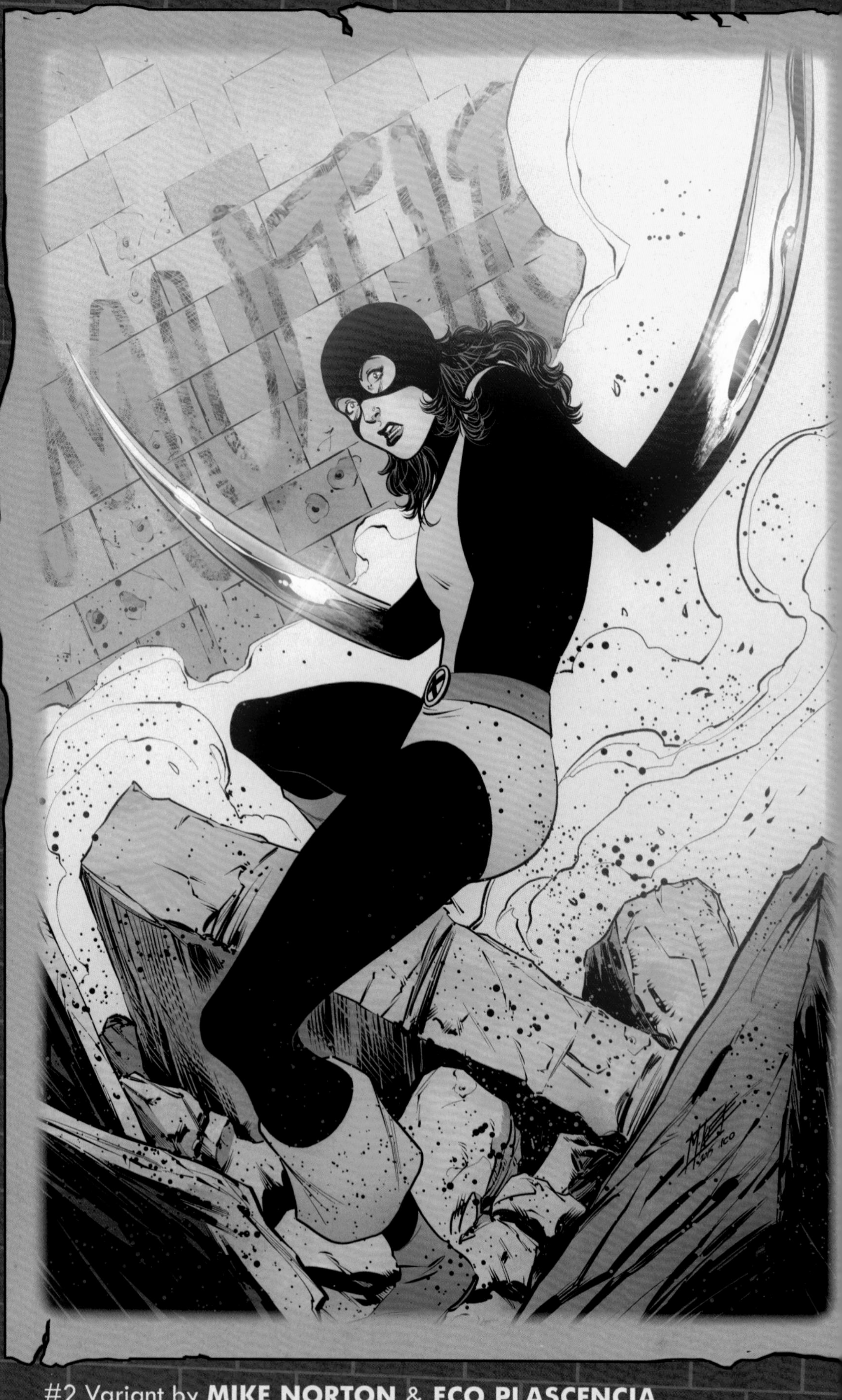

#2 Variant by **MIKE NORTON** & **FCO PLASCENCIA**

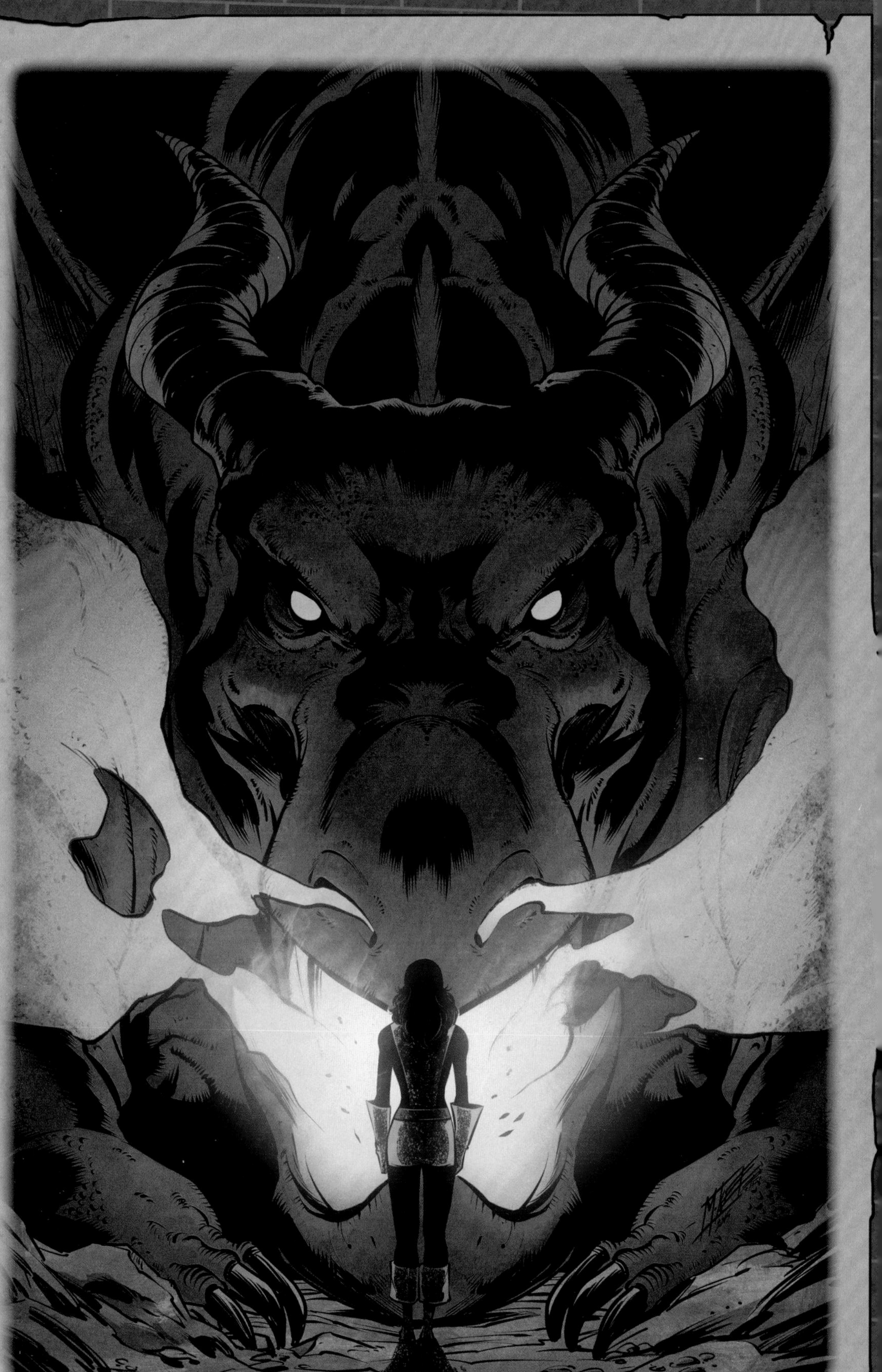

#3 Variant by **MIKE NORTON** & **FCO PLASCENCIA**

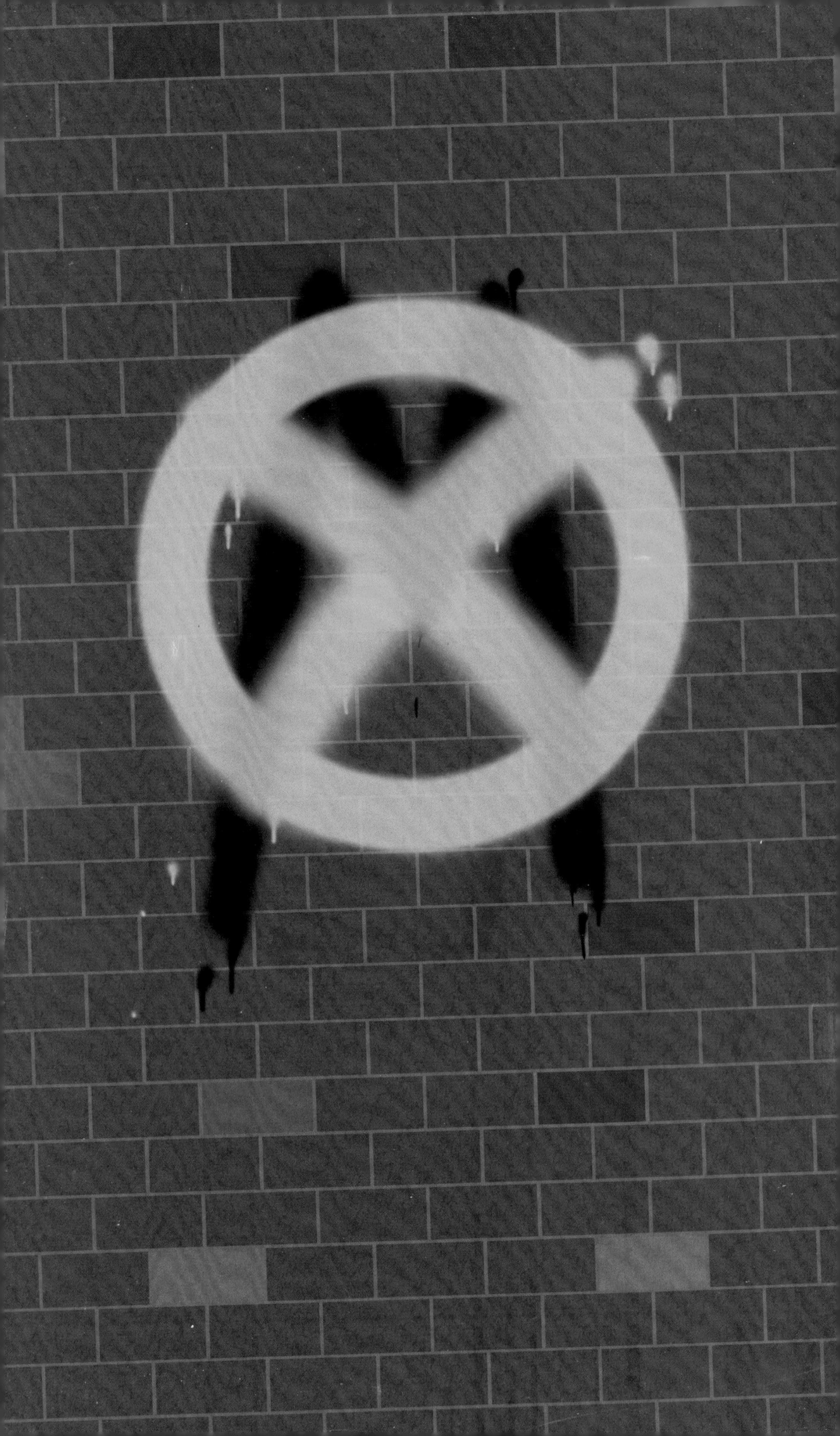